T0181701

IFIP Advances in Information and Communication Technology 653

Editor-in-Chief

Kai Rannenberg, Goethe University Frankfurt, Germany

Editorial Board Members

IFIP – The International Federation for Information Processing

IFIP was founded in 1960 under the auspices of UNESCO, following the first World Computer Congress held in Paris the previous year. A federation for societies working in information processing, IFIP's aim is two-fold: to support information processing in the countries of its members and to encourage technology transfer to developing nations. As its mission statement clearly states:

> IFIP is the global non-profit federation of societies of ICT professionals that aims at achieving a worldwide professional and socially responsible development and application of information and communication technologies.

IFIP is a non-profit-making organization, run almost solely by 2500 volunteers. It operates through a number of technical committees and working groups, which organize events and publications. IFIP's events range from large international open conferences to working conferences and local seminars.

The flagship event is the IFIP World Computer Congress, at which both invited and contributed papers are presented. Contributed papers are rigorously refereed and the rejection rate is high.

As with the Congress, participation in the open conferences is open to all and papers may be invited or submitted. Again, submitted papers are stringently refereed.

The working conferences are structured differently. They are usually run by a working group and attendance is generally smaller and occasionally by invitation only. Their purpose is to create an atmosphere conducive to innovation and development. Refereeing is also rigorous and papers are subjected to extensive group discussion.

Publications arising from IFIP events vary. The papers presented at the IFIP World Computer Congress and at open conferences are published as conference proceedings, while the results of the working conferences are often published as collections of selected and edited papers.

IFIP distinguishes three types of institutional membership: Country Representative Members, Members at Large, and Associate Members. The type of organization that can apply for membership is a wide variety and includes national or international societies of individual computer scientists/ICT professionals, associations or federations of such societies, government institutions/government related organizations, national or international research institutes or consortia, universities, academies of sciences, companies, national or international associations or federations of companies.

More information about this series at https://link.springer.com/bookseries/6102

Gilbert Peterson · Sujeet Shenoi (Eds.)

Advances in Digital Forensics XVIII

18th IFIP WG 11.9 International Conference
Virtual Event, January 3–4, 2022
Revised Selected Papers

Springer

Editors
Gilbert Peterson
Air Force Institute of Technology
Wright-Patterson AFB, OH, USA

Sujeet Shenoi
University of Tulsa
Tulsa, OK, USA

ISSN 1868-4238   ISSN 1868-422X (electronic)
IFIP Advances in Information and Communication Technology
ISBN 978-3-031-10080-2   ISBN 978-3-031-10078-9 (eBook)
https://doi.org/10.1007/978-3-031-10078-9

This Springer imprint is published by the registered company Springer Nature Switzerland AG
The registered company address is: Gewerbestrasse 11, 6330 Cham, Switzerland

Contents

Contributing Authors

Sani Mohammed Abdullahi is a Postdoctoral Researcher in Information Security at China Three Gorges University, Yichang, China. His research interests include digital forensics, biometric security, digital watermarking and deep learning.

Omoche Cheche Agada is a Ph.D. student in Information Technology at George Mason University, Fairfax, Virginia. His research interests include cyber security, digital forensics, data science and machine learning.

Andreas Attenberger is the Head of Research in Digital Forensics at the Central Office for Information Technology in the Security Sector, Munich, Germany. His research interests include extracting and interpreting data from embedded systems encountered in digital forensic investigations.

Harald Baier is a Professor of Digital Forensics at Bundeswehr University, Munich, Germany. His research interests include bulk data handling in digital forensics, data synthesis and random-access memory forensics.

Riskhan Basheer is an Assistant Professor of Computer Science at China Three Gorges University, Yichang, China. His research interests include big data, deep learning and digital forensics.

Josh Brunty is an Associate Professor of Digital Forensics at Marshall University, Huntington, West Virginia. His research interests include mobile device forensics, Internet of Things forensics and mobile application analysis.

Kam-Pui Chow, Chair, IFIP WG 11.9 on Digital Forensics, is an Associate Professor of Computer Science at the University of Hong Kong, Hong Kong, China. His research interests include information security, digital forensics, live system forensics and digital surveillance.

Andrew Clark IV is an M.S. student in Cyber Forensics and Security at Marshall University, Huntington, West Virginia. His research interests include digital forensics, reverse engineering and software development.

Yunyun Dong is a Lecturer of Computer Science at Yunnan University, Kunming, China. Her research interests include big data indexing, distributed computing and image steganography.

Gokila Dorai is an Assistant Professor of Computer and Cyber Sciences at Augusta University, Augusta, Georgia. Her research interests include mobile and Internet of Things forensics, targeted data extraction using applied machine learning and content-hiding application analysis.

Kevin Fairbanks is a Principal Cyber Operations Engineer at MITRE Corporation, McLean, Virginia. His research interests include digital forensics, computer security, software development and computer networking.

Pulkit Garg is a Ph.D. student in Computer Science and Engineering at the Indian Institute of Technology Jodhpur, Karwar, India. His research interests include image processing and computer vision, and their applications in document fraud detection.

Thomas Göbel is a Ph.D. student in Computer Science and a Researcher in the Research Institute of Cyber Defense at Bundeswehr University, Munich, Germany. His research interests include similarity hashing and realistic digital forensic data synthesis.

Patrik Goncalves is a Ph.D. student in Digital Forensics at Bundeswehr University, Munich, Germany, and a Doctoral Candidate Researcher at the Central Office for Information Technology in the Security Sector, Munich, Germany. His research interests include data synthesis and simulation in mobile forensics.

Yanan Gong is a Ph.D. student in Computer Science at the University of Hong Kong, Hong Kong, China. Her research interests include cryptocurrency and digital forensics.

Garima Gupta is an Independent Researcher in New Delhi, India. Her research interests include image processing and computer vision, and their applications in document fraud detection.

Gaurav Gupta, Vice Chair, IFIP WG 11.9 on Digital Forensics, is a Scientist E in the Ministry of Electronics and Information Technology, New Delhi, India. His research interests include mobile device security, digital forensics, web application security, Internet of Things security and security in emerging technologies.

Ibifubara Iganibo is a Ph.D. student in Information Technology and a Cyber Security Researcher at the Center for Secure Information Systems at George Mason University, Fairfax, Virginia. His research interests include computer and information security, attack surface measurement, security analytics and privacy.

Qian Jiang is an Associate Professor of Computer Science at Yunnan University, Kunming, China. Her research interests include neural networks, fuzzy sets, image processing and bioinformatics.

Xin Jin is an Associate Professor of Computer Science at Yunnan University, Kunming, China. His research interests include neural networks theory and applications, image processing, optimization algorithms and bioinformatics.

James Jones is an Associate Professor of Digital Forensics and Director of the Criminal Investigations and Network Analysis Center at George Mason University, Fairfax, Virginia. His research interests include digital artifact persistence, extraction, analysis and manipulation.

Ranjan Kumar is a Scientist E in the Ministry of Electronics and Information Technology, New Delhi, India, and the Director of the Asia-Pacific Advanced Network, New Delhi, India. His research interests include network traffic monitoring, dual stack access of Internet Protocol version 6 (IPv6) and Internet Protocol version 4 (IPv4), Internet of Things, network security and security in emerging technologies.

Divam Lehri is a Cyber Forensic Expert at the National Cyber Forensic Laboratory of the Indian Cyber Crime Coordination Center, New Delhi, India. His research interests include digital forensics, threat intelligence and critical infrastructure protection.

Martin Lukner recently received his M.S. degree in Computer Science from Bundeswehr University, Munich, Germany. His research interests include malware analysis and realistic digital forensic data synthesis.

Asad Malik is an Assistant Professor of Digital Forensics at Aligarh Muslim University, Aligarh, India. His research interests include multimedia forensics, information hiding and deep learning.

Rayna Mock is an M.S. student in Forensic Science at Marshall University, Huntington, West Virginia. Her research interests include digital forensics, crime scene investigations and DNA analysis.

Otabek Khudeybardiev is a Ph.D. student in Information Technology at Southwest Jiaotong University, Chengdu, China. His research interests include deep learning, digital forensics and computer vision.

Ce Liang is an M.Eng. student in Electronic Engineering at Guangxi Normal University, Guilin, China. His research interests include artificial intelligence, digital forensics and image processing.

Yuling Luo is a Professor of Electronic Engineering at Guangxi Normal University, Guilin, China. Her research interests include information security, image processing, chaos theory, artificial intelligence and embedded system implementation and optimization.

Sheng Qin is an M.Eng. student in Electronic Engineering at Guangxi Normal University, Guilin, China. His research interests include artificial neural networks, reinforcement learning and intelligent control systems.

Anyesh Roy is the Deputy Commissioner of Police of the National Capital Territory of Delhi, New Delhi, India. His research interests include cyber security, digital forensics, financial fraud investigations, disaster management, maritime security and electronic surveillance systems.

Somitra Sanadhya is a Professor of Computer Science and Engineering at the Indian Institute of Technology Jodhpur, Karwar, India. His research interests include cryptology, security, blockchain and quantum computation.

Ao Shen is a Ph.D. student in Computer Science at the University of Hong Kong, Hong Kong, China. Her research interests include natural language processing, social network forensics and threat intelligence.

Shuifa Sun is a Professor of Information Technology and Computer Vision at China Three Gorges University, Yichang, China. His research interests include digital forensics, intelligent information processing and computer vision.

Hing-Fung Ting is an Associate Professor of Computer Science at the University of Hong Kong, Hong Kong, China. His research interests include bioinformatics, design and analysis of algorithms, and computational complexity

Logan VanPutte is an M.A. student in Intelligence and Security Studies at Augusta University, Augusta, Georgia. Her research interests include threat intelligence, digital forensics, cyber security, investigation and analysis.

Nan Wu is an M.S. student in Computer Science at Yunnan University, Kunming, China. His research interests include neural networks and deepfake detection.

Shaowen Yao is a Professor of Computer Science at Yunnan University, Kunming, China. His research interests include neural network theory and applications, cloud computing and big data.

Siu-Ming Yiu is a Professor of Computer Science at the University of Hong Kong, Hong Kong, China. His research interests include cyber security, cryptography, digital forensics and bioinformatics.

Shunsheng Zhang is a Technical Staff Member in the School of Electronic Engineering at Guangxi Normal University, Guilin, China. His research interests include artificial intelligence, security, cryptographic algorithms and side-channel attacks.

Ya Zhang is an M.S. student in Computer Science at Yunnan University, Kunming, China. Her research interests include neural networks and deepfake detection.

Wei Zhou is a Professor of Computer Science at Yunnan University, Kunming, China. His research interests include distributed-data-intensive computing, image processing and bioinformatics.

Preface

Digital forensics deals with the acquisition, preservation, examination, analysis and presentation of electronic evidence. Computer networks, cloud computing, smartphones, embedded devices and the Internet of Things have expanded the role of digital forensics beyond traditional computer crime investigations. Practically every crime now involves some aspect of digital evidence; digital forensics provides the techniques and tools to articulate this evidence in legal proceedings. Digital forensics also has myriad intelligence applications; furthermore, it has a vital role in cyber security – investigations of security breaches yield valuable information that can be used to design more secure and resilient systems.

This book, *Advances in Digital Forensics XVIII*, is the eighteenth volume in the annual series produced by the IFIP Working Group 11.9 on Digital Forensics, an international community of scientists, engineers and practitioners dedicated to advancing the state of the art of research and practice in digital forensics. The book presents original research results and innovative applications in digital forensics. Also, it highlights some of the major technical and legal issues related to digital evidence and electronic crime investigations.

This volume contains eleven revised and edited chapters based on papers presented at the Eighteenth IFIP WG 11.9 International Conference on Digital Forensics, a fully-virtual event held on January 3-4, 2022. The papers were refereed by members of IFIP Working Group 11.9 and other internationally-recognized experts in digital forensics. The post-conference manuscripts submitted by the authors were rewritten to accommodate the suggestions provided by the conference attendees. They were subsequently revised by the editors to produce the final chapters published in this volume.

The chapters are organized into four sections: Forensic Data Collection, Mobile Device Forensics, Image and Video Forensics, and Novel Applications. The coverage of topics highlights the richness and vitality of the discipline, and offers promising avenues for future research in digital forensics.

This book is the result of the combined efforts of several individuals. In particular, we thank Kam-Pui Chow and Gaurav Gupta for their tireless work on behalf of IFIP Working Group 11.9 on Digital Forensics. We also acknowledge the support provided by the U.S. National Science Foundation, U.S. National Security Agency and U.S. Secret Service.

GILBERT PETERSON AND SUJEET SHENOI

I

FORENSIC DATA COLLECTION

Chapter 1

A DIGITAL BODY FARM FOR COLLECTING DELETED FILE DECAY DATA

Omoche Cheche Agada, Ibifubara Iganibo, James Jones and Kevin Fairbanks

Abstract   Recovering deleted data can be a time-consuming task during digital forensic investigations. As tedious as the task is, it may not produce useful results. New files written to locations containing previously-deleted file data may render some or even all of the deleted file unrecoverable. Insights into the factors that influence deleted file decay are required to enable digital forensic professionals to determine if attempting file recovery is a wise use of time. Significant research efforts have focused on deleted file decay, but gaps in knowledge still exist. This chapter discusses an attempt at collecting data to help discover how deleted file content decays over time in computing systems running the Microsoft New Technology Filesystem (NTFS). In particular, it describes the implementation of a digital body farm that uses differential analysis to monitor and record patterns of decay as deleted data are erased or overwritten on secondary storage media attached to a live system. The collection of realistic file decay data and relevant system parameters can be used to create a model that provides useful insights into the deleted file decay process.

Keywords: File decay data, digital body farm, data persistence, decay patterns

1.   Introduction

In forensic anthropology and related disciplines, a body farm is described as a facility that is dedicated to the study of the decomposition of human remains [28]. In a body farm, human remains are subjected to various conditions in a controlled environment in order to observe and understand the process of decay. Knowledge from such endeavors has been applied in several disciplines, including law enforcement inves-

© IFIP International Federation for Information Processing 2022
Published by Springer Nature Switzerland AG 2022
G. Peterson and S. Shenoi (Eds.): DigitalForensics 2022, IFIP AICT 653, pp. 3–20, 2022.
https://doi.org/10.1007/978-3-031-10078-9_1

tigations and forensic pathology. Experts in these disciplines are able to reason about human remains and paint an accurate or near-accurate picture about the circumstances surrounding the human remains, including body identification, time of death and cause of death. Numerous homicide cases have been solved by the diligent application of procedures developed after careful studies of the decay process of human remains.

During an investigation, a digital forensic professional may be tasked with unravelling the mystery surrounding data that may have been deleted deliberately to hide criminal activity. In such a situation, the professional attempts to recover the deleted files as evidence of wrong-doing. In other cases, data may have been deleted during the normal course of business or personal activities without malicious intent. In the two scenarios, attempts are made to recover deleted data to prosecute or exonerate an individual in civil or criminal proceedings. Depending on the circumstances surrounding the deletion process and the associated system, it may or may not be possible to recover deleted data. Deleted files decay just like human remains, but unlike the decay of human remains, deleted file decay is not a well-studied topic [7, 12]. This chapter describes the implementation of a digital body farm, a suite of applications that use differential analysis to monitor and record patterns of decay as file content is overwritten on secondary storage media.

2.   Background

Estimating the rate at which deleted files decay in digital media has always been of interest in digital forensic investigations. Understanding how file contents decay and the factors that affect the process are useful in making decisions about artifact recovery. They are also important in determining if a file was deleted during the normal course of computing activities or deliberately with malicious intent [12]. This research has sought to identify patterns pertaining to deleted file decay in computing systems that use the Microsoft New Technology Filesystem (NTFS).

When a file is deleted, the associated clusters are deallocated by the filesystem, but the data content remains intact on storage media. The data is, therefore, recoverable until it is erased by internal mechanisms of the storage device or is overwritten by the allocation of newly-created or existing data to the same storage area by the filesystem [3, 4].

Erasing or overwriting the memory blocks associated with a deleted file is referred to as decay in this context. Contrary to conventional understanding, when a computer file is deleted, it does not automatically cease to exist in the storage device. Instead, it is marked as deleted and the space it occupies on the drive is freed up to hold new files [14].

Although the filesystem designates the space as "free space," it still holds the data content of the deleted file. The data content persists until the space is allocated to a different file or the space is reclaimed by drive housekeeping activities. After this occurs, the file is partially or completely overwritten.

While the mechanisms that cause deleted file content decay are well known, the actual file decay behavior and patterns are not well understood, and it is difficult to predict with certainty if a deleted file can be recovered. Indeed, deleted file content recovery remains a hit or miss activity. No generalizable theory or even empirical data exist that can fully explain how and why deleted data may or may not persist [7, 12]. The rate at which data decays after deletion has not been quantified and, therefore, the expected success of recovery efforts is largely unknown. A methodology is needed for collecting and analyzing data in order to identify digital artifact decay patterns upon file deletion. The goal of this research is to develop a methodology and a validated tool for collecting data as deleted file content is erased or overwritten in digital storage devices.

3. Related Work

Artifact decay and artifact persistence are closely related concepts in the digital forensics literature. The concepts are, in fact, mutually exclusive, like the outcome of a coin toss where the presence of one outcome necessarily implies the absence of the other. Researchers tend to use the terms somewhat interchangeably because they are determined by the same underlying factors. For example, some authors focus on decay [8, 11, 14] whereas others consider persistence [7, 12]. Depending on the artifact in question, the presence or absence of certain factors in a computing system determine if and how the artifact decays or persists.

Fairbanks and Garfinkel [8] were the first to articulate the factors that determine decay – allocation status, reuse policy, media type, data type, media degradation and media errors. Other factors include filesystem design, fragmentation, pre-allocation strategies, filesystem size/utilization/age, drive usage patterns and implementation errors. Jones et al. [14] established that the sizes of deleted and newly-created files, overwriting frequency and sector/cluster sizes are significant to decay or persistence. Fairbanks [7] defines persistence as a property that depends on many factors, including the allocation status of the data in question.

Garfinkel et al. [9] formalized the concept of differential forensic analysis and demonstrated its application in multiple forensic analysis contexts. Differential forensic analysis considers the differences between a

pair of forensic artifacts. Jones [10] describes differential analysis as a
data science tool that can be applied to a variety of cyber security and
digital forensics problems. Laamanen and Nelson [15] have used it to
create a record of system states called diskprints. Jones et al. [13] have
used it to construct forensic artifact catalogs. Nelson [23] has employed
differential analysis to extract software signatures from the Windows
Registry. In contrast, the research described in this chapter uses differential analysis to monitor changes in individual drive sectors associated
with a deleted file, indicating that the sectors have been erased or overwritten.

Jones and Khan [12] studied deleted file persistence by applying differential analysis to multiple drive images from a single computer. Each
drive image represented a snapshot of the disk drive after a predeter-
mined set of activities took place. The research described in this chapter
monitors the decay process in running systems instead of drive images.
Measuring data decay in running systems provides an opportunity to
observe the effects of variation in computing environments and the factors that affect the decay process. This also ensures that the activities
that result in data deletion and subsequent data decay are not prede-
termined. The goal is to study a process that is as close as possible to
real-world situations.

The introduction of solid-state drives (SSDs) as an alternative to hard
disk drives (HDDs) has changed how digital forensic professionals and
researchers view data decay and data recovery. Solid-state drives have
overtaken hard disk drives as the storage media of choice in personal
computers, although server and storage farms still make heavy use of
hard disk drives primarily due to their lower cost [6]. While the two types
of media are alike in many respects and serve the same basic purpose,
their internal mechanisms and capabilities are very different. As a result,
the factors articulated in [8] as data decay catalysts may affect file decay
differently for solid-state drives as opposed to hard disk drives. The
important, albeit controversial, features related to data decay on solid-
state drives are garbage collection, TRIM commands and wear leveling.
While some researchers opine that these features have no significant
impact on digital forensic data recovery procedures [27], others believe
their combined effects have changed the practice forever [24]. The issue
of whether solid-state drives have changed the practice of digital forensics
recovery procedures is an ongoing conversation. This work is intended
to help advance the conversation.

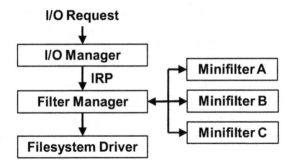

Figure 1. Minifilters managed by the filter manager [29].

4. Digital Body Farm Methodology

The digital body farm developed in this research is essentially a data collection and monitoring tool. It comprises multiple components, a filesystem filter driver, a Windows service application, a database and a script.

4.1 Digital Body Farm Components

At the heart of the digital body farm is a filesystem filter driver (minifilter or minifilter driver). The minifilter driver is a kernel mode application that intercepts and handles input/output requests targeted at the filesystem. The minifilter attaches to a legacy filter driver called the filter manager [21]. The filter manager is provided by default with a Windows installation and becomes active when it detects an attached minifilter driver.

The filter manager is designed to manage multiple minifilter drivers concurrently (Figure 1). An input/output request could be a request from an application to create, read, write or delete a file. When an input/output request is made by a user mode application, the request passes through a series of application programming interfaces (APIs) before arriving at the input/output manager in kernel space. The input/output manager creates an input/output request packet (IRP) and passes it to the filter manager. The filter manager calls an attached minifilter to deal with the request as appropriate. A filesystem filter driver does not handle system calls; instead, it intercepts system calls that trigger the execution of specific functions. It is the responsibility of the filesystem to see that the call is eventually executed. However, minifilters can manipulate or terminate calls before they reach the filesystem and prevent them from being executed [2, 16, 25].

To reduce the burden on filter driver developers, Microsoft provides driver samples that help speed up the development process [20]. The filesystem filter driver used in this work is called the delete filesystem minifilter driver. The original design, as provided by Microsoft, intercepts delete calls and extracts basic information such as the complete file path, file size and system call time. Several modifications were made to the delete filesystem minifilter driver obtained from Microsoft to augment its functions, which are very basic and insufficient for this research effort.

Another component of the digital body farm is the Windows service application, also known as a Windows service. A Windows service provides additional capability to an executable application. It enables the application to become a long-running executable that can run in its own Windows session [19]. The application runs in the background and does not require user input. Once started, it runs continuously and restarts automatically after a system reboot. Since the application does not display an interface, it does not directly interfere with the user's ability to use the system for other purposes. The application can be paused, stopped or restarted as needed. Unlike the minifilter, the Windows service runs in the user mode. It also runs in the listening mode, receiving and processing data from the minifilter. As such, it services the minifilter as well as the database component of the digital body farm.

The file data extracted by the minifilter is passed to the service application and stored in the database after processing. The database also holds important system information.

The script is the decay detection component of the digital body farm. It uses information from the database to check the data content of the deleted files on the drive. It updates the database whenever there are changes to the sector content of a deleted file.

4.2   Digital Body Farm Process

Figure 2 shows a graphical representation of the digital body farm process. When a file is deleted, the minifilter intercepts the delete system call in kernel space and extracts data about the file to be deleted before the delete call proceeds. It is important to intercept the delete system call before it is executed. This is because, once execution completes, it becomes difficult if not impossible to obtain file information. The extracted data, which includes the logical addresses (offsets) of the sectors occupied by the file on the drive, is passed on to the Windows service in user space along with the name and complete file path. Using the sector offsets received from the minifilter, the service application

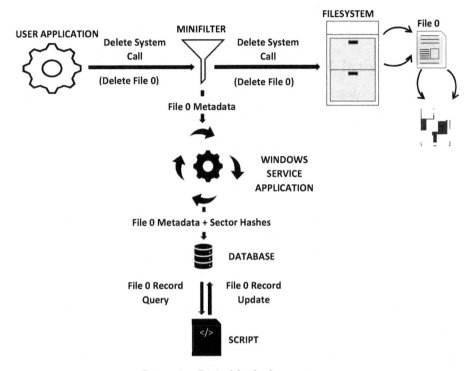

Figure 2. Digital body farm process.

computes the cryptographic hash values of the contents of the sectors associated with the deleted file. The hash values are stored in a database along with sector addresses and other data extracted from the file by the minifilter.

Although the file is deleted at the operating system and filesystem levels and the clusters are deallocated, the data content is still intact in the physical layer (on the drive). The content remains intact until it is partially or completely erased or overwritten. The script that checks if the sector content has changed is scheduled to run at a specified time each day. It applies differential analysis to record sector-level changes to the content of a previously-deleted file. Whenever the script executes, it uses sector addresses in the database to determine the locations of the file content on the drive. New hash values are computed for the current content of the sectors on the drive and are compared against the hash values of the corresponding sectors stored in the database. A match indicates that a sector is intact whereas a mismatch indicates that the sector has been erased or overwritten. This is used to measure the decay of the file content. The process continues until all the sectors associated with the file are completely overwritten or until a specified time has elapsed. Data about the decay – which has no actual file content – is collected and analyzed.

5.   Digital Body Farm Implementation

This section describes the implementation of the principal components of the digital body farm and discusses the limitations of the implementation.

5.1   Delete Filesystem Filter Driver

The delete minifilter (`delete.sys`) is implemented in C++. It registers itself with the filter manager as a filesystem filter driver upon installation. When the minifilter detects a delete system call targeted at a file, it intercepts the call, creates a hard link to the file, queries the filesystem for the file sector layout and notifies the Windows service about the deletion. The notification message includes the file path, hard link path and sector map.

The Windows service uses the information to compute the cryptographic hashes of the file sectors. MD5 was employed in this work, but any hashing algorithm (SHA-1, SHA-256, etc.) could be used. Computing sector hashes for a file requires time, which becomes more significant as the file size grows. The filesystem could erase or overwrite file data before the hash computations are complete, leading to data corruption. To prevent this from occurring, a hard link [18] is attached to the file, which gives the filesystem the impression that the file contents are still active. This ensures that the file data is not freed for deletion until the sector hashing is complete.

The hard link is deleted after the hash computations are complete or if it is determined that the file is not of interest and the hash computations are not necessary. The hard link, which is created in the same directory as the deleted file, appears as a file with the naming convention **XXX.YYY**. **XXX** is the driver initialization timestamp, which is unique to each session that begins when the driver is loaded and ends when the driver is unloaded. **YYY** is an incremental counter of hard links created by the driver in a given session.

Figure 3 shows the hard links created in a folder after files have been deleted. The delete minifilter implementation is available at GitHub [5]. The original version of the delete minifilter provided by Microsoft is also available at GitHub [17].

Microsoft does not permit the installation of unsigned third-party drivers on 64-bit versions of the Windows operating system. This is intended to prevent the installation of rogue or malicious drivers. How-

```
Name              Date Modified        Type      Size
496948.5          2/23/2021 4:35 PM    5 File    1,027 KB
496948.6          4/17/2020 6:31 AM    6 File    5,811 KB
496948.7          4/29/2020 11:09 AM   7 File    1,078 KB
496948.8          4/29/2020 11:09 AM   8 File    1,257 KB
496948.9          9/7/2020 10:02 PM    9 File      904 KB
496948.10         2/11/2015 1:19 PM    10 File     115 KB
496948.11         7/23/2020 5:01 PM    11 File   6,643 KB
496948.12         12/18/2020 9:06 AM   12 File   2,769 KB
496948.14         5/27/2021 2:16 PM    14 File   2,927 KB
```

Figure 3. Hard links created after file deletion.

ever, a signed driver neither guarantees bug-free driver code nor prevents system crashes; it only gives some confidence in the driver because it is published by Microsoft. Additionally, it gives no assurance that the code has not been changed since its release [29]. Different procedures apply to signing drivers during development and testing as opposed to signing them for public release [22]. During the development and testing efforts, driver signing was disabled or the system was placed in the test mode.

5.2 Windows Service

The Windows service (`bodyfarm.exe`) is a user mode application implemented in C++. It is bundled with and installed with the delete minifilter. The service also creates the database for storing information about deleted files. Once it is installed, the service runs continuously, sending and receiving messages to and from the minifilter using a bidirectional message queue.

The service waits in a queue to obtain notifications about deleted files. A notification includes the file path, hard link path, sector map and other file information. When the notification arrives, the service checks that the file is a user file instead of a system file. It also checks that the file size is within the allowable limits.

If the file type and size meet the criteria, the notification data is placed in the hash computation thread queue. A hash computation thread reads notification data from its queue. For every notification, it starts the hash computation loop in which it directly reads the device block from which the file was deleted using the sector map in the notification. An MD5 hash value is computed and inserted in the database for each file sector. Once this is done, the service notifies the driver so that all the resources allocated to the file can be released and the hard link removed. The service also notifies the driver if a file does not meet the type and size

Table 1. Database tables.

Table Name	Description
Decay	This table records the percentage of each file that remains intact as the file is overwritten. The data is only recorded after the checker script executes and there has been some decay in one or more files (i.e., at least one file sector has been overwritten).
Disk	This table holds data about the drives from which a file has been deleted. It does not contain data about every drive in the system. A drive is listed in the table if at least one file on the drive has been deleted.
Extent	This table holds data about the cluster runs occupied by a file. It also shows the file fragmentation data.
File	This table contains basic file data and the hash computation times for all the sectors of a deleted file.
PC	This table contains identifying information about the computing system that executed the program.
Sector	This table contains data about all the sectors associated with a file. Also, it contains the sector hash values.

criteria, in which case the allocated resources are also released and the hard link is removed.

The service stores the MD5 hash values of file names in the database instead of the file names themselves. This is done to prevent the release of a file name that may provide personally-identifiable information. After the file names are hashed, only the file extensions remain visible. The service also creates a log of all the deleted files, including system files. The logs, which are intended for troubleshooting, are only maintained locally on the system under study and may contain sensitive information, including personally-identifiable information.

5.3   Database

The database (`sector.db`) is a SQLite3 database. It is also bundled with the service and created upon installation of the service and minifilter. The database holds information about all the deleted files and also contains system parameters that provide context for the decay data. The database maintains six tables (Decay, Disk, Extent, File, PC and Sector). Table 1 describes the tables in `sector.db`.

5.4 Script

The script (`Body_Farm_Checker.exe`) is implemented in Python 3. It uses the sector addresses stored in the database to check if the file sectors on the drive are intact. The checking process begins upon obtaining all the sectors associated with a file in the database that have not been marked as overwritten. The sectors on the drive are hashed using MD5 and the hash values are compared against the hash values in the database. A match indicates that the data content in the sector is intact whereas a mismatch indicates sector content has been erased or overwritten. The database is updated after it is determined that the sector content has changed; subsequent checks are not performed on such sectors.

The script is compiled using `pyinstaller` version 4.5.1 [26] to produce a Python executable. Creating the executable eliminates the need to install Python on the system before running the script. It also facilitates running the script on a schedule.

The script requires administrative privileges because it accesses sensitive system resources. Not all task schedulers are able to run programs that require elevated privileges; Z-Cron version 5.8 [30], available as freeware for non-commercial use, was employed for this purpose.

5.5 Limitations

User files are the focus of forensic investigations. The current study is limited to user files with sizes between 1 KB and 10 MB. The file types and sizes can be adjusted as necessary.

6. Validation Tests and Results

This section describes the validation tests and results.

6.1 Validation Tests

The goal of the validation tests is to confirm that the data processed and stored by the digital body farm is a true representation of deleted file content on the storage media. The file sector hashes of allocated files were computed using the `C++Validator.exe` program, which was written for this work. The computed hash values were stored in the SQLite3 database `C++Validator.db` along with sector addresses and file names. The files were subsequently deleted and processed by the digital body farm. The resulting sector hash values were stored in a second database (`sector.db`). The two databases were compared using the `CompareSectors.py` Python script.

```
sectorAddr  sectorHash                            sectorAddr  sectorHash
279617536   af1a83d6b18bf3e065be82cf44246037  |   279617536   af1a83d6b18bf3e065be82cf44246037
279618048   d5cedca078545cbcb0b2a9b514f9b92d  |   279618048   d5cedca078545cbcb0b2a9b514f9b92d
279618560   457ee2f5dc6f95b09599fc3f479878b6  |   279618560   457ee2f5dc6f95b09599fc3f479878b6
279619072   a509c66cf89de0e3c2863107b72d5d50  |   279619072   a509c66cf89de0e3c2863107b72d5d50
279619584   eoe88bce4af9e1e3d6c8f5d6270993f7  |   279619584   eoe88bce4af9e1e3d6c8f5d6270993f7
279620096   118a5a15cb729foe6c61ac651161ad18  |   279620096   118a5a15cb729foe6c61ac651161ad18
279620608   c2ede9d52b3188c69f46c5f11b7f8f48  |   279620608   c2ede9d52b3188c69f46c5f11b7f8f48
279621120   9c30f5a08b98d87f272c5ffe526ea634  |   279621120   9c30f5a08b98d87f272c5ffe526ea634
279621632   ei9e6cc5adfdf5e2e798c9f995284f84  |   279621632   ei9e6cc5adfdf5e2e798c9f995284f84
279622144   cd2b72ae0214df0985cb4f34754e6a56  |   279622144   cd2b72ae0214df0985cb4f34754e6a56
279622656   5b9e3e21849ae2cfcaf5ee02b0767912  |   279622656   5b9e3e21849ae2cfcaf5ee02b0767912
279623168   f5a5f4596eba4512c2f1f5d6a1395a04  |   279623168   f5a5f4596eba4512c2f1f5d6a1395a04
279623680   d229a1685f5469012dab8a859a34322c  |   279623680   d229a1685f5469012dab8a859a34322c
279624192   4f36b924164bb7a913691854324d98de  |   279624192   4f36b924164bb7a913691854324d98de
279624704   3e61cb355ce8dda7a4d1264573090443  |   279624704   3e61cb355ce8dda7a4d1264573090443
279625216   5dbc4becbb443f5c16e8813ff2482199  |   279625216   5dbc4becbb443f5c16e8813ff2482199
279625728   9656e6d757e4a6c92e32609bd0cbfbac  |   279625728   9656e6d757e4a6c92e32609bd0cbfbac
279626240   ac8e3df92e6977f26e1e133e0b5660a3  |   279626240   ac8e3df92e6977f26e1e133e0b5660a3
```

Figure 4.   Comparison of file sector hash values before and after file deletion.

Figure 4 shows the two database files. The C++Validator.db data-base on the left was created before files were deleted. The sector.db database on the right was created after files were deleted. Twenty random files were used in the validation tests, each with a different size and, therefore, a different number of sectors.

```
======  RESTART:  C:\Users\chex2\Desktop\New folder\compareSectors.py  ======
Welcome to the compareSectors program

The result of comparing C++Validator.db and sector.db is as follows:
Total sectors:      61645
Matched sectors:       61645
Unmatched sectors: 0

NOTE: See log for details
```

Figure 5.   Comparison of file sector hash values using compareSector.py.

Figure 5 shows the comparison of 61,645 file sector hash values. Upon executing the compareSector.py script on the two database files, every corresponding sector pair was found to match, indicating that all the sectors were still intact after deletion.

6.2   Results

The digital body farm was tested using the four computing systems described in Table 2. A total of 20 files were deleted and monitored

Table 2. Computing systems used in the validation tests.

Parameter	PC 1	PC 2	PC 3	PC 4
Make	HP Laptop	HP Laptop	Dell Laptop	Microsoft Tablet/PC
Model	HP 15 Notebook PC	17t-cn000	Inspiron 3593	Surface Pro 4
Processor	3rd Gen Intel Core i5 @ 2.60 GHz	11th Gen Intel Core i5 @ 2.40 GHz	10th Gen Intel Core i7 @ 1.30 GHz	6th Gen Intel Core i5 @ 2.40 GHz
Disk	1 TB (5,400 rpm SATA) HDD (Seagate/ Samsung)	1 TB (5,400 rpm SATA) HDD (Western Digital)	512 GB (M.2 PCIe NVMe) SSD (Kioxia/ Toshiba)	256 GB (NVMe PCIe Gen3 x4) SSD (Samsung)
Disk Usage	4%	10.6%	49.4%	81.9%

for seven days. The methodology does not determine precisely when the sector contents of a deleted file were erased or overwritten, but the frequency with which checks are conducted determines a time range. For example, if the checker script is executed every hour, then a change would have occurred in a 60-minute window. The checks were executed once a day based on a common use case where a forensic investigation is initiated several days after an incident. The tests were conducted multiple times and the results were consistent.

Table 3 provides details of the test results. Figure 6 shows graphical representations of file decay in the four computing systems over the test period. Files monitored on PC 4 were completely overwritten shortly after deletion, typically within minutes. The system incorporated a solid-state drive with very aggressive garbage collection, TRIM commands and wear leveling mechanisms. At 80% capacity utilization, it is no surprise that deleted data was erased almost immediately.

In contrast, PC 3 was slower at erasing files after deletion, although it was only 50% full. Future work will investigate how these drives would behave if their utilizations are reversed. PC 1 and PC 2 are typical hard disk drives, but PC 2 displayed decay behavior similar to a solid-state drive, possibly because its logical to physical address mapping was different from that of PC 1. PC 2 was recognized as a hard disk drive

Table 3. Validation test results.

Day	Parameter	Validation Test Data			
	Computing System	PC 1	PC 2	PC 3	PC 4
	Number of Files	20	20	20	16
	Files with Complete Decay	2	19	10	16
Day 1	Files with Partial Decay	6	0	5	0
	Files Intact	12	1	5	0
	% Files with Decay	40	95	75	100
	% Files with Complete Decay	10	95	50	100
	% Files Intact	60	5	25	0
Day 2	% Files Intact	15	5	0	0
Day 3	% Files Intact	15	5	0	0
Day 4	% Files Intact	10	5	0	0
Day 5	% Files Intact	10	0	0	0
Day 6	% Files Intact	10	0	0	0
Day 7	% Files Intact	10	0	0	0

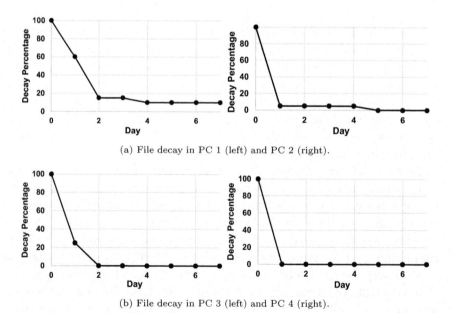

(a) File decay in PC 1 (left) and PC 2 (right).

(b) File decay in PC 3 (left) and PC 4 (right).

Figure 6. Percentages of entire files remaining on the test systems per day.

by the Windows operating system, but its features appear to be more like a hybrid drive or solid-state drive.

The results aggregate multiple files from each system, although the methodology preserves detailed sector-level and file-level decay data for subsequent analysis. As discussed earlier, data decay is not based only on drive type. The research did not account for user and non-user activities occurring on the computing systems throughout the observation period. PC 1 preserves more files than the other computing systems, but the rate of data decay is higher than expected for a 1 TB hard disk drive with 4% utilization. The rapid data decay could be due to other factors that were not considered, including the observer effect [1], because, in the test setup, the application wrote to two log files and a database file that were resident on the drive. Also, beyond the first day, data decay was measured in terms of the percentage of entire files remaining, but several partially-decayed files persisted for several days. Such residual fragments are often critical to investigations and future work will examine persistent fragments more thoroughly.

7.   Conclusions

The digital body farm described in this chapter is designed to help study the deleted file decay process on storage media in a live computing system with NTFS. The methodology was validated by conducting tests on four computing systems. The results demonstrate some consistency with previous research on the mechanics of deleted file decay.

The next phase of the research is to collect the decay patterns exhibited by individual files as opposed to groups of files. The digital body farm will also be deployed in non-laboratory environments to ensure that the data collected is representative of real-world situations. In addition to deleted file decay data, file ecosystem data such as system configuration and usage profile data will be collected to provide context for the observed decay process. The dataset obtained will be employed to create a statistical/machine learning model that predicts (in terms of a confidence interval) the time it would take for a file on digital storage media to decay completely given the prevailing circumstances.

This is an ongoing study and future work will focus on ensuring data integrity. To obtain accurate results, it will be necessary to identify and isolate changes induced by the experimental setup used for observation and data collection, followed by deep analysis of the collected data. It is hoped that this research will provide insights into the intent underlying deletion events that would better inform digital forensic investigations.

The views expressed in this chapter are those of the authors, and do not reflect the official policy or position of MITRE Corporation or U.S. Government. This document has been approved for public release, distribution unlimited (Case #21-4005).

Acknowledgement

The authors wish to thank Vishal Ghadge, Vladimir Fedorov and John Matthew Thompson for their contributions and insights in developing the programs used in this research.

References

[1] K. Baclawski, The observer effect, *Proceedings of the IEEE Conference on Cognitive and Computational Aspects of Situation Management*, pp. 83–89, 2018.

[2] H. Balinsky, D. Subiros Perez and S. Simske, System call interception framework for data leak prevention, *Proceedings of the Fifteenth IEEE International Conference on Enterprise Distributed Object Computing*, pp. 139–148, 2011.

[3] S. Bunting, *EnCase Computer Forensics: The Official EnCase Certified Examiner Study Guide*, John Wiley and Sons, Indianapolis, Indiana, 2012.

[4] E. Casey, *Handbook of Digital Forensics and Investigation*, Elsevier, Burlington, Massachusetts, 2010.

[5] chex2chex, Digital-Body-Farm (DBF), GitHub (`www.github.com/chex2chex/Digital-Body-Farm`), 2021.

[6] Datarecovery.com, Will magnetic storage ever become completely obsolete? Edwardsville, Illinois (`www.datarecovery.com/20 20/07/will-magnetic-storage-ever-become-completely-obso lete`), July 17, 2020.

[7] K. Fairbanks, A technique for measuring data persistence using the Ext4 filesystem journal, *Proceedings of the Thirty-Ninth Annual IEEE Computer Software and Applications Conference*, vol. 3, pp. 18–23, 2015.

[8] K. Fairbanks and S. Garfinkel, Column: Factors affecting data decay, *Journal of Digital Forensics, Security and Law*, vol. 7(2), article no. 1, 2012.

[9] S. Garfinkel, A. Nelson and J. Young, A general strategy for differential forensic analysis, *Digital Investigation*, vol. 9(S), pp. S50–S59, 2012.

[10] J. Jones, Differential analysis as a data science tool for cyber security, *Proceedings of the International Conference on Advances and Applications of Data Science and Engineering*, pp. 29–32, 2016.

[11] J. Jones, Deleted audio file decay on a digital voice recorder, *Proceedings of the AES International Conference on Audio Forensics*, 2017.

[12] J. Jones and T. Khan, A method and implementation for the empirical study of deleted file persistence in digital devices and media, *Proceedings of the Seventh Annual IEEE Computing and Communication Workshop and Conference*, 2017.

[13] J. Jones, T. Khan, K. Laskey, A. Nelson, M. Laamanen and D. White, Inferring previously uninstalled applications from digital traces, *Proceedings of the Eleventh Annual Conference on Digital Forensics, Security and Law*, pp. 113-130, 2016.

[14] J. Jones, A. Srivastava, J. Mosier, C. Anderson and S. Buenafe, Understanding deleted file decay on removable media using differential analysis, *Proceedings of the Twelfth Annual Conference on Digital Forensics, Security and Law*, pp. 153–165, 2017.

[15] M. Laamanen and A. Nelson, NSRL Next Generation – Diskprinting, presented at *Forensics@NIST 2014* (`www.nsrl.nist.gov/Documents/Diskprints.pdf`), 2014.

[16] M. Liu, Z. Xue, X. Xu, C. Zhong and J. Chen, Host-based intrusion detection system with system calls: Review and future trends, *ACM Computing Surveys*, vol. 51(5), article no. 98, 2018.

[17] Microsoft, Delete File System Minifilter Driver, GitHub (`www.github.com/microsoft/Windows-driver-samples/tree/master/filesys/miniFilter/delete`), 2021.

[18] Microsoft, Hard Links and Junctions, Microsoft Technical Documentation, Redmond, Washington (`www.docs.microsoft.com/en-us/windows/win32/fileio/hard-links-and-junctions`), January 7, 2021.

[19] Microsoft, Introduction to Windows Service Applications, Microsoft Technical Documentation, Redmond, Washington (`www.docs.microsoft.com/en-us/dotnet/framework/windows-services/introduction-to-windows-service-applications`), September 15, 2021.

[20] Microsoft, File System Driver Samples, Microsoft Technical Documentation, Redmond, Washington (`www.docs.microsoft.com/en-us/windows-hardware/drivers/samples/file-system-driver-samples`), December 14, 2021.

[21] Microsoft, Filter Manager Concepts, Microsoft Technical Documentation, Redmond, Washington (`www.docs.microsoft.com/en-us/windows-hardware/drivers/ifs/filter-manager-concepts`), December 14, 2021.

[22] Microsoft, Signing a Driver, Microsoft Technical Documentation, Redmond, Washington (`www.docs.microsoft.com/en-us/windows-hardware/drivers/develop/signing-a-driver`), December 14, 2021.

[23] A. Nelson, Software Signature Derivation from Sequential Digital Forensic Analysis, Ph.D. Dissertation, Department of Computer Science, University of California Santa Cruz, Santa Cruz, California, 2016.

[24] A. Nisbet and R. Jacob, TRIM, wear leveling and garbage collection on solid state drives: A prediction model for forensic investigators, *Proceedings of the Eighteenth IEEE International Conference on Trust, Security and Privacy in Computing and Communications and Thirteenth IEEE International Conference on Big Data Science and Engineering*, pp. 419–426, 2019.

[25] Open Systems Resources, An Introduction to Standard and Isolation Minifilters, Manchester, New Hampshire (`www.osr.com/nt-insider/2017-issue2/introduction-standard-isolation-minifilters`), 2020.

[26] Python Software Foundation, `pyinstaller 4.10`, Fredericksburg, Virginia (`www.pypi.org/project/pyinstaller`), March 5, 2022.

[27] J. Vieyra, M. Scanlon and N. Le-Khac, Solid state drive forensics: Where do we stand? *Proceedings of the International Conference on Digital Forensics and Cyber Crime*, pp. 149–164, 2018.

[28] Wikipedia Contributors, Body farm, *Wikipedia* (`en.wikipedia.org/wiki/Body_farm`), 2022.

[29] P. Yosifovich, *Windows Kernel Programming*, Lean Publishing, Victoria, Canada, 2019.

[30] Z-DBackup Professional Backup Software, Z-Cron Windows Task and Backup Scheduler, Berlin, Germany (`www.z-cron.com`), 2022.

Chapter 2

REALISTIC AND CONFIGURABLE SYNTHESIS OF MALWARE TRACES IN WINDOWS SYSTEMS

Martin Lukner, Thomas Göbel and Harald Baier

Abstract   Malware constitutes a long-term challenge to the operation of contemporary information technology systems. A tremendous amount of realistic and current training data is necessary in order to train digital forensic professionals on the use of forensic tools and to update their skills. Unfortunately, very limited training data images are available, especially images of recent malware, for reasons such as privacy, competitive advantage, intellectual property rights and secrecy. A promising solution is to provide recent, realistic corpora produced by dataset synthesis frameworks. However, none of the publicly-available frameworks currently enables the creation of realistic malware traces in a customizable manner, where the synthesis of relevant traces can be configured to meet individual needs.

   This chapter presents a concept, implementation and validation of a synthesis framework that generates malware traces for Windows operating systems. The framework is able to generate coherent malware traces at three levels, random-access memory level, network level and hard drive level. A typical malware infection with data exfiltration is demonstrated as a proof of concept.

Keywords: Forensic datasets, data synthesis framework, malware traces, `hystck`

1.   Introduction

Contemporary digital forensic investigations are encountering large amounts of increasingly complex traces that have to be analyzed [18]. Meanwhile, attackers are using sophisticated techniques to obfuscate their traces. As a result, it is becoming increasing necessary to employ tools that automate portions of digital forensic investigations. Simul-

© IFIP International Federation for Information Processing 2022
Published by Springer Nature Switzerland AG 2022
G. Peterson and S. Shenoi (Eds.): DigitalForensics 2022, IFIP AICT 653, pp. 21–44, 2022.
https://doi.org/10.1007/978-3-031-10078-9_2

taneously, digital forensic professionals need to be trained to deal with complex traces [19].

Developing a digital forensic tool requires considerable effort. In addition to providing the required capabilities, the tool and the results it yields must be accepted in judicial proceedings. This requires the tool to meet certain criteria [5]. An important criterion is testing, which ensures that the tool has been evaluated thoroughly. This requires a large amount of real-world data with adequate coverage.

Unfortunately, labeled data sets are rare in the cyber security domain as well as in specialized areas such as network security, biometrics and digital forensics [1, 11, 13]. A study by Abt and Baier [1] reveals that 70% of the published papers in network security rely on self-compiled datasets and only 10% of the datasets are released to the public.

A key problem with publicly-available datasets is that they are often constructed for special research studies and may not adequately represent real-world scenarios. Another problem is the paucity of datasets. Malware analysis is an important task in contemporary digital forensic investigations, but publicly-available corpora containing traces of executed malware are exceedingly rare [13]. This situation is primarily due to reasons such as privacy, competitive advantage, intellectual property rights and secrecy. What is needed is a configurable tool that can automatically generate malware-related forensic images for forensic tool testing as well as for training forensic professionals.

This chapter presents a concept, implementation and validation of a synthesis framework that generates malware traces for the Microsoft Windows operating system. The concept and implementation leverage the `hystck` framework [12], which is extended by a malware generation module. The extension is able to imitate characteristics of recent malware. Unlike current synthesis frameworks, it provides coherent digital forensic traces at three levels, random-access memory (RAM) images, network dumps and persistent hard drive images. The source code of the malware synthesis extension is available at GitHub [3].

The synthesis framework focuses on Windows-based malware because of the large global footprint of computing systems running Microsoft Windows operating systems. According to Statista [30], roughly 84% of the malware released during the first quarter of 2020 affected Windows operating systems. The framework relies on a client-server malware infrastructure model. It considers different types of communications between a remote access tool and command-and-control server. Configuration files are employed to create various, easily adaptable real-world scenarios with the respective ground truths. The validation reveals that the implementation is successfully integrated in the `hystck` framework

Table 1. Overview of related work on forensic data synthesis.

Tool or Authors	Year	Type	Active	Tool Code Available	Image Types and Traces
Carrier [6]	2010	Man	No	NA	R,P
Hadi [14]	2011	Man	No	NA	P,M
Garfinkel et al. [11]	2009-14	Man	No	NA	P
NIST [26]	≤2019	Man	Yes	NA	R,N,P,M
Honeynet [31]	2010-15	Man	No	NA	N,P,M
ID2T [8]	2015	Syn	No	Yes	N,M
FLAME [4]	2008	Syn	No	No	N,M
Forensic Image Generator Generator [22]	2011	Syn	No	No	P
Forensic Test Image Generator [33]	2015	Syn	No	Yes	P
EviPlant [29]	2017	Syn	No	Yes	P
TraceGen [10]	2021	Syn	Yes	No	P,N
hystck [12]	2020	Syn	Yes	Yes	R,N,P

and that the configured traces exist at the RAM, network and hard drive levels to provide coherent pictures of malware infections.

2. Related Work

This section discusses related work in the context of dataset generation and shows that no publicly-available, configurable data synthesis framework exists for generating forensically-relevant images for malware investigations.

Grajeda et al. [13] have discussed the availability of datasets for digital forensics and what is missing. A key gap exists with regard to framework-generated datasets where the framework code is publicly available and holistic views of the datasets are possible. Of particular interest are datasets that provide volatile, network and persistent images, and forensically-relevant traces of malware activity.

Table 1 provides an overview of related work on forensic data synthesis. The first column lists the tool or authors (researchers), the second column indicates when the tool or image was last updated and the third column specifies if the forensic image was created manually (Man) or if the work relates to a synthesis tool (Syn). The active and code available columns indicate current support of the tool or image and code availability, respectively. The sixth (last column) deals with the image type and malware traces. A generated image type is designated by R for RAM,

N for network and P for persistent. An M designates if malware traces are present in the image or may be generated.

Manual Image Generation.   Manually-generated forensic images are commonly used for digital forensic practice and training purposes. Such forensic images have been created by Carrier [6], Hadi [14], Garfinkel et al. [11] and NIST [26]. If a forensic image is created manually, it can be assumed that all the traces it contains are intended.

However, manually-generated forensic images are difficult to modify because the entire images have to be created anew. As a result, there are relatively few manually-generated images. Also, some forensic images, notably the images created by Garfinkel et al. [9, 11], are subject to access restrictions imposed by U.S. law [9, 35]. Additionally, manually-generated images quickly become outdated because they use old hardware, operating systems and/or versions of installed software.

The static nature of manually-generated forensic images poses another problem. When images are used for forensic training purposes or in forensic challenge competitions, the solutions are disseminated over the Internet, which negatively impacts learning and training. Techniques are available to address this problem [34]. However, it is much easier to automatically create individual images based on parameters that are set in a configuration file before the data synthesis process and determine the traces in the resulting forensic image.

Network Traffic Generation.   Traffic generators produce network dumps for digital forensic investigations. The ID2T framework [8] enables the creation of labeled datasets for testing intrusion detection systems. Packet captures of arbitrary networks are collected and malicious traffic is injected into them to simulate network attacks such as distributed-denial-of-service attacks. ID2T also supports modern protocols such as IPv6.

FLAME [4] works in a manner similar to ID2T, but it generates network flows. The network flows contain basic information about grouped packets in flows specified in the NetFlow format and IPFIX standard.

Drive Image Generation.   Drive image generators enable the creation of forensic images of persistent storage devices such as hard drives, solid-state drives and USB drives. The Forensic Image Generator Generator [22, 23] demonstrates the feasibility of developing generators of forensic images for students. The input to the generator comprises scripts written by an instructor and the output comprises a filesystem image and an automatically-generated report in human-readable form that defines the ground truth. The Forensic Image Generator Generator creates traces in a virtual machine (VM), enabling the system settings to be modified as required. However, the framework is out-of-date and is no longer maintained.

The Forensic Test Image Generator (ForGe) [33], unlike the Forensic Image Generator Generator, provides a user interface. Input instructions are provided in the form of database entries and the output contains drive images and information sheets. Although the tool is available at GitHub [32], it has not been updated since 2015 and does not provide network logs or RAM dumps.

The EviPlant framework [29] is a more recent image generator. The framework makes use of a base drive image, which can be downloaded. Additionally, challenges or traces are available in the form of `evidence packages`. In order to obtain a forensically-relevant drive image, a chosen evidence package has to be injected into the base image. However, injecting consistent traces is very difficult and the manual work involved in creating traces is barely reduced.

Multilevel Image Generation. Multilevel image generators provide at least two of the three levels of images, volatile, network and persistent images. TraceGen [10] is a recent framework that captures network traces as well as hard drive traces. However, the approach is currently published as a proof of concept, meaning that no code is available. To combine the advantages of manual and automatic trace generation, APIs such as `pywinauto` [20] are used to simulate user interactions with the graphical user interface. For example, setting a registry key via the interface generates different traces than when setting a registry key via a command line. This also solves the problem of evidence packages in the `EviPlant` framework. It appears that all available scenarios are in the form of Python scripts or all individual actions are in lists. This does not make it very user-friendly, especially for users with limited technical experience.

The `hystck` [12] framework can create traces in RAM, network logs and hard drive images. This is done automatically using Python scripts or via YAML configuration files. Automated synthesis makes it possible to create a variety of traces with little effort. The traces can be distributed efficiently in template and differential images.

Summary. Unfortunately, existing data synthesis frameworks support the creation of limited scenarios. Typical malware behavior may be replicated by certain commands, but important aspects such as infection vectors or RAM artifacts and important events, such as Syslog events, are missing. Frameworks that mimic malware techniques, such as MITRE's Caldera [21], have different goals than the synthesis frameworks discussed above. For example, Caldera can be used for red or blue team operations as well as for testing servers or security teams whereas frameworks such as `hystck` generate traces in template virtual machines in large quantities in an automated manner. Table 1 shows that no framework exists that combines the advantages of automated synthesis and malware trace generation. Moreover, the manually-created datasets containing RAM dumps, network captures and drive images are not coherent. In contrast, `hystck` is the only synthesis framework that provides coherent multilevel traces. This is where the work described in this chapter begins and it ultimately enables the creation of complex malware scenarios that are not generated by any other framework.

3.   Forensic Dataset Synthesis Framework

Instead of creating a new framework for synthesizing malware traces from scratch, it was decided to extend `hystck`, the existing framework with the best fit. The extended `hystck` framework must create digital forensic traces by simulating natural human-computer interactions. The generated traces are intended to be as indistinguishable as possible from real-world RAM snapshots, network traffic and hard drive images.

In order to have good control over the generated traces, `hystck` employs a virtualization solution that leverages KVM and QEMU. The actual implementation makes use of Python because a platform-independent programming language enables the creation of traces for different guest operating systems.

The `hystck` framework has a client-server architecture (Figure 1). The server is responsible for controlling the client, which runs in the background and controls the guest's graphical user interface via an interaction manager. To prevent control traffic and forensically-relevant Internet traffic from mixing, the client component communicates using two network cards, an Internet card and a local network card. The local network is only used for control traffic between the client and server. Packets are captured at the Internet network interface using the `tcpdump` tool and stored in a PCAP file.

A template file is used as a base for each image that is created. The Linux, Windows 7 and Windows 10 operating systems are supported at this time. Important settings, such as the number of virtual machines to be created, template file names, IP addresses and actions to be taken, are stored in a text-based configuration file and are easily adapted. The `hystck` generator component (Figure 2) facilitates the creation of large

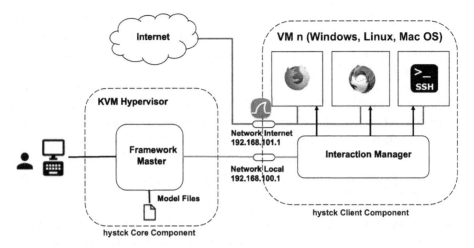

Figure 1. `hystck` architecture [12].

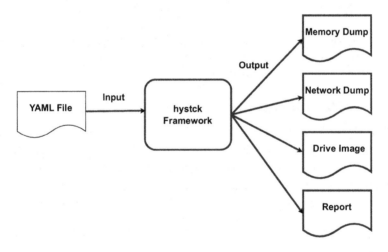

Figure 2. Generator component workflow [12].

amounts of traces using an easy-to-configure YAML file, eliminating the need to code complex Python scripts.

The actual creation of traces is accomplished by cloning the template virtual machine and establishing a connection with the guest virtual machine. Following this, sniffers are started on the corresponding interfaces and the desired actions are carried out by the agents on the virtual machines. Finally, the memory content is captured, the `tcpdump` tool is terminated and the captured contents are made available as RAM dumps and PCAP files. The PCAP files contain the forensically-relevant traces that should be explicitly generated as well as additional network traffic (e.g., realistic background noise corresponding to network communications of standard operating system services such as updates). In addition to creating PCAP files, `hystck` can create persistent drive images with the drive image generator. Several applications can be emulated and updated constantly due to the modular architecture. The applications are controlled via simple guest user interaction models. This makes it almost impossible to distinguish a generated image from an image created by real user interactions. Additional services such as email and file services required by the data synthesis process are provided by separate service virtual machines.

At the end of the data synthesis process, all the changes made, whether malicious or benign, are summarized by the reporting component. These are compiled into an XML-based report file that informs the user about all the generated traces.

4.   Malware Dataset Synthesis

This section describes the approach for creating a forensic image generation framework that provides malware traces at the volatile (RAM), network and persistent (hard drive) levels.

4.1   Requirements

The malware dataset synthesis approach relies on the `hystck` framework because it is the only currently-maintained framework that publishes its code, is configurable and enables the generation of traces at the three desired levels. The requirements are defined to enable the development of realistic, complex scenarios. The `hystck` extension should make it possible to create malware traces in RAM, network traffic and on the hard drive. During real malware analysis, a digital forensic professional is usually confronted with traces such as command-and-control communications patterns, various persistence mechanisms and other artifacts created by malware. A client-server architecture is required to generate all these types of artifacts.

In particular, the proof-of-concept implementation uses the Windows registry, the creation of a service and dynamic link library search-order hijacking for persistence mechanisms. From an analyst's point of view, the Windows registry has the advantage of occurring twice, volatile in the RAM dump and persistently on the hard drive. To simulate as many different scenarios as possible, several protocols that are typically encountered during malware infections are employed. One is HTTP, which enables the transfer of large files. A second protocol is raw TCP

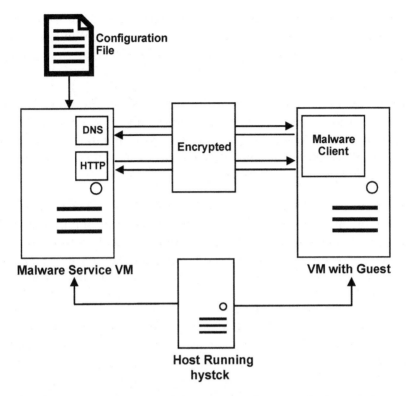

Figure 3. High-level architecture of the `hystck` malware synthesis extension.

transfer. A third is DNS, which is used less frequently by malware, but offers advantages in networks with firewalls because DNS traffic is often not filtered and is essential for a network to function. To create different levels of difficulty during forensic analyses, various encoding schemes and encryption methods are implemented. Indeed, the algorithms commonly used by malware authors are employed; these include Base64 as an encoding scheme and RC4 and AES for encryption. In order to focus forensic analysis on the various traces left by the malware as well as to realize different attack vectors, the client component must be delivered to the target system using different droppers in different ways.

4.2 Framework Architecture

Figure 3 shows the high-level architecture of the `hystck` malware synthesis extension. Several components are required to implement the desired functionality. The host needs a running instance of `hystck`. In order to use the malware synthesis component, the framework extension requires a server component and a client component. Since the malware service has to be implemented in C++ to use typical Windows libraries, it is necessary to integrate a second Windows service virtual machine (malware service VM), which serves as a command-and-control server, in addition to the existing Linux service virtual machine. The malware service virtual machine can be configured dynamically, which simplifies the integration of new scenarios. Additionally, the guest virtual machines of `hystck` are augmented with a corresponding malware client component. Communications between the client and server components employ the network protocols mentioned above.

Droppers and Delivery. Malware can be delivered by the client component in multiple ways. In the proof-of-concept implementation, a Microsoft Office macro is used as a dropper that downloads the entire malware. The dropper can be used as a normal variant and as a variant with special properties for bypassing antivirus software. To pass malware checks unhindered, VBA-stomping is employed, which exploits the undocumented property of VBA macros whereby only contained p-code is executed instead of the VBA macro code [7, 15, 16]. To create appropriate Microsoft Office documents, the EvilClippy tool available at GitHub [27] can be used. As an infection vector, the framework supports the delivery of malware in an automated manner via browser download, automated email delivery and automated download via the command line using `curl`.

Configurable Forensic Scenario Synthesis. In order to create as many different malware scenarios as possible and prevent digital forensic professionals from attaching importance to unimportant things, the server component for malware synthesis is generally first configured at startup using a JSON-like configuration file that is specific to each scenario. The advantage of a dynamically-configurable server component is also evident when, for example, multiple forensic images must be generated for machine learning algorithms. The configuration file enables a framework user to specify in advance exactly which commands should be executed during data synthesis. After the malware is launched on the target system, it gradually requests the commands to be executed.

Figure 4 shows the configurable malware scenario synthesis workflow. After all the commands in the configuration file have been executed, a special command is sent that finally terminates the malware on the victim machine. After the synthesis process, the intended traces should be present in the generated memory and hard drive images for subsequent forensic analysis. In addition, all the network traffic between the client

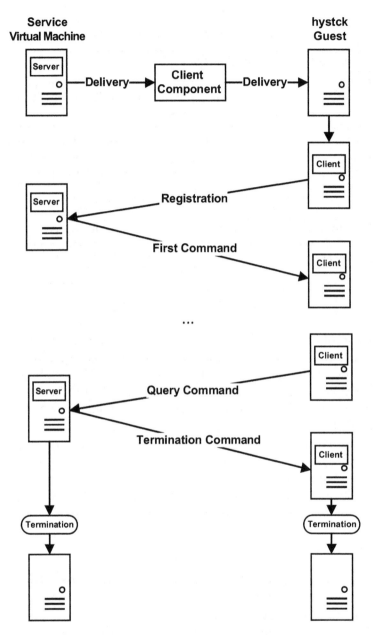

Figure 4. Configurable malware scenario synthesis workflow.

and server is stored in the PCAP files that are automatically generated by hystck.

Table 2. Malware synthesis commands.

Command	Explanation
Nothing	Does nothing and exists only for testing purposes
Execute	Executes arbitrary commands via the Microsoft Windows command line
Download	Downloads a file from the server to the client
Upload	Sends an arbitrary file from the client to the server
Hollow	Starts a new process via process hollowing
Inject	Loads a dynamic link library by injecting code into a running process
Persistence_Registry	Sets up a persistence mechanism by creating a registry key
Persistence_Service	Achieves persistence by creating a service
Change_Interval	Changes the query interval for new commands
Persistence_DLL	Creates a persistence mechanism by dynamic link library search-order hijacking

The proof-of-concept implementation has adequate commands for typical malware behavior as well as for leaving the corresponding traces in the memory and drive images. Table 2 describes the commands that are currently implemented for malware synthesis. In the future, new commands will be introduced to increase the functionality of the malware component.

Additional traces are created by droppers depending on the exact scenario configuration. For example, it is possible to download the main malware component at one time via a Microsoft Office macro or to download malware in multiple stages and then launch it by process hollowing. Depending on the configuration files, additional traces can be created in user accounts (e.g., user email accounts) as well as in the RAM and hard drive images during synthesis.

Communications and Encryption. Since a key requirement for the client and server components is to support multiple protocol types, the proof-of-concept implementation supports Base64 encoding and RC4 and AES encryption implemented via Microsoft's CryptoAPI in addition to the plaintext mode. The different protocol types enable a framework user to map different levels of difficulty to a scenario that would become apparent during subsequent forensic analysis.

The communications include client requests for commands, server commands in response and client notifications of command execution results. All encoding and encryption types can be used via HTTP as

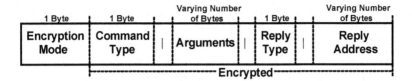

Figure 5. Malware control command structure.

well as DNS. In the case of HTTP, the initial request is made by a GET request; all subsequent requests are made by POST requests where the POST data contains the results. Communications via DNS use TXT records and domain names. The DNS server is implemented to respond to each request strictly according to the configuration file. When the client makes a request, a corresponding DNS response is created that contains a TXT record with the next command. The message about the execution status is specified by the domain name in the next request. Due to the protocol limitations, it may be necessary to append multiple TXT records [24]. In any case, regardless of the chosen protocol, all the commands have the form shown in Figure 5.

A separate protocol and encryption type can be chosen for each command. For example, it is possible to retrieve the first command via HTTP in plaintext and the second command Base64-encoded via DNS. In the case of HTTP, files for the upload and download commands are transferred via POST requests. In the case of DNS, a requested file is opened on the server side via the configuration file. It is then transferred to the client via TXT records. Again, the limitations of the DNS protocol must be considered, so it may be necessary to send more than one request per file. If a file is to be transferred from the client to the server, even more requests are necessary. The file is transferred in the requested domain name.

To avoid invalid characters, the HTTP and DNS protocols transfer files exclusively using Base64 encoding. This limits file uploads via DNS to about 40 bytes per request. However, normal Base64 is not used to avoid invalid characters. Since domain names do not support "=" and multiple dots, no trailing characters are introduced for padding purposes in an encoding; instead, it is adapted to the length during decoding. For the same reason, all the data encrypted using RC4 or AES is encoded with the same special Base64 variant.

Static keys exist for AES and DNS communications. Depending on the chosen configuration, the key can be extracted during subsequent forensic analysis from the executable located in the RAM dump, from the PCAP file or from the hard drive.

Notification and Validation. Notification of success or failure is done via POST data for HTTP and requested domain for DNS. In the case of HTTP, only the string `success` or `failed` is sent. In the case of DNS, a simple request is made to `SUCCESS.com` or `FAILED.com`. The success or failure message is then output via `stdout` so that the user of the synthesis framework is informed about the status of the generated image. Furthermore, the `hystck` reporting function is used to inform the user of the synthesis framework about all the automated user actions performed and, thus, about the underlying ground truth in the output images.

5.   Malware Synthesis Module Integration

The `hystck` framework makes it possible to create scenarios via test scripts and via its generator component [12]. Test scripts have the advantage that they are precisely configurable as Python scripts and can, therefore, also generate arbitrary scenarios that are not covered by the generator component. The generator, on the other hand, enables scenarios to be configured using YAML files, which allows less technical users to create scenarios. The malware synthesis extension supports image generation using test scripts and the generator component.

5.1   Data Synthesis Using Test Scripts

In order not to block the main thread and to enable data synthesis, the login to the service virtual machine and the start of the server component should be executed in separate threads. The server component can then be started with the configuration file via SSH as shown in Figure 6. For simplicity, the configuration file is already present in the server in the example workflow. However, it is also possible to transfer the configuration file to the server via the SSH connection before malware synthesis starts. The thread in which the server component is started does not end until the server component is terminated.

To better understand the workflow in Figure 6, it is necessary to clarify selected persistence mechanism search-order hijacking. In the passed configuration file, the malware is requested to download a dynamic link library suitable for persistence and to set up a persistence mechanism in the client. The command-and-control server terminates automatically, which ends the thread. The main thread waits for this thread to terminate and then shuts down the virtual machine to test the persistence mechanism. Before restarting the virtual machine, the server component of the malware is restarted in a thread using the same function. This time, however, there is a different configuration file with different control

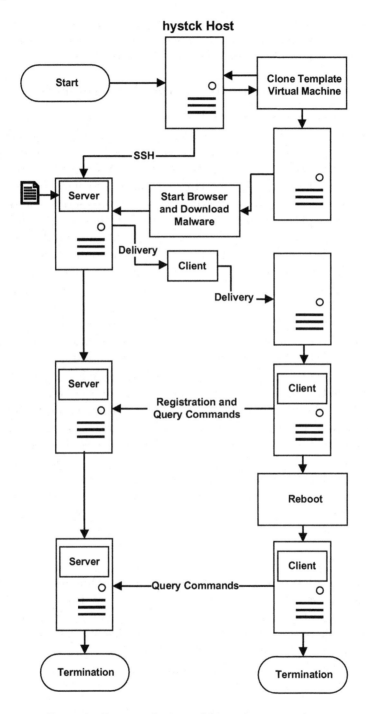

Figure 6. Data synthesis workflow using test scripts.

commands. Thus, if the malware is started again on the client due to the persistence mechanism, it connects to the server and executes the commands stored in the configuration file and terminates.

5.2   Data Synthesis Using the Generator

Aside from the test scripts that have to be programmed manually, the generator is the most important component of the hystck framework. The generator enables a user with limited technical skills to easily configure the data synthesis process using a YAML file, automatically generating a large number of traces rapidly and with relatively little effort. This is only partially the case with test scripts because they sometimes require several hundred lines of Python code to achieve the same functionality. In addition to the actual commands executed on the client, the YAML configuration file specifies information such as the service virtual machine (command-and-control server) address, email to be synthesized (e.g., for a phishing scenario), exact download paths and ports.

An important point has to be considered to integrate malware functionality in the generator. During the normal execution of the generator, the order of actions to be performed is shuffled randomly before execution, so it is not known which functions have completed and which have not. While this is not a problem when accessing a large number of websites, it can be problematic to obtain the correct malware component functionality. For example, before each scenario, it is necessary to ensure that malware has been downloaded or that a persistence mechanism has been created. Otherwise, an attempt could be made to execute the malware before it is delivered to the target system. The configuration settings passed to the YAML file are, therefore, only executed on restart if a persistence mechanism was previously set up or after the malware was downloaded. Figure 7 shows the data synthesis workflow using the generator.

The configuration files passed in a YAML file look very similar to the configuration files of the server component. Only special commands are added, for example, to trigger a restart. Within the YAML file, new collection types for the configuration files and application types are added for the malware component. This makes it possible to configure various parameters such as server IP addresses and download paths. Figure 8 shows an example YAML file.

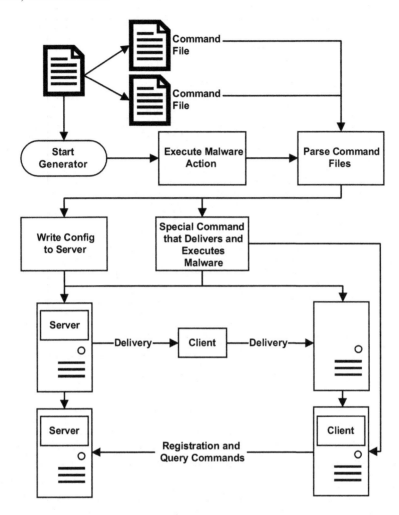

Figure 7. Data synthesis workflow using the generator.

6. Generated Dataset Validation

The dataset generated via data synthesis was validated by examining volatile RAM dumps, PCAP network traffic files and persistent drive images. Multiple evaluation phases were performed that focused on where and how traces could be found during a forensic investigation. This proved the existence of traces after data synthesis and, thus, validated the correct functioning of the proof-of-concept implementation.

RAM Dump. To find relevant traces in a RAM dump, it is necessary to first locate the malicious process. The traces differ depending on

```
 1. name: hystck example
 2. author: Lukner, Goebel, Baier
 3. collections:
 4.    c-malware-1:
 5.       type:          malware
 6.       commands:      /data/hystck/examples/generator/
                            collections/malware1.txt
 7.       email:         /data/hystck/examples/data/
                            email_hay.xml
 8. applications:
 9.    malware-1:
10.       type:          malware
11.       service-vm:    192.168.122.219
12.       name:          MalwareBot.exe
13.       dnsServer:     192.168.122.219
14.       webServer:     192.168.122.219
15.       webPort:       7777
16.       service-port:  8080
17.       beacon:        3
18.       path:          C:\users\hystck\Desktop
19. hay:
20. needles:
21.    h-malware-2:
22.       application:   malware-1
23.       collection:    c-malware-1
```

Figure 8.   Example YAML file.

when the RAM dump was created and which commands were executed. It is important to record handles and open network connections that are only valid during command execution. It can be difficult to acquire data from RAM at exactly the right time. Therefore, the query interval was extended and an automated RAM capture feature was incorporated in hystck.

Depending on the executed commands, a suspicious process can be detected by various characteristics in a RAM dump, such as open network connections and the process list. Depending on the chosen configuration of the malware synthesizer, certain anomalies may occur. First, an investigation could determine that an unknown process was started by dumping the process list regardless of the process name. Second, the process may appear in the open network connections linked to a UDP connection and to a TCP connection. A UDP connection could be suspicious because it would not belong to the DNS server in the system and a TCP connection could look suspicious because of the port used. Third, strings such as http://192.168.122.219:8080/MalwareBot.exe that provide information about the process origin would be discovered. After a malicious process is found, it can be extracted from memory using the Volatility tool and analyzed to discover its true functionality. By reverse engineering the executable, even the keys used in communications could be recovered. Fourth, traces of persistence mechanisms can be found in the process list based on the associated parent processes and the paths of the loaded dynamic link libraries of the processes.

Since malware can execute arbitrary code using `cmd` commands and download additional code and files, any number of additional traces can be created in RAM during data synthesis. If the malware performs operations such as uploads and downloads, then it is possible that handles to the corresponding files would still be open in memory. This information enables conclusions to be drawn about the exfiltrated data and downloaded malware code.

When the Inject command is executed, memory is allocated in the target process and the name of the dynamic link library to be loaded is written to the memory area. With the help of the `malfind` plugin, which recognizes such memory areas based on page permissions, the dynamic link library injection could be found. Another code injection technique that is not detected by `malfind` is process hollowing, when a process is started in the suspended mode and its executable is replaced by another executable. However, this can be detected using another Volatility plugin that is available at GitHub [25].

Network Traffic. Depending on the scenario and encoding or encryption method used, network traffic can be easy or rather difficult to analyze. The traces that can be extracted from network traffic include exfiltrated data in addition to the control commands sent. An infection can be detected in several ways, including a running malicious process in RAM, network anomalies or traces on a hard drive.

Suspicious DNS behavior in the proof-of-concept implementation may involve a large number of DNS requests with many TXT records occurring during a file transfer, especially when the requests are directed to a server that is not set as the DNS server for the system. The associated IP address would be of considerable interest during further analysis. Depending on the selected configuration, the entire malicious executable could be extracted and analyzed or at least the amount of exfiltrated data could be estimated from the capture. By choosing static keys, it would be possible to recover the RC4 and AES encryption keys by reverse engineering and thus decrypt the transmitted commands and identify the exfiltrated data.

Persistent Drive Image. Depending on the chosen malware settings, malware would leave various traces in the filesystem, browser download history and user email program. The ability to execute arbitrary code using `hystck` functions enables a large number of traces to be created. Examples include hiding traces by setting file attributes or generating arbitrary email for synthesizing a supply chain attack. Furthermore, persistence mechanisms could create additional traces. These traces would be found in the filesystem, for example, when using dynamic link library search-order hijacking or in the Windows Registry (e.g., a key under `HKCU\Software\Microsoft\Windows\CurrentVersion\Run`) or due to execution via an autostart service.

Reporting. The malware components on the client and server output information via `stdout` for each executed command. In the case of the malware client, this is more for testing purposes because the output is not sent to the server; instead, the server is only informed whether or not the action was successful. This avoids additional network traffic, which should be kept to a minimum in the case of malware.

During automated execution, the server output is available to a framework user on the console during runtime and in a `hystck` report. This includes information about the success or failure of the last operation, beacon data and the next command sent to the malware. It would not be possible to validate the traces retroactively because implementing a command to execute arbitrary `cmd` commands would produce almost any number of traces. As a result, it would not be possible to validate the traces on the fly. However, in most cases, it can be assumed that the desired traces are present when the server receives feedback that execution was successful.

7.   Conclusions

The extension of the `hystck` data synthesis framework developed in this research generates coherent malware traces for Windows operating systems at the RAM, network and hard drive levels. This enables the creation of realistic corpora that are needed to train digital forensic professionals on the use of forensic tools and to update their skills.

The new malware module integrated in `hystck` works with the generator component as well as test scripts. The new module makes it possible to create targeted malware scenarios as well as combine new malware features with existing `hystck` components. The server and client malware components are configured using JSON-like configuration files that contain large sets of implemented commands that generate malware traces.

The extended `hystck` data synthesis framework was validated using test scenarios for which coherent malware traces were created in RAM dumps, PCAP files and hard drive images. The validation reveals that the malware module is successfully integrated in the `hystck` framework and that configured traces exist at the RAM, network and hard drive levels to provide coherent pictures of malware infections. The framework incorporates a report module that records all the actions performed during data synthesis and, thus, all the generated artifacts. The resulting report provides the labeled ground truth and enables users to get a holistic picture of all the relevant traces existing in the generated RAM, network and hard drive images.

Future research will extend the data synthesis framework with additional malware-specific commands, network protocols, encryption types and persistence mechanisms to provide more configurable options for the data synthesis process, including obfuscating malicious control traffic and providing a variety of persistence techniques. In some places, constants are already reserved for extensions such as reserved flags for using raw TCP and providing full IPv6 support.

A limitation of the current framework is that the only dropper available is a Microsoft Office macro. Therefore, future work will implement additional droppers to represent alternative infection vectors, including a PDF document dropper.

Due to problems arising from the connectionless nature of the DNS protocol, it will be necessary to include sequence numbers in DNS communications to prevent file transfers from failing and transmitted commands from being lost. Additionally, the current implementation only uses the standard DNS port 53, which will be expanded.

References

[1] S. Abt and H. Baier, Are we missing labels? A study of the availability of ground truth in network security research, *Proceedings of the Third International Workshop on Building Analysis Datasets and Gathering Experience Returns for Security*, pp. 40–55, 2014.

[2] I. Baggili and F. Breitinger, Data sources for advancing cyber forensics: What the social world has to offer, *Proceedings of the AAAI Spring Symposia – Sociotechnical Behavior Mining: From Data to Decisions?* pp. 6–9, 2015.

[3] Biometrics and Information Security Group (`dasec`), `hystck-malware-module`, GitHub (`github.com/dasec/hystck-malware-module`), 2022.

[4] D. Brauckhoff, A. Wagner and M. May, FLAME: A flow-level anomaly modeling engine, *Proceedings of the Conference on Cyber Security Experimentation and Test*, article no. 1, 2008.

[5] B. Carrier, Open Source Digital Forensic Tools: The Legal Argument, @stake, Cambridge, Massachusetts, 2002.

[6] B. Carrier, Digital Forensics Tool Testing Images (`www.dftt.sourceforge.net`), 2010.

[7] R. Cole, A. Moore, G. Stark and B. Stancill, STOMP 2 DIS: Brilliance in the (visual) basics, Mandiant, Reston, Virginia (`www.mandiant.com/resources/stomp-2-dis-brilliance-in-the-visual-basics`), February 5, 2020.

[8] C. Cordero, E. Vasilomanolakis, N. Milanov, C. Koch, D. Hausheer and M. Muhlhauser, ID2T: A DIY dataset creation toolkit for intrusion detection systems, *Proceedings of the IEEE Conference on Communications and Network Security*, pp. 739–740, 2015.

[9] Digital Corpora, Home (`www.digitalcorpora.org`), 2021.

[10] X. Du, C. Hargreaves, J. Sheppard and M. Scanlon, TraceGen: User activity emulation for digital forensic test image generation, *Digital Investigation*, vol. 38(S), article no. 301133, 2021.

[11] S. Garfinkel, P. Farrell, V. Roussev and G. Dinolt, Bringing science to digital forensics with standardized forensic corpora, *Digital Investigation*, vol. 6(S), pp. S2–S11, 2009.

[12] T. Göbel, T. Schäfer, J. Hachenberger, J. Türr and H. Baier, A novel approach for generating synthetic datasets for digital forensics, in *Advances in Digital Forensics XVI*, G. Peterson and S. Shenoi (Eds.), Springer, Cham, Switzerland, pp. 73–93, 2020.

[13] C. Grajeda, F. Breitinger and I. Baggili, Availability of datasets for digital forensics – And what is missing, *Digital Investigation*, vol. 22(S), pp. S94–S105, 2017.

[14] A. Hadi, Digital Forensic Challenge Images (Datasets), Champlain College, Burlington, Vermont (`www.ashemery.com/dfir.html`), 2011.

[15] N. Harbour, Flare-On 7 challenge solutions, Mandiant, Reston, Virginia (`www.mandiant.com/resources/flare-7-challenge-solutions`), October 23, 2020.

[16] S. Hegt, Evil Clippy: MS Office maldoc assistant, *Outflank Blog*, Amsterdam, The Netherlands (`www.outflank.nl/blog/2019/05/05/evil-clippy-ms-office-maldoc-assistant`), May 5, 2019.

[17] J. Huang, A. Yasinsac and P. Hayes, Knowledge sharing and reuse in digital forensics, *Proceedings of the Fifth IEEE International Workshop on Systematic Approaches to Digital Forensic Engineering*, pp. 73–78, 2010.

[18] D. Lillis, B. Becker, T. O'Sullivan and M. Scanlon, Current challenges and future research areas for digital forensic investigations, *Proceedings of the Eleventh Annual Conference on Digital Forensics, Security and Law*, 2016.

[19] J. Liu, Ten-year synthesis review: A baccalaureate program in computer forensics, *Proceedings of the Seventeenth Annual Conference on Information Technology Education and the Fifth Annual Conference on Research in Information Technology*, pp. 121–126, 2016.

[20] M. McMahon and Contributors, What is `pywinauto`? (`pywinauto.readthedocs.io/en/latest`), 2018.

[21] MITRE Corporation, Caldera, GitHub (`github.com/mitre/caldera`), 2021.

[22] C. Moch and F. Freiling, The Forensic Image Generator Generator (Forensig^2), *Proceedings of the Fifth International Conference on IT Security Incident Management and IT Forensics*, pp. 78–93, 2009.

[23] C. Moch and F. Freiling, Evaluating the Forensic Image Generator Generator, *Proceedings of the International Conference on Digital Forensics and Cyber Crime*, pp. 238–252, 2011.

[24] P. Mockapetris, Domain Names – Implementation and Specification, RFC 1035, 1987.

[25] `monnappa22`, HollowFind, GitHub (`github.com/monnappa22/HollowFind`), 2016.

[26] National Institute of Standards and Technology, The CFReDS Project, Gaithersburg, Maryland (`www.cfreds.nist.gov`), 2019.

[27] Outflank, Evil Clippy, GitHub (`github.com/outflanknl/EvilClippy`), 2021.

[28] Quarkslab, LIEF Project, GitHub (`github.com/lief-project/LIEF`), 2022.

[29] M. Scanlon, X. Du and D. Lillis, EviPlant: An efficient digital forensics challenge creation, manipulation and distribution solution, *Digital Investigation*, vol. 20(S), pp. S29–S36, 2017.

[30] Statista, Operating systems most affected by malware as of 1st quarter 2020, New York (`www.statista.com/statistics/680943/malware-os-distribution`), April 11, 2022.

[31] The Honeynet Project, Challenges (`www.honeynet.org/challenges`), 2022.

[32] H. Visti, ForGe, Forensic Test Image Generator, GitHub (`github.com/hannuvisti/forge`), 2015.

[33] H. Visti, S. Tohill and P. Douglas, Automatic creation of computer forensic test images, in *Computational Forensics*, U. Garain and F. Shafait (Eds.), Springer, Cham, Switzerland, pp. 163–175, 2015.

[34] K. Woods, C. Lee, S. Garfinkel, D. Dittrich, A. Russell and K. Kearton, Creating realistic corpora for security and forensic education, *Proceedings of the Sixth Annual Conference on Digital Forensics, Security and Law*, 2011.

[35] Y. Yannikos, L. Graner, M. Steinebach and C. Winter, Data corpora for digital forensics education and research, in *Advances in Digital Forensics X*, G. Peterson and S. Shenoi (Eds.), Springer, Berlin Heidelberg, Germany, pp. 309–325, 2014.

II

MOBILE DEVICE FORENSICS

Chapter 3

SMARTPHONE DATA DISTRIBUTIONS AND REQUIREMENTS FOR REALISTIC MOBILE DEVICE FORENSIC CORPORA

Patrik Goncalves, Andreas Attenberger and Harald Baier

Abstract   Mobile devices such as smartphones are carried and used constantly by people in their daily lives and, therefore, play important roles in forensic investigations. As a result, digital forensic professionals are confronted with large numbers of devices with data that has to be extracted and analyzed. The education and training of forensic experts and the development and evaluation of smartphone forensic tools require copious amounts of realistic data. Unfortunately, secrecy and privacy considerations limit the availability of real digital forensic data. Smartphone datasets for training and testing are sparse and unrealistic, and knowledge about data distributions in real smartphones is limited.

   This chapter presents the results of a survey of law enforcement professionals from two countries that sought to understand the typical data residing in smartphones encountered in criminal investigations, with the goal of supporting the creation of publicly-available forensic datasets. The typical data extracted from smartphones using current forensic tools is presented; this data is divided into two forensic classes, relevant and irrelevant. Additionally, the chapter discusses current problems encountered by mobile device forensic professionals and opportunities for future research.

Keywords: Smartphones, investigations, datasets, data distributions

1.   Introduction

Mobile devices such as smartphones, tablets, wearable computers and Internet of Things devices are carried and used by people in their daily lives and, therefore, play important roles in forensic investigations. In fact, law enforcement professionals encounter increasing numbers of portable devices compared with stationary devices such as desktop comput-

G. Peterson and S. Shenoi (Eds.): DigitalForensics 2022, IFIP AICT 653, pp. 47–63, 2022.
https://doi.org/10.1007/978-3-031-10078-9_3

ers in forensic investigations [2]. Since smartphones incorporate embedded sensors and enable users to adapt their functionality by installing custom applications, they contain valuable information about user activities and their contexts (e.g., business, social and criminal contexts) [13].

Law enforcement professionals employ a number of forensic tools to extract and analyze relevant information from smartphones. Since the results are included in final reports presented in court proceedings, it is mandatory that the forensic tools are validated against realistic test datasets to minimize false positives and false negatives. Unfortunately, using real datasets drawn from confiscated devices to validate forensic tools is not an option due to ongoing investigations [15] and data protection regulations such as the European Union's General Data Protection Regulation [5]. Some researchers have clearances or authorizations that enable them to use real data, but this is a very small group and the results may not be available for public use. As a result, the only options available to the digital forensics community are to use data from public sources or create their own training and testing datasets.

Synthetic forensic data, like real forensic data encountered in investigations, should convey scenarios involving criminal and non-criminal activities. Defining realistic scenarios is not easy because it requires detailed knowledge about criminal and non-criminal behavior and how smartphones are used in these contexts. Realistic scenarios are best created by interacting with experts, especially law enforcement professionals with extensive experience extracting and analyzing data from seized smartphones.

Complex forensic scenarios are typically created and published by dedicated working groups that draw on the knowledge and experience of experts. A key drawback of published datasets is that their scenarios and contents do not change. Researchers with resources and time often create their own forensic datasets to suit their needs. However, Grajeda et al. [8] report that such datasets are shared in a limited manner or not shared at all.

A digital forensic professional uses various forensic tools to obtain all the information that is available to answer a set of investigative questions. Some of the information is labeled as relevant and the rest is labeled as irrelevant. The labeling process is not simple; it depends greatly on the specific investigation and the information recovered in the investigation. Thus, a researcher who seeks to create a synthetic forensic dataset must know what constitutes typical relevant and irrelevant information and where the information resides in smartphones.

An important use case for a forensic dataset is to validate forensic tools against the ground truth. The ground truth is expressed by correctly-labeled data corresponding to the categorization of digital artifacts into task-relevant and task-irrelevant data. Unfortunately, Abt and Baier [1] note that publicly-available datasets often do not provide ground truth data. This missing labeled data problem hinders research and development efforts focused on novel forensic tools and methods. The absence of labeled data also hinders the comparability and repeatability of results.

Technological advances make it particularly challenging to keep up with the data content of smartphones. Smartphone content can be categorized by file class (picture, video or document file) or entry class found in one or more files (contacts, chat messages, browser log entries or geospatial data). Having collected all the content in a smartphone, it is possible to state that the device contains certain numbers of files and entries with certain statistical distributions. Abt and Baier [1] note that statistical properties may be used to assess the quality of synthetic data sets with respect to real data. The statistical properties may also be extended to assess manually-created data sets.

Employing a statistical approach requires knowledge about the data distributions in smartphones, but this knowledge is currently missing. In order to address the problem, this research focuses on acquiring knowledge about smartphone data distributions. Specifically, a survey was conducted of law enforcement professionals to obtain detailed information about smartphone data content. All the survey participants were digital forensics experts who actively worked on extracting and analyzing smartphone data.

The survey focused on the contents of a representative smartphone that would be acquired and analyzed by a law enforcement professional to gain insights into data statistics. The representative contents were labeled into typical task-relevant and task-irrelevant content. The survey also attempted to understand the problems encountered by the participants while conducting forensic examinations of smartphones with the goal of articulating law enforcement needs related to mobile device forensics.

The research results are intended to assist the mobile device forensics community in creating synthetic datasets and employing statistical properties to compare the synthetic datasets against the data contained in real mobile devices. The insights gained into the problems encountered by law enforcement professionals are intended to enable the mobile device forensics community to help address current and future law enforcement needs.

2.   Related Work

This section discusses work published between 2010 and 2021 on assessing the problems encountered by digital forensic professionals and their needs related to mobile device forensics. The section also discusses efforts focused on creating realistic mobile device datasets for forensic tool testing and evaluation. The literature review leveraged four leading research publisher databases and two scientific research search engines:

- **IEEE Xplore** (`ieeexplore.ieee.org`).

- **ACM Digital Library** (`dl.acm.org`).

- **Elsevier ScienceDirect** (`www.sciencedirect.com`).

- **Springer Link** (`link.springer.com`).

- **Google Scholar** (`scholar.google.com`).

- **ResearchGate** (`www.researchgate.net`).

In 2010, Garfinkel [6] published his seminal work on the state of the art of digital forensics and the future of digital forensics research. He described the challenges that existed and how to make future research in digital forensics more efficient. A key finding was the absence of standardized file formats and forensic tools, which needed to be addressed by collaborative efforts involving practitioners, researchers and industry. However, while this work mentioned mobile device forensics, it did not address the need to understand and process large amounts of diverse mobile device data.

Motivated by the challenges faced by network forensic practitioners, Woods et al. [15], in 2011, published their experience creating the M57-Patents dataset comprising realistic traffic involving multiple networked devices. The M57-Patents dataset was the result of a workshop attended by several experts who created a realistic scenario with criminal activity. The primary objectives were to provide answer keys (ground truths of scenarios) with realistic digital artifacts generated from applications, networking and background processes. The resulting disk images, traffic dumps, RAM dumps and other evidentiary data were published to advance network forensics education and training. The work of Woods and colleagues has motivated this research focused on smartphone data content and distributions.

In 2016, Lillis et al. [9] identified technical challenges in the digital forensics domain based on an extensive review of the contemporary literature. A key problem for digital forensic professionals was coping with the numbers, heterogeneities and data volumes of mobile devices. They also discussed the need to address the interactions of mobile devices with other data sources such as Internet of Things devices and cloud resources. However, Lillis and colleagues did not consider smartphone content and the statistical distributions of smartphone data.

In 2018, Luciano et al. [11] described the results of a workshop attended by digital forensic professionals that sought to identify important research issues over the next five years. Their findings included limited research funding, absence of standards, limited multidisciplinary knowledge and approaches, lack of information sharing and collaborative activities, use of outdated techniques and tools, and the need to advance the reputation of digital forensics as a discipline.

In 2018, Barmpatsalou et al. [2] published a review of the contemporary literature on mobile device forensics. They noted that data encryption was more prevalent and that it was much harder to decrypt data. Also, the diversity of devices, operating systems and software was creating incompatibilities with commercial forensic tools, requiring digital forensic professionals to pursue manual efforts or use third-party software. Additionally, they encouraged tool developers to focus on the standardization of forensic file formats and tool interoperability. A key critique was that researchers were not focusing on automated methods for evidence classification. The gaps included data and artifact classification, user behavior pattern detection, automated malicious activity detection, multi-source data correlation and criminal activity detection by analyzing data patterns.

Also in 2018, Camacho et al. [3] published a review of contemporary mobile device forensics. They identified the lack of standardized methodologies and the need to use large numbers of forensic tools to achieve investigative goals. Additionally, they noted the need to integrate browser applications that support instant messaging, social networking, email, video and audio analysis.

3. Survey Methodology

This research sought to capture the knowledge and experience of law enforcement professionals related to the forensic extraction and analysis of data from seized smartphones and specify the contents of a representative smartphone encountered in criminal investigations.

Goals. A representative smartphone would provide digital forensic researchers with valuable insights pertaining to the forensic analysis of devices seized in criminal investigations. These include the type and amount of data at the file-class level (e.g., databases, pictures, videos, audio and text documents) as well as the data structures encountered in multiple file classes (e.g., accounts, contacts, messenger apps, calls and geospatial data). The survey focused not on the actual file extensions (e.g., PNG, JPG and GIF in the case of pictures), but the types of content that are represented (e.g., when file carving is used to determine file types [10]).

To cope with the data labeling problem [1], the survey participants were asked to classify content into two classes, typical task-relevant information and typical task-irrelevant information. The survey participants were also interviewed to identify the problems encountered while conducting mobile device forensic tasks and law enforcement needs. In summary, the three goals of the survey were:

- **Goal 1:** Gain insights into the data distributions in a representative contemporary smartphone.

- **Goal 2:** Determine notable files and apps that contain large amounts of task-relevant and/or task-irrelevant information.

- **Goal 3:** Identify the problems encountered by law enforcement professionals while conducting mobile device forensic tasks and their needs related to mobile device forensics.

Achieving the first and second goals would assist the digital forensics community in creating realistic smartphone datasets for training and tool testing. Additionally, the representative content provided by the survey participants would support statistical analyses of smartphone datasets and comparisons of data from real devices against synthetic or manually-generated datasets. Achieving the third goal would provide insights into current challenges related to mobile device forensics and steer mobile device forensics research and development efforts.

Survey Design.   Interviews were chosen as a qualitative method to assess the knowledge and experience of experts in mobile device forensics [12]. The interviewees were provided with a set of potential questions in advance of the interviews to give them time to prepare their responses. The semi-structured interviews were designed to emphasize extensive discussions and reduce the need for a large survey population. This was deemed necessary because it is difficult to recruit experts in mobile device forensics for research studies due to their high workloads.

Survey Method.   Active professionals from different law enforcement agencies whose tasks involved extracting and analyzing smartphone data were selected as survey participants. The interviews were conducted over an online videoconferencing system to facilitate access. Each interviewee provided a list of crimes that were typically encountered. The interviews were terminated after six participants because thematic saturation of the types of crimes covered was attained.

Survey Questions. The survey had four parts: (i) introduction, (ii) assessing the contents of typical seized smartphones, (iii) assessing the data distributions in a representative smartphone and (iv) open discussion.

During the introduction part, it was ascertained that the participant matched the desired focus group based on occupation, affiliation and personal experience working on smartphone forensics. Also, the forensic tools that were typically used by the participant were identified.

The second part of the survey covered the typical contents of a seized smartphone. Specifically, each participant was asked to identify the data and/or file extensions encountered in large amounts of task-relevant and task-irrelevant content.

The third part of the survey acquired statistical information about the distribution of data in a representative smartphone with respect to 11 categories: (i) account entries (Acc), (ii) contact entries (Con), (iii) messenger apps (Msgr), (iv) text/email messages (Msg), (v) calls made (Call), (vi) geospatial data entries (Geo), (vii) database files (DB), (viii) picture files (Pic), (ix) video files (Vid), (x) audio files (Aud) and (xi) document files (Doc).

The final part of the survey involved an open discussion of topics in mobile device forensics. This included general comments, problems encountered and potential solutions related to mobile device forensics.

Data Collection. During the interviews, all the comments and answers provided by the participants were transcribed directly. The list of questions provided to the participants in advance guided the interviews and facilitated the collection of detailed data. The list also maximized the amount of data collected during the interviews.

Survey Limitations. The interviews were restricted to law enforcement professionals from regional and national agencies in Germany and Switzerland. Surveys of law enforcement professionals from other countries would have to be conducted in the future for validation and generalization. Additionally, the survey responses related to the problems encountered by law enforcement professionals are expected to have a country bias.

Table 1. Statistics of data in a representative smartphone.

	Acc	Con	Msgr	Msg	Call	Geo	DB	Pic	Vid	Aud	Doc
Mean	28	1,161	6	34,759	829	10,232	1,713	182,000	1,571	3,613	8,983
Median	24	270	7	32,253	180	535	825	77,500	788	2,545	8,600
Minimum	10	44	1	10	10	200	200	10,000	50	10	6,000
Maximum	60	4,300	7	150,000	8,000	100,000	12,000	1,300,000	5,000	22,000	15,000

Data Analysis. Responses involving numerical values, such as the data distributions in a typical seized smartphone, were specified as ranges instead of exact values; the means of these ranges were used to simplify subsequent computations. The computed statistical parameters included the mean, median, minimum value and maximum value. The non-numerical responses and comments were accumulated across all the interviews and analyzed in a qualitative manner.

4. Survey Results

Interviews were conducted with six German and Swiss law enforcement officers from different regional/national agencies to obtain a diverse coverage of criminal activities. The crimes investigated by the survey participants included drug crimes, theft, Internet fraud, illegal immigration, property damage, crimes against the state/public, terrorism, weapons, explosives, organized crime, internal affairs, money laundering, murder, homicide and others. This section describes the survey results and compares the collected data against published smartphone datasets.

4.1 Typical Smartphone Content

During the survey, each participant provided data size ratings for 11 data categories: (i) account entries (Acc), (ii) contact entries (Con), (iii) messenger apps (Msgr), (iv) text/email messages (Msg), (v) calls made (Call), (vi) geospatial data entries (Geo), (vii) database files (DB), (viii) picture files (Pic), (ix) video files (Vid), (x) audio files (Aud) and (xi) document files (Doc). The individual ratings were used to compute the mean, median, minimum value and maximum value of each data category. When participants provided intervals instead of single values, the midpoints of the intervals were employed to compute the statistics. The exceptions were computing the minimum and maximum values as the low and high points of the intervals, respectively.

Table 1 summarizes the data distributions in a representative seized smartphone. For instance, the smartphone contains 28 accounts on average. The median is 24 accounts and the minimum and maximum numbers of accounts are 10 and 60, respectively.

The survey participants emphasized that the data distributions are highly dependent on the specific smartphones. Some smartphones contain little or no data, especially those used exclusively for criminal activities, which might only contain a few text messages. Another factor is the type of crime tied to a seized smartphone. For example, smartphones used for human trafficking, Internet fraud and document forgery tend to have large numbers of stored contacts and messages.

Geospatial data deserves special mention. According to the survey participants, locally-stored geospatial data is very useful in investigations, but popular cloud services such as Google Cloud also store valuable geospatial data. In fact, online services store about 80 times more geospatial data than is stored in a typical smartphone.

4.2 Labeling Typical Content

The survey participants noted that labeling data content as task-relevant and task-irrelevant is not trivial and is highly dependent on the specific case. For example, if the location of a crime is not relevant in a case, then geospatial data is labeled as task-irrelevant. However, in the vast majority of cases, geospatial data is task-relevant.

The survey participants were asked about the data categories that usually contain task-relevant information and those that mostly contain task-irrelevant information. Specifically, the participants had to identify the typical apps and locations of relevant and irrelevant information, respectively. Table 2 summarizes the relevant and exclusively irrelevant content in a representative smartphone as provided by the survey participants.

It is important to note that relevant and irrelevant content are not mutually exclusive; instead, relevant information is a proper subset of irrelevant information. Thus, if a participant deems some type of content to be relevant, then there is a high probability that the content belongs to one of the listed types. On the other hand, if a participant deems some content to be exclusively irrelevant (i.e., absolute complement of relevant information), then the content likely belongs to an exclusively irrelevant type.

The survey participants stated that irrelevant information is often in system and app files; this is typically content that does not change. Furthermore, relevant information is rarely found in general apps used for recreation (e.g., gaming). According to the participants, pictures and videos may be labeled as relevant and irrelevant. Subsets of pictures

Table 2. Relevant and exclusively irrelevant content in a representative smartphone.

	Relevant	Exclusively Irrelevant
Data Files/ Structures	Text/email messages, Chats, Calls, Contacts, Geospatial data, Pictures, Videos, Audio (voice messages), Databases	Private/erotic pictures/videos, System/app databases
Apps/ System	Messenger apps, Browser logs, Social media, App usage logs, Wi-Fi logs, Power logs, Search queries, Health/fitness apps, Personal notes	Gaming apps, Cookies, System data, Template files
Additional File Types	HEIC (iOS), SQL (DB, SQLITE3), PLIST, PDF, DOC, Arbitrary types (0, DATA, ...)	None

and videos used exclusively for recreation are mainly shared with social network contacts. These files may have erotic (excluding illegal pornography), humorous or informative content and are mostly task-irrelevant.

In contrast, media files (pictures, videos, audio, documents), app databases and content created by user interactions (calls, stored contacts, messages, app usage, geospatial data, notes, search queries and others) often contain task-relevant information. The survey participants stated that geospatial data plays an important role in forensic investigations. They provided examples where analyzing logs containing geospatial data entries provided conclusive evidence in investigations. This information was often found in fitness and health applications or at cloud service providers that tracked and stored smartphone locations and movements.

4.3   Mobile Device Problems and Needs

The survey also focused on the problems faced by the participants while conducting their forensic tasks and solicited information about their needs related to mobile device forensics. The principal findings relate to content extraction, forensic tools and content analysis.

Content Extraction. According to the survey participants, content extraction from smartphones and other mobile devices is often hindered by data encryption or password/PIN locks. A typical example is a seized smartphone whose screen is turned off and a password or PIN is required to unlock the device.

Another problem is that some forensic tools require root access, but this is not always possible due to operating system security mechanisms. Social media applications and cloud services store user credentials on local device storage, but encryption prevents access to the credentials.

Forensic Tools. At this time, no single forensic tool can extract and analyze content in all types of smartphones. The diversity of hardware and operating systems forces digital forensic professionals to use forensic tools from different vendors, each tool with its own proprietary file formats. The smartphone forensic tools used by the survey participants come from Cellebrite (Physical Analyzer, Reader, Pathfinder, UFED, etc.), MSAB (XRY and XAMN), Oxygen Forensics (Oxygen Forensic Detective), Magnet Forensics (AXIOM), X-Ways (X-Ways Forensics), Grayshift (GrayKey) and SQLite Consortium (SQLite). Additionally, the survey participants employ self-developed hardware and software tools for extracting and analyzing smartphone content.

The survey participants noted that tool diversity results in forensic reports being produced in different formats with limited interoperability with other tools. Additionally, the participants, regardless of their affiliations, complained that forensic software, even software procured from leading vendors, tends to have bugs and critical security problems for which patches are rarely provided. This is a concern because the quality and validity of forensic reports could be questioned in court.

The needs of the survey participants include high-quality forensic tools that provide better filtering mechanisms, enable the discovery of correlations in data and support the verification of results (e.g., providing qualitative and/or quantitative evaluations via enhanced user interfaces).

Content Analysis. The survey participants, without exception, stated that they encounter increasing numbers of devices with large volumes of data that have to be extracted and analyzed. Problems are also posed by devices created for use in foreign countries for which content in various languages had to be translated manually prior to analysis. This leads to additional costs for translation as well as delays because survey participants have to wait for translations before they can determine the relevance of content to their investigations.

A related problem involved apps that are commonly used in foreign countries as well as by expatriates in other countries. In many instances, the survey participants were unaware of the app functionality and the information the apps might hold. Even worse, the foreign apps often are not supported by common forensic tools. An example is WeChat, a multi-purpose app from Tencent, that is widely for social networking, instant messaging and mobile payments in East Asia.

Another problem is that common forensic tools support popular apps (mainly communications apps), but may not support other app types such as online booking, shopping and package tracking apps; thus, valuable information in the unsupported apps is not automatically integrated in the final reports produced by forensic tools. Yet another problem encountered by the survey participants is recovering and recreating information from deleted encrypted files and deleted SQLite database entries.

Finally, the survey participants observed that criminals deliberately inject files with false content in their smartphones. The anti-forensic files, which come from various sources, mimic content created by the smartphones, deceiving forensic professionals to classify the files as false positives and covering criminal activity. One example given by a survey participant was the injection of pictures that apparently show illegal weapons. The pictures of the weapons, obtained from public sources, were recreated on the smartphone using its camera app to show that the suspect was at the locations where the pictures were originally taken.

5.   Discussion

This section discusses the principal findings of the survey. Also, it compares the statistical properties of the data categories in the representative smartphone created by the survey against the statistical properties of the data categories in a published dataset.

5.1   Key Findings

The assessment of the problems and needs with regard to mobile device forensics pointed out the deficiencies in current forensic tools. The problems mentioned by the survey participants were similar to those identified by the digital forensics community in the past. Problems related to forensic tools that persist are the lack of standardized forensic file formats and interoperability between forensic tools [2, 6, 9, 11], bugs in forensic tools and long update cycles [6, 11] and lack of tool support for efficient identification of relevant information (e.g., data correlation and pattern detection) [6, 9].

Validation and verification of forensic tool results based on qualitative and/or quantitative feedback are also problems that persist [6]. Current commercial tools are still black boxes without any documentation about their internal algorithms. Absent adequate validation and verification, forensic professionals and courts are forced to blindly trust commercial tools although validation and verification are important components of forensic investigations [4].

The survey also identified that smartphones contain valuable data that is not analyzed automatically because forensic tools do not support less popular apps. Some crimes are committed using specific types of apps. For example, stolen credit card information is used to purchase goods from online shops that are sent to dummy addresses. Online shopping and package tracking apps would contain valuable information in such investigations, but forensic professionals have to search such apps manually because they are not supported by forensic tools.

Another gap in contemporary forensic tools involves their handling of foreign apps. The survey indicated that the absence of documentation about foreign app functionality is problematic. Additionally, manual translation of the extracted app information from foreign languages can be expensive and leads to delays because information can be labeled only after it is translated.

From a technical point of view, the survey indicated that the extraction of data from smartphones continues to be problematic. The retrieval of user credentials from internal smartphone databases would be useful in investigations. It would also be useful to obtain deleted SQL entries and encrypted files. Recent research has demonstrated advances in restoring deleted SQLite entries [14].

5.2 Data Content Comparison

This section compares the representative smartphone content created as a result of the survey against the content of a published smartphone dataset analyzed by Goncalves et al. [7]. The published smartphone dataset content covers the same 11 data categories as the representative smartphone content.

The log-scale bar chart in Figure 1 shows the means of the data categories in the representative smartphone and in the published smartphone dataset. The lighter bars correspond to the representative smartphone whereas the darker bars correspond to the published dataset. The number above each data category is the variance corresponding to the representative smartphone relative to the mean distribution in the published dataset. Specifically, a value lower than one indicates that the published

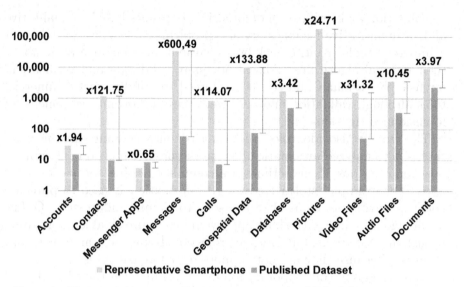

Figure 1. Representative smartphone content versus published dataset content.

dataset contains more files or entries in the particular data category compared with the representative smartphone whereas a value greater than one indicates that the published dataset contains less files or entries compared with the representative smartphone.

The number of messenger apps is lower by about one-third for the representative smartphone compared with the published dataset. For the other data categories, the representative smartphone has more content than the published dataset by factors ranging from two to about 600. Specifically, the representative smartphone contains about twice the number of accounts, 122 times more stored contacts, 600 times more text/email messages, 114 times more calls, 134 times more geospatial data, three times more database files, 25 times more picture files, 31 times more video files, ten times more audio files and four times more text documents than in the published dataset.

The amount of content corresponding to each data category in the published dataset was rated according to the minimum and maximum values of the representative smartphone shown in Table 1. Table 3 shows the published dataset content ratings. A data category in the published dataset is rated low (respectively, high) if its content is less than the minimum value (respectively, higher than the maximum value) of the representative smartphone. The data category in the published dataset is rated good if its content is within the minimum and maximum values of the representative smartphone.

Table 3. Published dataset content ratings based on a representative smartphone.

Low Rating	Good Rating	High Rating
Contacts	Accounts	Messenger apps
Calls	Text/email messages	
Geospatial data	Databases	
Pictures	Video files	
Documents	Audio files	

Only the number of messenger apps in the published dataset is greater than the number in the representative smartphone whose content corresponds to the contents of a real smartphone. Accounts, text/email messages, databases, video and audio files in the published dataset are rated good, although their numbers are very low compared with the representative smartphone. The remaining data categories have low ratings and, therefore, do not constitute realistic representations of real smartphones. The key finding is that the public dataset does not capture the complexity of real devices, which brings into question the realism of the published dataset and the quality of the forensic tools validated using the published dataset and other similar datasets.

The most notable difference between public and real datasets are the numbers of files and their contents. A possible explanation is that real devices are not only used to perform specific (criminal) acts, but are also constantly used in daily activities. This generates greater numbers of entries in the various smartphone databases which, in turn, results in forensic professionals encountering more files in smartphones. In contrast, public datasets are typically generated based on the specific scopes of the experiments instead of realistic user behavior.

6.   Conclusions

The survey study of law enforcement professionals from Germany and Switzerland provides valuable information about the data in a representative smartphone encountered in a criminal investigation. Comparison of the distributions of data types in the representative smartphone against those in a published smartphone dataset revealed that real smartphones contain much more data than published datasets, which may be considered to be not very realistic; this calls into question validations of smartphone forensic techniques and tools based on the published datasets. The data distributions and the subsequent labeling of smartphone content as task-relevant and task-irrelevant assist researchers in creating more realistic datasets.

The survey reveals that the problems encountered by law enforcement professionals are similar to those identified in previous studies. Specifically, problems that persist include the lack of standardized forensic file formats and tool interoperability, bugs in forensic tools and long update cycles and absence of tool support for efficiently identifying relevant information. From the technical perspective, effective techniques and tools must be developed to access locked devices and encrypted content; an alternative solution is to encourage companies to install backdoor capabilities for law enforcement agencies. Forensic tool development efforts should focus on reducing bugs and vendors should provide tool support and release updates and patches on good schedules. Additionally, techniques should be developed to combat anti-forensic approaches that are increasingly being implemented in seized devices.

At this time, law enforcement professionals employ forensic techniques and tools that do not meet strict forensic examination requirements, and they often have to manually search for relevant information in seized devices. It is imperative that the digital forensics community institutes collaborative efforts to develop efficient techniques and cutting-edge tools as well as realistic forensic corpora that can help validate that the techniques and tools and the evidence proffered in court meet the highest standards.

References

[1] S. Abt and H. Baier, Are we missing labels? A study of the availability of ground truth in network security research, *Proceedings of the Third International Workshop on Building Analysis Datasets and Gathering Experience Returns for Security*, pp. 40–55, 2014.

[2] K. Barmpatsalou, T. Cruz, E. Monteiro and P. Simoes, Current and future trends in mobile device forensics, *ACM Computing Surveys*, vol. 51(3), article no. 46, 2018.

[3] J. Camacho, K. Campos, P. Cedillo, B. Coronel and A. Bermeo, Forensic analysis of mobile devices: A systematic mapping study, in *Information and Communication Technologies of Ecuador*, M. Botto-Tobar, L. Barba-Maggi, J. Gonzalez-Huerta, P. Villacres-Cevallos, O. Gomez and M. Uvidia-Fassler (Eds.), Springer, Cham, Switzerland, pp. 57–72, 2018.

[4] E. Casey and C. Rose, Forensic analysis, in *Handbook of Digital Forensics and Investigation*, E. Casey (Ed.), Elsevier, Burlington, Massachusetts, pp. 21–62, 2010.

[5] European Parliament and Council, Regulation (EU) 2016/679, *Official Journal of the European Union*, vol. 59(L 119), pp. 1–88, 2016.

[6] S. Garfinkel, Digital forensics research: The next 10 years, *Digital Investigation*, vol. 7(S), pp. S64–S73, 2010.

[7] P. Goncalves, K. Dolovs, M. Stebner, A. Attenberger and H. Baier, Revisiting the Dataset Gap Problem – On Availability, Assessment and Perspectives of Mobile Forensic Corpora, Unpublished Manuscript, Cyber Defense Research Institute, Bundeswehr University, Munich, Germany, 2021.

[8] C. Grajeda, F. Breitinger and I. Baggili, Availability of datasets for digital forensics – And what is missing, *Digital Investigation*, vol. 22(S), pp. S94–S105, 2017.

[9] D. Lillis, B. Becker, T. O'Sullivan and M. Scanlon, Current challenges and future research areas for digital forensic investigations, *Proceedings of the Eleventh Annual Conference on Digital Forensics, Security and Law*, 2016.

[10] X. Lin, Chapter 9: File carving, in *Introductory Computer Forensics*, Springer, Cham, Switzerland, pp. 211–233, 2018.

[11] L. Luciano, I. Baggili, M. Topor, P. Casey and F. Breitinger, Digital forensics in the next five years, *Proceedings of the Thirteenth International Conference on Availability, Reliability and Security*, article no. 46, 2018.

[12] M. Meuser and U. Nagel, The expert interview and changes in knowledge production, in *Interviewing Experts*, A. Bogner, B. Littig and W. Menz (Eds.), Palgrave Macmillan, London, United Kingdom, pp. 17–42, 2009.

[13] A. Mylonas, V. Meletiadis, B. Tsoumas, L. Mitrou and D. Gritzalis, Smartphone forensics: A proactive investigation scheme for evidence acquisition, in *Information Privacy and Research*, D. Gritzalis, S. Furnell and M. Theoharidou (Eds.), Springer, Berlin Heidelberg, Germany, pp. 249–260, 2012.

[14] D. Pawlaszczyk and C. Hummert, Making the invisible visible – Techniques for recovering deleted SQLite data records, *International Journal of Cyber Forensics and Advanced Threat Investigations*, vol. 1(1-3), pp. 27–41, 2021.

[15] K. Woods, C. Lee, S. Garfinkel, D. Dittrich, A. Russell and K. Kearton, Creating realistic corpora for security and forensic education, *Proceedings of the Sixth Annual Conference on Digital Forensics, Security and Law*, 2011.

Chapter 4

FORENSIC ANALYSIS OF THE SNAPCHAT iOS APP WITH SPECTACLES-SYNCED ARTIFACTS

Logan VanPutte, Gokila Dorai, Andrew Clark IV, Rayna Mock and Josh Brunty

Abstract   The Spectacles wearable smart glasses device from Snapchat records snaps and videos for the Snapchat service. A Spectacles device can sync data with a paired smartphone and upload recorded content to a user's online account. However, extracting and analyzing data from a Snapchat app is challenging due to the disappearing nature of the media. Very few commercial tools are available to obtain data from Snapchat apps.

This chapter focuses on the extraction and analysis of artifacts from Snapchat and, specifically, Spectacles devices paired with Apple iPhones. A methodology is presented for forensically imaging Apple iPhones before and after critical points in the Spectacles and Snapchat pairing and syncing processes. The forensic images are examined to reveal the effects of each step of the pairing process. Several photos, videos, thumbnails and metadata files originating from Spectacles devices were obtained and tied to specific times, devices and locations. The research provides interesting insights into evidence collection from Spectacles devices paired with Apple iPhones.

Keywords: Wearable devices, Snapchat, Spectacles, iOS apps, iPhones, evidence

1.   Introduction

Snapchat, originally launched as Picaboo [8, 11], is a social-media mobile messaging application with related desktop and web applications [22, 24] that is used for multimedia instant messaging and communications. Manufactured by Snap of Santa Monica, California, Snapchat is a very popular application – as of 2020, it had more than 347 million global users active each month, the vast majority of them in India and

© IFIP International Federation for Information Processing 2022
Published by Springer Nature Switzerland AG 2022
G. Peterson and S. Shenoi (Eds.): DigitalForensics 2022, IFIP AICT 653, pp. 65–81, 2022.
https://doi.org/10.1007/978-3-031-10078-9_4

the United States [27, 29]. Since 2018, Snapchat has been ranked as the most critical social media application by teens in the United States, followed by TikTok and Instagram [28].

After creating an account, a Snapchat user can take and send pictures and videos called snaps and text messages called chats to individual friends, group chats, all Snapchat friends using My Story and publicly using Our Story. By default, snaps are deleted unless they are saved to memory; however, the length of time before automatic deletion depends on how the snaps were shared. In the default settings, snaps sent to friends are deleted after all the recipients view them or after 30 days; snaps sent to group chats, My Story and Shared Stories are deleted after 24 hours; snaps sent to Public Stories do not have a set amount of time before they are deleted [25]. Chats are automatically deleted after all the recipients view them [25]. According to Snapchat Support [23], snaps saved in chats are not saved to user devices, but to Snapchat servers [23].

In 2016, Snap released the first generation of Spectacles [10]. Following this, the second-generation of Spectacles and the third generation, Spectacles 3, were released. The most recent fourth-generation Spectacles has augmented reality capabilities. Spectacles are Bluetooth-enabled glasses with two camera lenses on the outside of each eye, enabling Snapchat users to take snaps with the glasses and share the snaps in their Snapchat accounts via the app.

Social media is widely used around the world – Statista [26] reports that almost 50% of Internet users use social media at least once a month. As a result, it is not surprising that social media may contain evidence of criminal activity. The top three areas of content and account violations on Snapchat during the last half of 2020 were sexually-explicit content by a large margin, followed by sales and distribution of regulated goods, and threatening, violent or harmful content [21]. Given these statistics and reports about child exploitation, restricted or banned drug sales and money laundering conducted on and via Snapchat and other similar apps [2, 12, 20], research into the evidence found in Snapchat and accessories would be very useful to digital forensic professionals.

Previous research on mobile device artifacts from Snapchat has focused on smartphones running Android operating systems. Limited research has been conducted on iPhones running iOS. Currently, Google's Android and Apple's iOS have more than 99% of the global mobile operating system market share, with Android controlling most of the global market [17]. About 90% of U.S. residents have access to smartphones and 46.9% of them use Apple iPhones [16].

This research focuses on the extraction and analysis of artifacts from Snapchat and, specifically, Spectacles devices paired with Apple iPhones running iOS. Cellebrite UFED and Magnet AXIOM Process were employed for physical acquisition and iTunes backup was used for logical acquisition. Macroplant iExplorer, Cellebrite Physical Analyzer and Magnet AXIOM Examine were employed for forensic examinations and analyses. The experimental findings are reported and various implications related to user data privacy are discussed.

2. Related Work

Alyahya et al. [1] conducted forensic analyses of Snapchat on Android devices using the Magnet AXIOM Examine and Autopsy tools. Using Magnet AXIOM Examine, they were able to examine Snapchat event logs and metadata about Snapchat friends, sent snaps, chat messages and one of the received snaps. They were also able to see previews of some of the photo snaps using the two tools. However, they were only able to process video snaps using Autopsy.

Malley [14] examined Snapchat video files on Android and iPhone devices to see if the files were modified when transferred by Gmail, Dropbox and text messages, and to see if images sent from an iPhone to an Android device, and vice versa, would leave artifacts that tied the images to their original senders. In the case of Android devices, files transferred by Gmail and Dropbox were not altered based on hash value computations. However, files transferred by text messages were compressed, which altered their hash values. In the case of iPhones, files sent via Dropbox were not altered whereas those sent via Gmail or text messages were compressed, altering the files. Nevertheless, regardless of the compression encountered in the two types of devices, it was still possible to trace images back to the originating smartphone, based on the presence of Android data in video files and "core media" (an iOS-specific artifact) in images sent by iPhones.

Wu et al. [31] analyzed data from various messaging apps on iOS and Android devices. The goal was to determine the data and artifacts that could be gathered from apps such as Snapchat and Burner due to their increased use by criminals. Analyses of Snapchat apps using Cellebrite and AccessData Forensic Toolkit revealed that information such as timestamps, contact information and message IDs could be collected from iOS devices whereas the most recently received snaps could be obtained from Android devices, albeit in duplicate. Both types of devices provided logs that included the names of the most recently sent snaps, which could be used to link senders and receivers. However, it was not possible to determine the length of time after which snaps were removed by Snapchat.

Walnycky et al. [30] attempted to reconstruct data gathered from the Snapchat app. However, Snapchat encrypts network traffic, so it was not possible to obtain audio, video and image sharing data, and packet inspection was unsuccessful.

Raji [19] loaded Snapchat on a rooted Android device in order to analyze the available artifacts. The Paraben E3 tool was used to identify recent chat messages, user account and friend list data, sent and received snaps with timestamps, and whether or not messages had been opened. The largest artifact that was not recoverable by the Paraben E3 tool was a preview of what a snap looked like. Since the experiments focused solely on an Android device, it is not clear what artifacts could be collected from an iOS device.

Chamberlain and bin Azhar [9] analyzed three mobile ephemeral messaging applications on an iOS device. Subsequently, they examined three other mobile ephemeral messaging applications on an Android device along with one application that was previously analyzed on the iOS device [6]. The Oxygen tool was used to examine the iOS and Android devices, MOBILedit Forensics Express to examine the iOS device, and Andriller, FTK Imager and Autopsy to examine the Android device. Snapchat and Facebook Messenger were selected for the iOS and Android devices due to their popularity, and two other applications were chosen due to their use of encrypted messaging, three in the case of the Android device with one shared application between the two devices. Analysis of Snapchat using Oxygen revealed the Snapchat user name, indications that offensive words were detected in messages, indications of messages between two users, evidence that a user deleted a message and general application data [9]. The MOBILedit Forensics Express tool found the same general application data as Oxygen, but additionally, obtained the accounts that logged into Snapchat, contact list, and location of the PLIST file containing contact information [9].

Matthews et al. [15] conducted a study on the usability of Snap Map, a Snapchat platform that shows publicly-available snaps by their locations on a live heat map to support closed-circuit TV footage in a distributed surveillance system. They determined that the web version of Snap Map was better than the mobile app version for this purpose because snaps and related metadata could be saved as JSON objects. Using the snaps and related metadata, Matthews and colleagues concluded that Snap Map could support law enforcement objectives related to closed-circuit TV systems. However, they discovered that the extent to which the objectives could be met depended on the accuracy of the location metadata, length of availability and quality of the snaps. They also noted that additional research regarding data reliability and accuracy

Table 1. Device details.

Device	Type	Operating System
Spectacles that Snap! (Coral) First Generation (S1)	Wearable IoT	Spectacles v1.11.5
Spectacles 2 (Original Onyx) Second Generation (S2)	Wearable IoT	Spectacles v2.15.2
Spectacles 2 (Original Onyx) Second Generation (S3)	Wearable IoT	Spectacles v2.15.2
iPhone 11 (P1)	Smartphone	iOS 14.6
iPhone 12 (P2)	Smartphone	iOS 14.6
Alienware 13 R3 (D1)	Laptop	Windows 10 Home v21H1
Computer (D2)	Computer	Windows 10 Enterprise v20H2
USB Cables	Connector	NA

was needed and whether or not the data could be collected and analyzed automatically [15].

3. Methodology

This section describes the methodology for forensically imaging Apple devices before and after critical points in the Spectacles and iPhone Snapchat pairing and syncing processes. Specifically, it describes the experimental environment and experimental procedure.

3.1 Experimental Environment

Table 1 describes the devices used in the experiments. One first generation Spectacles wearable glasses (S1) and two second generation Spectacles wearable glasses (S2 and S3) were employed. Two iOS devices, an Apple iPhone 11 (P1) and an Apple iPhone 12 (P2), both running iOS 14.6, were used. It was decided to focus on iPhones in the experiments because the vast majority of the research in Snapchat forensics has concentrated on Android devices and the Apple's iOS is the second most commonly used mobile operating system after Google's Android [17]. Two iPhone models were employed in the experiments to determine if any differences exist in the artifacts recovered from the two devices.

Figure 1 presents an overview of the methodology. After setting up the devices and conducting experimental trials, iTunes was used to perform unencrypted and encrypted backups. Cellebrite UFED and Magnet AXIOM Process were used to obtain forensic images. The forensic images were analyzed using Macroplant iExplorer, Cellebrite Physical Analyzer and Magnet AXIOM Examine. Acquisition and analysis of the iPhone

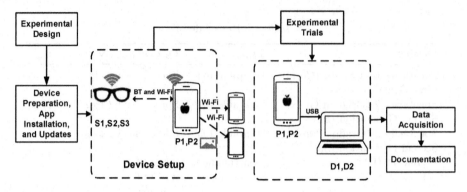

Figure 1. Overview of the methodology.

images were conducted using a laptop running Windows 10 Home OS Build 19043.1081 to 19043.12.37 and a computer running Windows 10 Enterprise OS Build 19042.1288. The Apple File System (APFS) is the default filesystem for iOS 10.3 and later versions [3, 4]; therefore, the iPhones running iOS 14.6 used APFS. The two Windows machines were used for ease of access and due to the physical distance between research team members.

Table 2. Software details.

Software	Version	Devices
Cellebrite Physical Analyzer	7.36.0.42	Computer
Cellebrite UFED	7.49.0.2	Computer
iExplorer	4.4.2	Laptop
iTunes	12.11.3.17	Laptop
Magnet AXIOM Process and Examine	5.3.0.25803	Laptop, Computer
Magnet AXIOM Process and Examine	5.5.1.26621	Laptop, Computer
Snapchat App for iOS	11.34.1.34-5	iPhone 11, iPhone 12

Table 2 lists the software used in the experiments. A mix of open-source and commercial digital forensic tools were employed. An official Snapchat app for iOS 11.34.1.35 was downloaded from the Apple App Store for each test iPhone, which had a dedicated phone number. An iCloud account was created for each test iPhone.

3.2 Experimental Procedure

After setting up the iPhones, installing updates, downloading the Snapchat app and setting up the Snapchat accounts, friends and the default Team Snapchat were setup on the iPhones. The Snapchat account of iPhone P1 had four friends, default Team Snapchat, iPhone P2 Snapchat account and two other friends. The Snapchat account of iPhone P2 had three friends, default Team Snapchat, iPhone P1 Snapchat account and one shared friend. Each Spectacles device (S1, S2 and S3) was paired to its iPhone using Bluetooth, enabling the device to sync its data with the Snapchat app. Note that an iPhone must be connected to Wi-Fi or cellular in order to pair the phone with a Spectacles device. After snaps were taken using the Spectacles devices and they were paired, thumbnails of the snaps showed up under Memories. However, the snaps could not be viewed or shared until they were imported from the Spectacles devices by connecting to them via Bluetooth and selecting import.

The research goal was to conduct forensic analyses of the iPhones to identify and examine the data and artifacts related to their Snapchat applications and Spectacles devices. Several experimental trials were conducted with the iPhones and Spectacles devices. During each trial, the dates, times, locations of all actions, observations and results were documented.

Several steps were involved in each trial after the Snapchat app was downloaded and configured, and the Spectacles devices were charged, updated and configured.

Each experimental trial involved messaging and sharing snaps in the following order. First, several snaps were taken with the Spectacles devices and it was confirmed that the snaps taken with the Spectacles devices appeared in the Snapchat applications on the iPhones. Next, the snaps taken with the Spectacles devices were shared with another Snapchat account. Following this, several additional snaps were taken. However, these snaps were taken with the iPhone cameras using the Snapchat app and the snaps were shared with another Snapchat account. The final step was to connect each iPhone to a laptop with a USB cable and create a backup of the iPhone using iTunes. The trials swapped iPhones and Spectacles devices for error checking purposes and to determine if different artifacts remained for different iPhone-Spectacles combinations.

The following information was recorded during each experimental trial:

- iPhone test device
- Spectacles test device
- Type of iPhone-Spectacles connectivity
- Device connected to the iPhone test device
- Physical location of the experiment

Table 3.   Main Snapchat data locations.

Directory Folder		Subfolder
App	com.toyopagroup.picaboo (F1)	/Documents (SF1)
		/Library (SF2)
App Group	group.snapchat.picaboo (F2)	/Library/Preferences (SF3)
		/WidgetExention (SF4)
App Plugin	com.toyopagroup.picaboo.homeWidget (F3)	
	com.toyopagroup.picaboo.notification (F4)	
	com.toyopagroup.picaboo.share (F5)	
	com.toyopagroup.picaboo.today (F6)	

- Date and time each snap was taken
- Type of each snap (picture or video)
- Device taking each snap (Spectacles device or iPhone camera)
- Description of each snap

During the experiments, it was observed that, when the snaps taken with a Spectacles device were shared, the snaps were rounded and, when they were shared with a friend, thumbnails of the shared snaps were shown. However, when snaps taken with an iPhone camera in Snapchat were shared, the snaps were not shown and only messages appeared to indicate that the snaps were delivered.

Forensic acquisitions were conducted on the iTunes backups using the Cellebrite UFED and Magnet AXIOM Process tools. The iTunes backups and other images were analyzed forensically using iExplorer, Cellebrite Physical Analyzer and Magnet AXIOM Examine.

4.   Experimental Results and Findings

This section describes the experiment results and discusses the experimental findings.

The iExplorer tool was used to access the iPhone filesystems. The filesystems were organized into ten parts with most of the data in the Backup Explorer folder. The Backup Explorer folder was divided into 21 sections.

Table 3 shows the locations of Snapchat-related data. Other artifacts and indications of artifacts related to Snapchat were found with iExplorer and in the file tree section of Magnet AXIOM Examine under folders F2 through F6. Two files were found in folder F1, a PLIST file in subfolder SF2 with the same name as folder F1 and **snapcode** in subfolder SF4. All the folders belonging to the App Plugin directory shown in Table 3 were empty except for the same three subfolders, Documents (SF1), Library (SF2) and Library/Preferences (SF3). Most of these artifacts did not change after the experimental trials or were not related to the Spectacles devices.

The majority of altered artifacts of interest were found in folder F1. Figure 2 shows the file tree for folder F1. Folder F1 contains two subfolders, Documents (SF1) and Library (SF2). In the Documents subfolder (SF1), the subfolders, gallery, gallery_data_object, gallery_encrypted_db, global_scoped and persisted_events only contained empty folders; the subfolder user_scoped was completely empty.

Data from Snapchat and Spectacles related to snaps were stored in the F1 folder. Images, video, thumbnails and metadata files were stored in subfolder SF1 in a file named `laguna` using unique identifiers. The majority of the time, each identifier had corresponding MOV, THM, JPG, IMU and MDA files with the same identifier. When using iExplorer, thumbnail files for some of the snaps taken with Spectacles S1 were viewable.

The directory also contained a file named `device-list-archive.dat`, a PLIST file with information about the Spectacles device and files transferred between the iPhone and Spectacles device. Data about the Spectacles device included the firmware version, device name, pairing information, Wi-Fi password (if enabled on the Spectacles device), timestamps, setup information, etc.

Image and video metadata were found in the PLIST file under SCSpectaclesDevicecontentStorecontentkeys. A SCSpectaclesContent key exists for each picture and video imported from a Spectacles device. The keys store location information (if available), timestamps, size, duration, as well as the filenames of images, videos, thumbnails and metadata.

Image, video and thumbnail files were found on the iPhone device after importing. Using the data found in `device-list-archive.dat`, a certain image, video or thumbnail can be tied to a time, Spectacles device, iPhone and (if available), a location (Figure 3). Thumbnails for all the images and videos taken with a Spectacles device were found on the iPhone. A file was present for the most recent video and mentioned in `device-list-archive.dat`, but the file turned out to be empty. It was confirmed that the MOV file was the most recent video based on the timestamps in `device-list-archive.dat`. However, playable MOV files were found for older videos taken with Spectacles. More research needs to be done to determine if importing, saving to Memories or uploading videos results in Spectacles videos being saved on the device or removed.

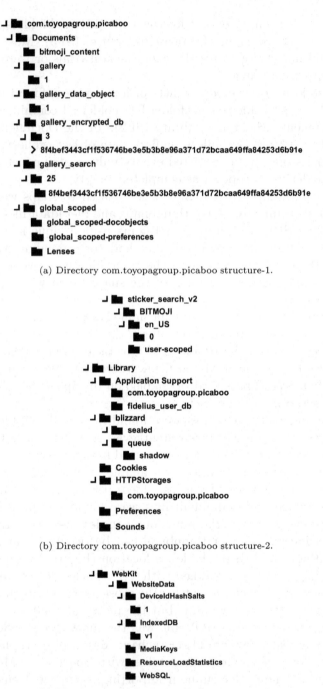

(a) Directory com.toyopagroup.picaboo structure-1.

(b) Directory com.toyopagroup.picaboo structure-2.

(c) Directory com.toyopagroup.picaboo structure-3.

Figure 2.   Directory com.toyopagroup.picaboo structure.

```
contentStore : SCSpectaclesContentStore = {
content : NSArray = {
    SCSpectaclesContent = {
        location : AsciiString = Null
        contentName : AsciiString = 0000000300000001
        thumbnailFile : SCSpectaclesFile = {
        pictureFile : AsciiString = Null
        multisnapGroupID : AciiString = 0030000
        mediaFormat : integer = 4
        videoDuration : real = 10.5
        hdVideoFile : SCSpectaclesFile = {
            remoteFileName : AsciiString =
                0000000300000001.MOV
            localFilename : AsciiString =
                00000003-0000-0001-832F-E0B7B45A8E6
            B_HD.MOV
            remoteFileSize : integer = 10682649
        buttonSide : integer = 0
        genericAssetFiles : AsciiString = Null
        synced : boolean = False
        type : integer = 0
        UUID: AciiString = 00000003-0000-0001-832F-
            E0B7B45A8E6B
        mediaType : integer = 5
        sdVideoFile : SCSpectaclesFile = {
        timeOfCapture : NSDate = 10/4/2021 7:19:07 PM
        batchID : NSUUID = 1f6f3f30-b754-8c40-444264d09ced
        metadataFile : SCSpactaclesFile = {
            remoteFileName : AsciiString =
                0000000300000001.MDA
            localFilename : AsciiString =
                00000003-0000-0001-832F-E0B7B45A8E6B.MDA
            remoteFileSize : integer = 527
        imuDataFile : SCSpectaclesFile = {
        genericAssetMetadata : AsciiString = Null
        IV : data = B9 CA D5 57 FD 74 10 49 D1 10 00 18
            9A 0A 3B
        key : data = 6F 70 E4 37 08 BF 6D 19 B6 66 26
            04 86 8D 71 6F 4B 4A 8C 20 A5 45 64 4A 98
            4E F3 6A 7D F0 29 6E
```

Figure 3. Image and video files transferred from a Spectacles device.

Other files changed after the Spectacles pairing, namely the PLIST file iPhone/mobile/Containers/Data/Application/com.toyopagroup. picabo-o/Library/Preferences/com.toyopagroup.picaboo.plist. This file was updated to include several keys related to Spectacles data such as the key SPECTACLES_IOS_HERMOSA_INTEGRATION. The file also appears to update information in the Spectacles updates and release notes. Three other PLIST files were found in the same folder, app.aifactory.-splendidSDK.plist, com.apple.EmojiCache.plist

```
{
    "app_travel_mode":false,
    "session_id":"f.ZkS2m5+oSPo1DWQ2",
    "os_type":"iOS",
    "event_sampling_rate":1,
    "device_storage":99,
    "app_startup_type":"WARM",
    "event_name":"SPECTACLES_DEVICE_STATUS",
    "app_version":"11.35.0.34",
    "user_id":"loganv6886",
    "AMPEvent.isCritical":false,
    "video_count":6,
    "device_id":"832FE0B8B45A8E6B",
    "user_guid":"ff93a73b-1d77-4312-8ac7-2d64e97156ca",
    "firmware_version":"v2.13.1",
    "client_ts":1633458074.439924,
    "log_queue_sequence_id":21,
    "locale":"en",
    "log_queue_name":"shadow",
    "frame_color":"ONYX",
    "hardware_version":"4.0",
    "device_battery":0,
    "app_build":"",
    "connection_download_bandwidth_bps":0,
    "os_version":"14.6",
    "device_model":"iPhone13,2",
    "device_connectivity":"UNREACHABLE",
    "client_id":"CC009CFB-3A4D-B118-E8779329B600",
    "user_sampling_rate":1,
    "has_bitmoji":false,
}
```

Figure 4.   JSON file retrieved after iPhone-Spectacles pairing.

and `com.mapbox.event-s.plist`. Other files that were updated after pairing included JSON files found in com.toyopagroup.picaboo/Library/ blizzard/sealed/queue-/gce_best_-effort and in com.toyopagroup.picaboo /Library/blizzard/seale-d/queue/shadow. These files, which contained references to Spectacles device and iPhone information, were created after pairing with and syncing data from the Spectacles device.

The majority of the Snapchat and Spectacles data was found in the /App/com.toyopagroup.picaboo/laguna directory and in the PLIST and JSON files in the /App/com.toyopagroup.picaboo/Library directory (Figure 4).

5.   Limitations and Challenges

Only two experiment trials were performed using Spectacles device S1 due to poor battery life, lack of charging equipment, difficulty importing snaps and unpredictable usage availability. Most of the snaps taken with the Spectacles device S1 on the iPhone 11 (P1) displayed thumbnails in the Snapchat application; however, it was possible to import only the first four snaps. As reported by Buxton [7], first-generation Spectacles devices such as S1 have several mechanical problems due to design flaws. The two trials involving Spectacles device S1 were conducted only on iPhone 11 (P1) and it was only possible to examine the backups using iExplorer because access was not available to the Cellebrite and Magnet AXIOM tools at the time. As a result, most of the analysis conducted using iExplorer, Cellebrite and Magnet AXIOM and the associated results came from images and backups of iPhone 11 (P1) and iPhone 12 (P2) using the second-generation Spectacles devices S2 and S3.

A jailbroken iPhone would likely have contained artifacts and data that were more accessible. Several folders that appeared to be promising were discovered, but they turned out to be empty. An article by Magnet Forensics [13] providing support for Magnet AXIOM says that obtaining encryption keys from a jailbroken device could help with uncovering more artifacts and decrypting Snapchat Memories and Snapchat My Eyes Only content.

In summary, images, videos, thumbnails and metadata files originating from Spectacles devices were stored in the /App/com.toyopagroup.pi cab-oo/Documents/laguna directory. This directory also contained the `device-list-archive.dat` file that provided data and insights about the Spectacles devices and transferred files. The Spectacles device data included the firmware version, device name, pairing information, Wi-Fi password (if enabled on the Spectacles device), timestamps and setup information. The file also contained location information (if available), timestamps, sizes, durations and the filenames of the images, videos, thumbnails and metadata originating from the Spectacles device.

6. Conclusions

This chapter has described the process of examining and analyzing forensic artifacts from Snapchat iOS apps that relate to the use of Spectacles devices. Non-jailbroken iPhone 11 and iPhone 12 smartphones with the Snapchat app installed and paired with first- and second-generation Spectacles devices were used to share snaps taken within the apps and with the iPhone cameras. Logical and physical acquisitions were conducted to obtain forensic images for analysis. Analysis of the forensic images using Macroplant iExplorer, Cellebrite Physical Analyzer and Magnet AXIOM Examine enabled the recovery of several photos, videos, thumbnails and metadata files originating from Spectacles devices that were tied to specific times, iPhone devices and locations. The results provide interesting insights into evidence collection during each step of the Spectacles-iPhone pairing process.

Research on forensic analyses of wearable devices [5] and the presence of sensitive user data from smartwatch devices [18] indicate that future research should examine the Spectacles devices themselves. Since this research only considered iPhones that sent snaps, it would be worthwhile to also look at iPhones that received snaps. Additionally, due to the different default deletion times in Snapchat [25] and the option to change when snaps are deleted, it would be valuable to conduct experiments that image iPhones several times over an extended period after snaps are created, shared, sent and received. Future research will also examine other glasses and wearable devices to understand and extract the stored evidence and evaluate its admissibility.

Acknowledgement

This research was supported by the National Science Foundation under the CyberCorps Scholarship for Service (SFS) Program Grant no. DGE 2043302.

References

[1] T. Alyahya and F. Kausar, Snapchat analysis to discover digital forensic artifacts on Android smartphones, *Procedia Computer Science*, vol. 109, pp. 1035–1040, 2017.

[2] M. Anderson, I-TEAM — Ambushed by images: An investigation into online child sexual abuse, *WRDW-TV*, Atlanta, Georgia (`www.wrdw.com/2021/10/07/i-team-ambushed-by-images-an-investigation-into-online-child-sexual-abuse`), October 7, 2021.

[3] Apple Developer Program, About Apple File System, Apple, Cupertino, California (`developer.apple.com/documentation/foundation/file_system/about_apple_file_system`), 2021.

[4] Apple Developer Program, File System Basics, Apple, Cupertino, California (`developer.apple.com/library/archive/documentation/FileManagement/Conceptual/FileSystemProgrammingGuide/FileSystemOverview/FileSystemOverview.html`), 2021

[5] I. Baggili, J. Oduro, K. Anthony, F. Breitinger and G. McGee, Watch what you wear: Preliminary forensic analysis of smart watches, *Proceedings of the Tenth International Conference on Availability, Reliability and Security*, pp. 303–311, 2015.

[6] H. bin Azhar, R. Cox and A. Chamberlain, Forensic investigations of popular ephemeral messaging applications on Android and iOS platforms, *International Journal on Advances in Security*, vol. 13(1-2), pp. 41–53, 2020.

[7] M. Buxton, The pipeline: The Snapchat Spectacles engineer who embraces failure, *Yahoo! News* (`www.yahoo.com/news/pipeline-snapchat-spectacles-engineer-embraces-173500431.html`), July 26, 2018.

[8] B. Caddy, Picaboo: How to send naughty photos without getting caught, *ShinyShiny* (`www.shinyshiny.tv/2011/09/how-to-send-naughty-photos-without-getting-caught.html`) September 16, 2011.

[9] A. Chamberlain and H. bin Azhar, Comparisons of forensic tools to recover ephemeral data from iOS apps used for cyberbullying, *Proceedings of the Fourth International Conference on Cyber-Technologies and Cyber-Systems*, pp. 88–93, 2019.

[10] K. Chaykowski, Snapchat leaps into hardware, rebrands as 'Snap Inc.', *Forbes*, September 24, 2016.

[11] J. Colao, The inside story of Snapchat: The world's hottest app or a $3 billion disappearing act? *Forbes*, January 19, 2014.

[12] Europol, Money muling, The Hague, The Netherlands (`www.europol.europa.eu/activities-services/public-awareness-and-prevention-guides/money-muling`), December 1, 2021.

[13] Magnet Forensics, Decrypt app data using the iOS Keychain and GrayKey, Herndon, Virginia (`support.magnetforensics.com/s/article/Decrypt-app-data-using-the-iOS-Keychain-GrayKey`), April 18, 2022.

[14] A. Malley, A Comparison Analysis of Saved Snapchat Video Files on Androids vs. iPhones, M.S. Thesis, Recording Arts Program, College of Arts and Media, University of Colorado Denver, Denver, Colorado, 2021.

[15] R. Matthews, K. Lovell and M. Sorell, Ghost protocol – Snapchat as a method of surveillance, *Digital Investigation*, vol. 36(S), article no. 301112, 2021.

[16] S. O'Dea, iPhone users as share of smartphone users in the United States 2014-2021, Statista, New York (`www.statista.com/statistics/260811/social-network-penetration-worldwide`), 2021.

[17] S. O'Dea, Market share of mobile operating systems worldwide 2012-2021, Statista, New York (`www.statista.com/statistics/260811/social-network-penetration-worldwide`), 2021.

[18] N. Odom, J. Lindmar, J. Hirt and J. Brunty, Forensic inspection of sensitive user data and artifacts from smartwatch wearable devices, *Journal of Forensic Sciences*, vol. 64(6), pp. 1673–1686, 2019.

[19] M. Raji, Digital Forensic Tools and Cloud-Based Machine Learning for Analyzing Crime Data, M.S. Thesis, Department of Information Technology, Georgia Southern University, Statesboro, Georgia, 2018.

[20] S. Ray, Snapchat promises crackdown on sale of illicit drugs amid Fentanyl scare, *Forbes*, October 7, 2021.

[21] Snap, Transparency Report, July 1, 2020 – December 31, 2020, Santa Monica, California (`snap.com/en-US/privacy/transparency/2020-12-31`), 2021.

[22] Snapchat Support, About Snap Map, Snap, Santa Monica, California (`support.snapchat.com/en-US/article/snap-map-about`), 2021.

[23] Snapchat Support, Saving and deleting snaps, Santa Monica, California (`support.snapchat.com/en-US/a/saving-snaps`), 2021.

[24] Snapchat Support, Snap Camera FAQ, Snap, Santa Monica, California (`support.snapchat.com/en-US/article/snap-camera-faq`), 2021.

[25] Snapchat Support, When does Snapchat delete snaps and chats? Snap, Santa Monica, California (`support.snapchat.com/en-US/a/when-are-snaps-chats-deleted`), 2021.

[26] Statista, Social network penetration worldwide from 2017 to 2025, New York (`www.statista.com/statistics/260811/social-network-penetration-worldwide`), 2020.

[27] Statista, Countries with the most Snapchat users 2021, New York (`www.statista.com/statistics/315405/snapchat-user-region-distribution`), 2021.

[28] Statista, Favorite social networks of U.S. teens 2012-2020, New York (`www.statista.com/statistics/250172/social-network-usage-of-us-teens-and-young-adults`), 2021.

[29] Statista, Snapchat: Number of global users 2018-2024, New York (`www.statista.com/statistics/626835/number-of-monthly-active-snapchat-users`), 2021.

[30] D. Walnycky, I. Baggili, A. Marrington, J. Moore and F. Breitinger, Network and device forensic analysis of Android social-messaging applications, *Digital Investigation*, vol. 14(S1), pp. S77–S84, 2015.

[31] C. Wu, C. Vance, R. Boggs and T. Fenger, Forensic analysis of data transience applications in iOS and Android, Poster Presentation, Forensic Science Graduate Program, Marshall University, Huntington, West Virginia (`www.marshall.edu/forensics/files/Wu-Poster.pdf`), 2013.

III

IMAGE AND VIDEO FORENSICS

Chapter 5

SPOOFED FINGERPRINT IMAGE DETECTION USING LOCAL PHASE PATCH SEGMENT EXTRACTION AND A LIGHTWEIGHT NETWORK

Sani Mohammed Abdullahi, Shuifa Sun, Asad Malik, Otabek Khudeyberdiev and Riskhan Basheer

Abstract   Fingerprint spoofing is one of the most successful attacks on fingerprint biometric systems. It involves the presentation of a fake fingerprint to a biometric sensor, which recognizes it as the original template and consistently uses it to authenticate an impostor as the genuine owner of the template.

   This chapter presents a methodology for combating fingerprint spoofing that employs local phase patch segment extraction and a lightweight triple-dense network. The methodology segments an input fingerprint image using local phase patch segment extraction, which also assists in extracting texture information so that each segment contains a consistent number of patches and each patch contains adequate minutiae information. The segmented image is fed to the lightweight triple-dense network, which is designed to generate discriminative information that helps distinguish between live and spoofed fingerprint images. This ensures optimum recognition accuracy and fast processing time while eliminating overfitting. Experimental evaluations using the LivDet 2013 and LivDet 2015 fingerprint datasets reveal that the methodology accurately classifies live and spoofed fingerprint images with an overall accuracy of 95.5%. Intra-class variation and inter-class similarity are eliminated by generalization without any accuracy degradation.

Keywords: Fingerprint spoofing detection, neural network, local phase quantization

1.   Introduction

   As biometric recognition systems are increasingly used for authentication, passcodes and cards are rapidly becoming obsolete. However, the

© IFIP International Federation for Information Processing 2022
Published by Springer Nature Switzerland AG 2022
G. Peterson and S. Shenoi (Eds.): DigitalForensics 2022, IFIP AICT 653, pp. 85–105, 2022.
https://doi.org/10.1007/978-3-031-10078-9_5

vulnerability of biometric authentication systems to fingerprint spoofing attacks has raised concerns due to their deployment in systems for secure mobile transactions, border security checks, smartphone locks and myriad user identity and authentication applications [20].

Fingerprints have been spoofed using replicas of original fingerprints made from inexpensive materials such as Ecoflex, silicone, latex, gelatin, Play-Doh and wood glue. Meanwhile, advanced 3D printing techniques are increasingly used to produce high-quality spoofed fingerprints.

Fingerprint liveness detection, which analyzes live and spoofed fingerprints from diverse sources, is a recognized countermeasure against fingerprint spoofing. The two main classes of countermeasures involve hardware and software solutions [5, 18, 20]. A hardware-based fingerprint authentication system typically incorporates sensors (usually integrated in a fingerprint reader) that detect the liveness condition or vitality characterization of the skin by considering features such as blood flow, pulse, temperature and distortion. Fingerprint authentication systems that rely on special vitality characterization sensors are able to circumvent spoofing attacks. However, they are complex and upgrades can be expensive, leading to degradation in accuracy.

A software-based fingerprint authentication system uses features extracted from captured fingerprint images to differentiate between live and spoofed fingerprints. These solutions do not require the integration of special vitality characterization sensors. As a result, they are easier to update and more cost-effective while ensuring accuracy.

This chapter presents a software-based methodology for combating fingerprint spoofing that employs local phase patch segment extraction and a lightweight triple-dense network. The methodology segments an input fingerprint image using local phase patch segment extraction, which also assists in extracting texture information so that each segment contains a consistent number of patches and each patch contains adequate minutiae information. The segmented image is fed to the lightweight triple-dense network, which is designed to generate more discriminative information for distinguishing between live and spoofed fingerprint images. This ensures optimum recognition accuracy and fast processing time while avoiding overfitting.

2.   Literature Review

Traditional software solutions employ techniques that rely on anatomical features of fingerprints (e.g., pores), physiological features (e.g., perspiration) and/or texture features. Marasco and Sansone [19] exploit robust morphological features and perspiration of presented fingerprints to measure their vitality. Ghiani et al. [6] leverage the insensitivity of local phase quantization to blurring effects to distinguish between live and spoofed fingerprints; their approach yields promising results, but it lacks a generalization capability. Nikam and Agarwal [24] have proposed a technique that uses local binary pattern histograms to capture texture details in fingerprint images such as orientation, smoothness, roughness and regularity; although the technique provides good classification results, it cannot identify spoofed fingerprints. Jiang and Liu [16] improved the technique of Nikam and Agarwal [24] using a uniform local binary pattern in a spatial pyramid; the method achieves good invariance and better accuracy.

Gragnaniello et al. [12] employ a local contrast phase descriptor generated from local amplitude contrast and behavior information to enhance feature selection; a support vector machine based linear kernel classifier is employed to differentiate between live and spoofed fingerprint images. Xia et al. [29] employ a Weber local binary descriptor that utilizes differential excitation and gradient orientation components from intensity variance and orientation features, respectively; experiments performed on two fingerprint liveness detection datasets yielded good accuracy. Gonzalez-Soler et al. [10] combine three image representation approaches by integrating local and global fingerprint information in the same feature space. The technique yields much better results compared with other texture-based approaches, including the ability to detect unknown spoofed fingerprints.

A limitation of texture-feature-based extraction techniques is their inability to generalize between live and spoofed fingerprints when unknown samples from different sensors are introduced. Deep learning approaches have been applied to address this limitation; they provide robust generalization capabilities by learning from high-level semantic features. Nogueira et al. [25], Pala and Bhanu [26] and Jang et al. [14] have employed convolutional neural networks for liveness detection. Their approaches yield reasonable detection accuracy, but they fall short of achieving a full generalization capability [4]. Chugh et al. [3] attempted to address the limitation using a convolutional neural network that exploits centered and aligned local patches through the use of fingerprint minutiae; the technique yields much better detection accuracy than its predecessor approaches.

Jung et al. [17] developed a novel approach for matching fingerprint templates and their corresponding probe samples using a convolutional neural network instead of merely classifying live and spoofed fingerprints. Their approach, which uses two sequential networks, yields good detection accuracy without much increase in computational time. Yuan et al. [30] proposed an improved convolutional neural network with image scale quantization to learn high-level semantic features through supervised learning. Their approach can handle scaling problems by transforming scaled images to a fixed scale, preserving the texture and quality information of features. However, the preservation of high-level information drastically reduces the generalization capability.

A major limitation of deep learning techniques is their high computational complexity and inability to efficiently work with fine-tuned network models because they are designed for digital images instead of fingerprints. To overcome these challenges, Zhang et al. [33] proposed a light-dense network that leverages the attention-pooling layer to overcome the shortcomings of global average-pooling. The technique, which integrates a residual path in dense blocks, achieves good generalization capability with low complexity. In other work, Zhang et al. [34] proposed the novel Slim-ResCNN architecture that incorporates a stacked series of improved residual blocks designed for fingerprint liveness detection. Finally, Park et al. [27] have proposed a tiny fully-convolutional network based on the SqueezeNet fire module structure with few parameters. Their approach achieves good detection accuracy, but it is not well-tuned to fingerprint images.

This research attempts to address the limitations in previous work by leveraging the advantages of texture-based solutions from handcrafted software techniques to fine-tune networks designed for digital images. Local phase patch segment extraction is applied to segment fingerprint images and extract level 1 texture features such as ridge valley patterns and orientation information. Next, the segmented region, identified as the region of interest (RoI) with rich information including minutiae, is input to a lightweight convolutional neural network architecture that leverages pooling and dense layers to ensure that the segmented minutiae regions assist in eliminating overfitting. This improves detection accuracy while providing a generalization capability and reduced computational complexity.

3.   Proposed Methodology

The proposed methodology employs local phase patch segment extraction based on features generated from minutiae locations and orientations. High-level global semantic features are extracted using a lightweight custom network named FinSpoofNet. Since most convolutional neural network models [14, 17, 25] are built to accept input images that require fixed-length inputs of larger sizes, they may not be suitable for biometric images such as fingerprints. Therefore, re-

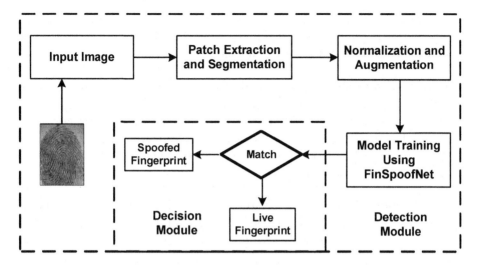

Figure 1. Fingerprint liveness detection methodology.

searchers attempt to resize input samples via pre-processing operations such as cropping and scaling. However, these operations come with shortcomings. Cropping results in the loss of some texture information, which renders the original images incomplete. Scaling compresses images, leading to geometric distortions and reduction in image resolution. To address these shortcomings, after extracting the vital minutiae information, the methodology segments images to 112×112 pixels using local phase extraction so that the input images fit into the network structure. The idea of local phase patch segment extraction comes from local phase quantization [7], which extracts rich texture information and eliminates geometric distortions using the short-term Fourier transform. This concept inspired the use of phase segmentation, which ensures that the input images fit well into the architecture without losing vital information.

Figure 1 summarizes the fingerprint liveness detection methodology. Of all the anti-spoofing techniques based on convolutional neural networks, techniques that extract local patches around minutiae have proved to be efficient and robust against fabricated fingerprints. Therefore, the methodology is designed such that each segment contains a sufficient number of patches and each patch contains minutia information regardless of the minutia position in the patch.

3.1   Local Phase Feature Extraction

The term local phase patch segment extraction is drawn from local phase quantization, which is mainly applied in software-based liveness detection techniques. Since generalized level feature extraction [2] is sought, local phase patch segment extraction begins by extracting the locations and orientations of minutiae features before segmentation.

Minutiae Extraction. The minutiae extraction algorithm specified in [1] is employed to detect minutiae information. Specifically, invariance operations are applied based on the reference minutiae $m_r = \{p_r, q_r, \theta_r\}$ where the set of minutiae locations from the given reference minutiae is $[p_i, q_i, \theta_i | i = 1, 2, \ldots, N]$ in which p_i, q_i and θ_i denote a minutia location and orientation, respectively.

Local Phase Patch Extraction. Local phase patch extraction employs a short-term Fourier transform based on local phase quantization, which is computed over each minutia patch of the local neighborhood M_{P_x} at each minutia location of the image I_x. The short-term Fourier transform is given by:

$$ST_F(f, x) = \sum_{y \in M_{P_x}} V_w \cdot I(x - y) \partial^{-2\Pi k f^N y}$$

where $x_i = p_i, q_i, \theta_i$. Note that x_i denotes the spatial coordinates (p_i, q_i) and its orientation (θ_i) and f is the frequency for defining the window vector V_w that is used to determine the patch phase neighborhood M_{P_x}. The patch neighborhood also contains all the x_i samples for each image $I_x = x^2$, which is given by:

$$M_{P_{x^2}} = [M_{P_{x_1^2}}, M_{P_{x_2^2}}, \ldots, M_{P_{x_n^2}}].$$

For effective segmentation of the phase patch extraction and to achieve the aforementioned invariance, the minutiae patch segments are set at $\partial^{-2\Pi k f^N x}$ for all the frequencies in $f = f_1, f_2, \ldots, f_n$. Subsequently, eight local coefficients are considered to repeatedly compute the eight corresponding Fourier phase-frequency points on all the segments. Thus, the phases are given by:

$$f_1 = [\varphi_{(c_1)}, 0]^T, f_2 = [0, \varphi_{(c_2)}]^T, f_3 = [\varphi_{(c_1)}, \varphi_{(c_2)}]^T, f_4 = [\varphi_{(c_2)}, \varphi_{(c_1)}]^T,$$
$$f_5 = [\varphi_{(c_3)}, 0]^T, f_6 = [0, \varphi_{(c_4)}]^T, f_7 = [\varphi_{(c_3)}, \varphi_{(c_4)}]^T, f_8 = [\varphi_{(c_4)}, \varphi_{(c_3)}]^T$$

where $\varphi_{(c_n)}$ is a scalar phase in the patch corresponding to the transforms given in all the frequencies of a particular segment. Also, for each minutia orientation, the following vector representation of all the patch invariance is extracted:

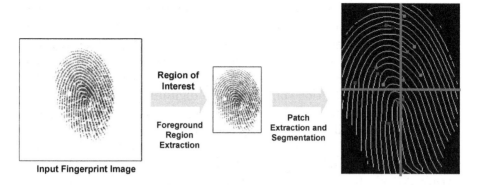

Figure 2. Local phase patch segment extraction process.

$$V_\eta = [ST_F(f_1, x), ST_F(f_2, x), ST_F(f_3, x), \ldots, ST_F(f_8, x)].$$

Consequently, each phase patch $\varphi_{(c_i)}$ is set at a corresponding minutia location from all the patch neighborhoods $M_{P_{x_i^2}}$ and aligned with respect to the minutia orientation $\theta_i(V_\eta)$. Following this, the selected segment of the minutia region is resized as:

$$\varphi_{(c_i)} = \sqrt{2P_{(p,q)}V_\eta}.$$

Phase Patch Segmentation and Normalization. Phase patch segmentation uses the extracted local patch for foreground area selection. This drastically reduces the execution time of the convolutional neural network because only the discriminative part that is rich in information is considered and used in training. The reduction in the amount of input information reduces the model size (number of parameters). This ensures that valid fingerprint information contained in the segmented patch is fully retained by the network architecture and is adequate for classification.

Figure 2 shows the steps involved in local phase patch segment extraction. Before training the segmented local patches using the convolutional neural network, the patches undergo a series of data enhancement processes that perform normalization to eliminate inconsistencies that may have been introduced during segmentation. Following this, data augmentation is performed to increase the number of samples required for training; this also helps get rid of overfitting.

FinSpoofNet Architecture. Several fingerprint liveness detection techniques such as VGG19 [25], FeatherNets [32], SqueezeNet [27] and

MobileNetV2 [28] use transfer learning techniques to fine-tune convolutional neural networks. A major drawback with fine-tuning a convolutional neural network architecture is that the final size and number of layers of the trained model are too large. This is because the original design is not intended for fingerprint images, which contain different levels of condensed information compared with digital images. As a result, the architecture cannot be implemented on low-end devices such as mobile phones; additionally, it has weak generalization capability. In contrast, the lightweight FinSpoofNet architecture developed in this research is designed from scratch with convolution, pooling and dense layers (called triple-dense). It can be implemented in lightweight mobile device applications and exhibits high spoofing detection efficiency.

Inspired by the advantages of DenseNets [13, 15], such as feature reuse, feature propagation strength and substantial reduction in the number of parameters, the last two blocks of the FinSpoofNet architecture incorporate three layers of dense networks. This is followed by attention-pooling in the fourth block before the final softmax function. The input size is decreased in each initial convolution layer while keeping the kernel size constant. All these layers incorporate the ReLU6 activation function, except for the last layer that uses the sigmoid activation function.

Conventional practice is to apply drop-out exclusively in the dense layers. However, in the FinSpoofNet architecture, drop-out is also applied in the convolution layers because the overall accuracy is increased significantly. Moreover, because overfitting has been shown to occur most commonly in the preceding network layers, a dropout value of 0.5 was adopted for the convolution layers and a dropout value of 0.2 was adopted for the equivalent dense layers in the third and fourth blocks.

Input image sizes of $112 \times 112 \times 3$ pixels and $64 \times 64 \times 3$ pixels were tested on different training sets to determine the optimum size for spoofed fingerprint detection. Eventually, a decision was made to use $112 \times 112 \times 3$ pixels, which were subsequently reduced in terms of convolutions. A 112-size 3×3 kernel with stride 1 was used on each input, yielding 64×64 feature maps of size 16. Max-pooling with 3×3 kernel size and stride 2 was then used to filter the maximum activations from the preceding 64 feature maps. In addition, a convolutional layer of filter size 3×3 and average-pooling with stride 1 was used, yielding 28 16×16 feature maps. Another average-pooling with kernel size 3×3 and stride 1 was then applied to help filter less important discriminative features. Finally, the softmax function was applied at the output step to recognize the two classes (live and spoofed fingerprints) according to the classification problem.

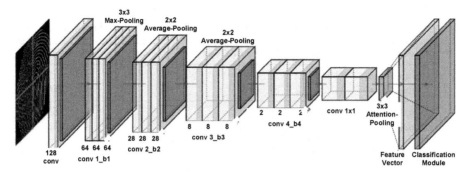

Figure 3. FinSpoofNet architecture.

In summary, after the first two-dimensional convolution layer, four major blocks were applied, each block constituting a transition layer with a 1 × 1 conv in the first three blocks. This was followed by max-pooling, average-pooling, average-pooling and attention-pooling layers with strides 1, 2, 1 and 1, respectively. To ensure robust and discriminatory information extraction from the network, [4 × 4 conv] × 3 conv filters were incorporated in all the blocks. This ensured the retention of important information previously extracted by local phase quantization (via local phase patch segment extraction). The final classification layer constituting attention-pooling and softmax assisted with the live and spoofed categorization of input patches. Figure 3 shows the FinSpoofNet architecture. Table 1 provides the detailed specification of the FinSpoofNet architecture.

The ReLU6 activation function was chosen to obtain superior performance in terms of fast processing capability, quantization friendliness due to the elimination of precision loss caused by various approximations and, of course, nonlinearity reduction. ReLU6 was used in all the layers of the FinSpoofNet architecture, except for the first and last layers. This helps maintain the lightness of the architecture. Additionally, all the features were adequately retained without a drop in resolution.

4. Experimental Results and Evaluation

This section presents an in-depth evaluation of the proposed fingerprint liveness detection methodology. First, the evaluation metrics are specified, and the datasets and training and testing strategies used in the experiments are described. Finally, the performance of the proposed methodology is compared against the performance of several state-of-the-art fingerprint liveness detection techniques.

Table 1.   Tabular representation of the FinSpoofNet architecture.

Layers	Output	FinSpoofNet	Stride	Parameters
Input Image	112×112	$32 \times 32 \times 1$		
Convolution	112×112	$32 \times$ conv	1	55,405
Block 1	64×64	$[4 \times 4 \text{ conv}] \times 3$		86,625
Transition	64×64	1×1 conv		24,353
Layer 1	32×32	3×3 max-pooling	2	
Block 2	28×28	$[4 \times 4 \text{ conv}] \times 3$		82,284
Transition	28×28	1×1 conv		27,192
Layer 2	16×16	32×2 average-pooling	1	
Block 3	8×8	$[4 \times 4 \text{ conv}] \times 3$		80,788
Transition	8×8	1×1 conv		24,557
Layer 3	4×4	2×2 average-pooling	1	
Block 4	2×2	$[4 \times 4 \text{ conv}] \times 3$		71,305
Classification	1×1	3×3 attention-pooling	1	
Layer		Softmax		
Total Parameters				452,509

4.1   Evaluation Metrics

The performance of the proposed methodology is primarily evaluated using the average classification error (ACE) metric, which is recommended as the standard evaluation metric in the Fingerprint Liveness Detection (LivDet) Competitions [8]. The ACE metric is computed as:

$$ACE = \frac{FMR(Ferrlive) + FNMR(Ferrfake)}{2}$$

where the FMR(Ferrlive) denotes the total average false match rate of misclassified live fingerprint images and FNMR(Ferrfake) denotes the total average false non-match rate of misclassified spoofed fingerprint images.

FMR(Ferrlive) and FNMR(Ferrfake) are computed as:

$$FMR(Ferrlive) = \frac{\text{Number of misclassified live images}}{\text{Number of live images}}$$

$$FNMR(Ferrfake) = \frac{\text{Number of misclassified spoofed images}}{\text{Number of spoofed images}}$$

For better performance, ACE is generally represented as a small value with respect to the pre-defined threshold value of $\gamma = 0.5$. Images are classified as live fingerprints when $\gamma > 0.5$ and spoofed fingerprints when $\gamma \leq 0.5$.

4.2   Datasets

The publicly-available LivDet 2013 [9] and LivDet 2015 [21] datasets were employed to evaluate the performance of the proposed fingerprint liveness detection methodology. The spoofed fingerprint images in the two datasets were collected from fabricated fingerprints created with materials such as Ecoflex, gelatin, latex, Modasil and wood glue.

The LivDet 2013 dataset contains fingerprint images collected using Biometrika and Italdata fingerprint readers for training purposes, and images collected from Biometrika, Crossmatch, Italdata and SwipeTest fingerprint readers for testing purposes. The experimental evaluations only employed the Biometrika and Italdata data for training and testing. This is because anomalies discovered in Crossmatch readers discourage their use for evaluation purposes [8] and SwipeTest readers have relatively low resolutions of about 96 dpi compared with other readers. The Biometrika and Italdata images in the LivDet 2013 have sizes of 315×372 pixels and 640×480 pixels with resolutions of 569 dpi and 500 dpi, respectively. The training/testing image splits were 1,000/1,000 for live and spoofed Biometrika and Italdata images; the images were selected without subject cooperation.

The LivDet 2015 dataset contains fingerprint images collected using Biometrika, Digital Persona, Green Bit and Crossmatch fingerprint readers. The images have resolutions of 500 dpi, except for the Biometrika images that have 1,000 dpi resolutions. The training/testing splits were 1,000/1,000 for live images and 1,000/1,500 for spoofed images for all the fingerprint readers except Crossmatch, whose training/testing splits were 1,510/1,473 for live images and 1,500/1,448 for spoofed images. All the images were selected with subject cooperation. The spoofed images collected using the Biometrika, Digital Persona and Green Bit fingerprint readers employed two additional materials, Liquid Ecoflex and RTV, than those used to create the LivDet 2013 dataset. The Crossmatch spoofed images were collected from fabricated fingerprints created using Body Double, Ecoflex, Play-Doh, OOMOO and gelatin materials.

Figure 4 shows sample live and spoofed fingerprint images from the LivDet 2013 and LivDet 2015 datasets. Figures 4(a) and 4(b) show sample LiveDet 2013 images taken by Biometrika and Italdata fingerprint readers, respectively. Figures 4(c) and 4(d) show sample LiveDet 2015 images taken by Digital Persona and Green Bit fingerprint readers, respectively.

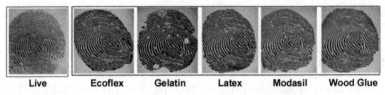

(a) Sample LiveDet 2013 images captured by Biometrika fingerprint readers.

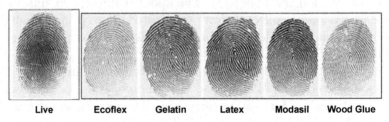

(b) Sample LiveDet 2013 images captured by Italdata fingerprint readers.

(c) Sample LiveDet 2015 images captured by Digital Persona fingerprint readers.

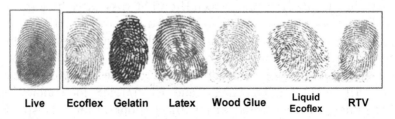

(d) Sample LiveDet 2015 images captured by Green Bit fingerprint readers.

Figure 4.   Fingerprint images from the LiveDet 2013 and LiveDet 2015 datasets.

Table 2 presents a comprehensive description of the LivDet 2013 and LivDet 2015 datasets used in the experimental evaluations. Note that the datasets contain images with different sizes (column 4). The image size diversity makes it imperative to apply the patch segment extraction to create input images with fixed (common) size. This eases convolutional neural network adaptation during the training phase, contributing to efficiency as well as improved accuracy.

Table 2. Summary of the LiveDet 2013 and LiveDet 2015 datasets used in the experimental evaluations.

Dataset	Fingerprint Reader	Model	Image Size, Resolution (dpi)	Cooperative Subject	Live/Spoofed Images (Training/Testing)	Spoofing Materials
LiveDet 2013 [9]	Biometrika	FX2000	315 × 372, 569	No	1,000/1,000, 1,000/1,000	Ecoflex, Gelatin, Latex, Modasil, Wood Glue
	Italdata	ET10	640 × 480, 500	No	1,000/1,000, 1,000/1,000	
LiveDet 2015 [21]	Biometrika	HiScan-PRO	1000 × 1000, 1000	Yes	1,000/1,000, 1,000/1,500	Ecoflex, Gelatin, Latex, Wood Glue, Liquid Ecoflex, RTV
	Digital Persona	U.are.U 5160	252 × 324, 500	Yes	1,000/1,000, 1,000/1,500	
	Green Bit	DactyScan26	500 × 500, 500	Yes	1,000/1,000, 1,000/1,500	
	Crossmatch	L Scan Guardian	640 × 480, 500	Yes	1,510/1,473, 1,500/1,448	Body Double, Ecoflex, Play-Doh, OOMOO, Gelatin

4.3   Performance Evaluation

The performance evaluation examined the classification accuracy of the proposed fingerprint liveness detection methodology for each training set and validation set drawn from the LivDet 2013 and LivDet 2015 datasets.

Robustness Comparison.   Three fingerprint liveness detection scenarios were developed to investigate the robustness of the proposed methodology against unknown spoofing materials and different sensors. The three scenarios are: (i) known materials and known sensors, (ii) unknown materials and known sensors and (iii) known materials and unknown sensors.

Known Materials and Known Sensors Scenario.   In the first evaluation scenario, the materials used to create spoofed fingerprints and sensors used to capture the fingerprint images were known, i.e., they were used for training and testing. The spoofed fingerprint materials were mainly used for testing purposes whereas all the captured fingerprint images (live and spoofed) were utilized for training and testing purposes. The scenario was designed to evaluate the robustness of the proposed methodology against other light architectures for detecting spoofed fingerprints, specifically, Slim-ResCNN [34], fPADnet [23], TripleNet [26] FDLNet [33] and DRN [31]. To ensure inclusion, FinSpoofNet is also evaluated against traditional software (non-deep learning) techniques, specifically, WLBD [29], FPAD [10] and LCPD [11].

Table 3 shows that the proposed FinSpoofNet methodology generally outperforms most of the state-of-the-art techniques with average ACE metric values of 0.31% and 2.26% for the LivDet 2013 and LivDet 2015 datasets, respectively. In contrast, Slim-ResCNN, fPADnet and LCPD yield average ACE metric values of 1.74%, 1.10% and 1.25%, respectively, for the LivDet 2013 dataset. Also, Slim-ResCNN, fPADnet and FPAD yield average ACE metric values of 3.11%, 3.58% and 2.82%, respectively, for the LivDet 2015 dataset. The proposed FinSpoofNet methodology yields the best overall average ACE metric value of 1.62% whereas WLBD has the worst overall average ACE metric value of 6.68%.

Unknown Materials and Known Sensors Scenario.   In the second evaluation scenario, the materials used to create spoofed fingerprints for testing were not used for training, but the sensors used to capture the fingerprint images were used for training and testing. Robustness was evaluated using the LivDet 2015 dataset in a cross-material fashion

Table 3. ACE comparison against lightweight deep-learning techniques and traditional software techniques.

Technique	LivDet 2013			LivDet 2015					Overall Avg.
	Biometrika	Italdata	Avg.	Biometrika	Digital Person	Green Bit	Crossmatch	Avg.	
Deep-Learning-Based									
Slim-ResCNN [34]	0.47	3.01	1.74	3.10	2.37	2.64	4.32	3.11	2.65
fPADnet [23]	0.90	1.30	1.10	4.10	8.50	1.40	0.30	3.58	2.75
TripleNet [26]	0.65	0.50	0.56	–	–	–	–	–	–
FLDNet [33]	0.36	1.35	0.86	2.95	3.61	0.53	1.78	2.22	1.76
DRN [31]	2.00	1.80	1.90	6.24	6.80	4.77	3.46	5.32	4.18
Software-Based									
WLBD [29]	0.40	0.95	0.68	9.64	13.72	4.53	10.82	9.68	6.68
FPAD [10]	0.50	0.10	0.30	3.20	4.60	1.20	2.28	2.82	1.98
LCPD [11]	1.20	1.30	1.25	–	–	–	–	–	–
FinSpoofNet	0.38	0.27	0.31	2.88	3.42	1.35	1.41	2.26	1.62

Table 4. Robustness comparison against the LivDet 2015 and LivDet 2017 winners.

Technique	LivDet 2015 Dataset	Unknown Materials and Known Sensors				
		Ferrlive (%)	Ferrfake (%)	Ferrfake- unknown (%)	Ferrfake- known (%)	ACE
Winner	Biometrika	8.50	3.73	2.70	5.80	5.64
LivDet	Digital Persona	8.10	5.07	4.60	6.00	6.28
2015 [21]	Green Bit	3.50	5.33	4.30	7.40	4.60
	Crossmatch	0.93	2.90	2.12	4.02	1.90
	Average	4.78	4.27	3.48	5.72	4.49
Winner	Biometrika	3.35	4.23	2.44	7.72	2.98
LivDet	Digital Persona	4.28	4.78	3.73	6.40	4.58
2017 [22]	Green Bit	2.22	2.65	2.42	3.11	2.19
	Crossmatch	1.72	3.91	3.18	4.58	2.99
	Average	3.14	3.89	2.99	5.45	3.18
FinSpoofNet	Digital Persona	3.75	2.94	2.55	4.83	3.42
	Green Bit	1.36	1.56	1.39	1.95	1.35
	Biometrika	2.04	3.88	2.42	6.01	2.88
	Crossmatch	1.13	2.74	1.97	4.25	1.41
	Average	2.07	2.78	2.08	4.26	2.26

because the LivDet 2015 testing dataset comprises spoofed fingerprint images created using six unknown materials.

Table 4 compares the robustness of the proposed FinSpoofNet methodology against the LivDet 2015 [21] and LivDet 2017 [22] competition winners. Note that the percentages of misclassified spoofed images created using known and unknown materials are identified as Ferrfakeknown and Ferrfakeunknown, respectively. Also, Ferrfake denotes the misclassified spoofed fingerprints under the number of samples in the Ferrfakeknown and Ferrfakeunknown categories.

Table 4 shows that the proposed FinSpoofNet methodology generally outperforms the other techniques in terms of the ACE metric values. However, the LivDet 2015 winner yields slightly better robustness for Crossmatch images in the Ferrlive and Ferrfakeknown categories.

To ensure further generalization capability, the LivDet 2013 dataset was used for a second set of cross-material tests while adopting the protocol employed by Nogueira et al. [25]. Table 5 presents the results of the comparison. The proposed FinSpoofNet methodology has a lower error rate than the FSB [3], TripleNet [26] and VGG19 [25] techniques, demonstrating that FinSpoofNet has the best efficiency and robustness.

Table 5. Cross-material robustness comparison against state-of-the-art techniques.

Dataset	Training Materials	Testing Materials	FSB [3]	TripleNet [26]	VGG19 [25]	FinSpoofNet
Biometrika	Wood Glue,	Modasil	1.30	2.10	4.90	0.75
Italdata	Ecoflex	Gelatin, Latex	0.60	1.25	6.30	1.22
Average			0.95	1.68	5.60	0.98

Table 6. Cross-sensor comparison against state-of-the-art techniques.

Training Dataset (Testing Dataset)	FSB [3]	TripleNet [26]	FLDNet [33]	FinSpoofNet
Biometrika (Italdata)	4.30	1.55	2.10	1.96
Italdata (Biometrika)	3.50	3.80	2.90	2.98
Average	3.90	2.68	2.50	2.47

Known Materials and Unknown Sensors Scenario. In the third evaluation scenario, the materials used to create spoofed fingerprints were used for training and testing. However, different sensors were employed to capture fingerprint images in the training and testing sets. This scenario primarily evaluates the discrimination ability of fingerprint liveness detection techniques under environmental and sensor variations. The protocol used in the second scenario [25] was adopted to select the training and testing sets. Table 6 shows that the proposed FinSpoofNet methodology has better discrimination capabilities than the FSB [3], TripleNet [26] and FLDNet [33] techniques.

4.4   System Setup and Processing Time

The experiments employed a MATLAB VerR2018b implementation with a Corei7-3.00 GHz processor and 16 GB RAM for local phase patch segment extraction and a Keras deep learning framework with a GTX 1080 GPU to implement the FinSpoofNet architecture and perform evaluations. The processing time for a single batch of 50 patches in the FinSpoofNet methodology was about 0.8 ms, which outperformed most of the state-of-the-art techniques. Thus, the proposed FinSpoofNet methodology meets the real-time processing requirements of the best-performing fingerprint liveness detection techniques.

5.   Conclusions

The novel fingerprint liveness detection methodology developed in this research incorporates local phase patch segment extraction (coined from local phase quantization) and a custom lightweight convolutional neural network architecture. Local phase patch segment extraction ensures local patch segmentation and the extraction of minutiae and local texture features from fingerprint images, which are subsequently trained and validated by the convolutional neural network. This leads to the extraction of additional discriminative and semantic feature information, following which the final softmax classifier differentiates between live and spoofed fingeprint images. The lightweight FinSpoofNet architecture enables fingerprint liveness detection to be deployed in real-time applications on devices with limited computational resources.

Experimental evaluations involving comparisons against state-of-the-art deep learning and software-based techniques demonstrate that the proposed fingerprint liveness detection methodology has superior classification accuracy. Additionally, the methodology demonstrates good robustness and discrimination characteristics in three key scenarios involving known materials and known sensors, unknown materials and known sensors, and known materials and unknown sensors. The experimental results also demonstrate the overall efficiency of the fingerprint liveness detection methodology.

Future work will attempt to incorporate a matching algorithm in the convolutional neural network architecture using a fusion approach. This will provide improved generalization and robustness characteristics when identifying spoofed fingerprints created using unknown materials.

Acknowledgement

This research was supported by China Three Gorges University High-Level Talent Funding under Grant No. 1910103.

References

[1] J. Abraham, P. Kwan and J. Gao, Fingerprint matching using a hybrid shape and orientation descriptor, in *State of the Art in Biometrics*, J. Yang and L. Nanni (Eds.), IntechOpen, London, United Kingdom, pp. 25–56, 2011.

[2] A. Alshdadi, R. Mehboob, H. Dawood, M. Alassafi, R. Alghamdi and H. Dawood, Exploiting level 1 and level 3 features of fingerprints for liveness detection, *Biomedical Signal Processing and Control*, vol. 61, article no. 102039, 2020.

[3] T. Chugh, K. Cao and A. Jain, Fingerprint spoof buster: Use of minutiae-centered patches, *IEEE Transactions on Information Forensics and Security*, vol. 13(9), pp. 2190–2202, 2018.

[4] T. Chugh and A. Jain, Fingerprint spoof detector generalization, *IEEE Transactions on Information Forensics and Security*, vol. 16, pp. 42–55, 2021.

[5] J. Galbally, S. Marcel and J. Fierrez, Biometric antispoofing methods: A survey in face recognition, *IEEE Access*, vol. 2, pp. 1530–1552, 2014.

[6] L. Ghiani, A. Hadid, G. Marcialis and F. Roli, Fingerprint liveness detection using local texture features, *IET Biometrics*, vol. 6(3), pp. 224–231, 2017.

[7] L. Ghiani, G. Marcialis and F. Roli, Fingerprint liveness detection by local phase quantization, *Proceedings of the Twenty-First International Conference on Pattern Recognition*, pp. 537–540, 2012.

[8] L. Ghiani, D. Yambay, V. Mura, G. Marcialis, F. Roli and S. Schuckers, Review of the Fingerprint Liveness Detection (LivDet) Competition Series: 2009 to 2015, *Image and Vision Computing*, vol. 58, pp. 110–128, 2017.

[9] L. Ghiani, D. Yambay, V. Mura, S. Tocco, G. Marcialis, F. Roli and S. Schuckers, LivDet 2013 Fingerprint Liveness Detection Competition 2013, *Proceedings of the International Conference on Biometrics*, 2013.

[10] L. Gonzalez-Soler, M. Gomez-Barrero, L. Chang, A. Perez-Suarez and C. Busch, Fingerprint presentation attack detection based on local feature encoding for unknown attacks, *IEEE Access*, vol. 9, pp. 5806–5820, 2021.

[11] D. Gragnaniello, G. Poggi, C. Sansone and L. Verdoliva, An investigation of local descriptors for biometric spoofing detection, *IEEE Transactions on Information Forensics and Security*, vol. 10(4), pp. 849–863, 2015.

[12] D. Gragnaniello, G. Poggi, C. Sansone and L. Verdoliva, Local contrast phase descriptor for fingerprint liveness detection, *Pattern Recognition*, vol. 48(4), pp. 1050–1058, 2015.

[13] G. Huang, Z. Liu, L. van der Maaten and K. Weinberger, Densely connected convolutional networks, *Proceedings of the IEEE Conference on Computer Vision and Pattern Recognition*, pp. 2261–2269, 2017.

[14] H. Jang, H. Choi, D. Kim, J. Son and H. Lee, Fingerprint spoof detection using contrast enhancement and convolutional neural networks, *Proceedings of the International Conference on Information Science and Applications*, pp. 331–338, 2017.

[15] W. Jian, Y. Zhou and H. Liu, Densely connected convolutional network optimized by genetic algorithm for fingerprint liveness detection, *IEEE Access*, vol. 9, pp. 2229–2243, 2021.

[16] Y. Jiang and X. Liu, Uniform local binary pattern for fingerprint liveness detection in the Gaussian pyramid, *Journal of Electrical and Computer Engineering*, vol. 2018, article no. 1539298, 2018.

[17] H. Jung, Y. Heo and S. Lee, Fingerprint liveness detection by a template-probe convolutional neural network, *IEEE Access*, vol. 7, pp. 118986–118993, 2019.

[18] E. Marasco and A. Ross, A survey of antispoofing schemes for fingerprint recognition systems, *ACM Computing Surveys*, vol. 47(2), article no. 28, 2015.

[19] E. Marasco and C. Sansone, Combining perspiration- and morphology-based static features for fingerprint liveness detection, *Pattern Recognition Letters*, vol. 33(9), pp. 1148–1156, 2012.

[20] S. Marcel, M. Nixon, J. Fierrez and N. Evans (Eds.), *Handbook of Biometric Anti-Spoofing: Presentation Attack Detection*, Springer, Cham, Switzerland, 2019.

[21] V. Mura, L. Ghiani, G. Marcialis, F. Roli, D. Yambay and S. Schuckers, LivDet 2015 Fingerprint Liveness Detection Competition, *Proceedings of the Seventh IEEE International Conference on Biometrics Theory, Applications and Systems*, 2015.

[22] V. Mura, G. Orru, R. Casula, A. Sibiriu, G. Loi, P. Tuveri, L. Ghiani and G. Marcialis, LivDet 2017 Fingerprint Liveness Detection Competition 2017, *Proceedings of the International Conference on Biometrics*, pp. 297–302, 2018.

[23] T. Nguyen, E. Park, X. Cui, V. Nguyen and H. Kim, fPADnet: Small and efficient convolutional neural network for presentation attack detection, *Sensors*, vol. 18(8), article no. 2532, 2018.

[24] S. Nikam and S. Agarwal, Texture and wavelet-based spoof fingerprint detection for fingerprint biometric systems, *Proceedings of the First International Conference on Emerging Trends in Engineering and Technology*, pp. 675–680, 2008.

[25] R. Nogueira, R. Lotufo and R. Machado, Fingerprint liveness detection using convolutional neural networks, *IEEE Transactions on Information Forensics and Security*, vol. 11(6), pp. 1206–1213, 2016.

[26] F. Pala and B. Bhanu, Deep triplet embedding representations for liveness detection, in *Deep Learning for Biometrics*, B. Bhanu and A. Kumar (Eds.), Springer, Cham, Switzerland, pp. 287–307, 2017.

[27] E. Park, X. Cui, T. Nguyen and H. Kim, Presentation attack detection using a tiny fully convolutional network, *IEEE Transactions on Information Forensics and Security*, vol. 14(11), pp. 3016–3025, 2019.

[28] M. Sandler, A. Howard, M. Zhu, A. Zhmoginov and L. Chen, MobileNetV2: Inverted residuals and linear bottlenecks, *Proceedings of the IEEE/CVF Conference on Computer Vision and Pattern Recognition*, pp. 4510–4520, 2018.

[29] Z. Xia, C. Yuan, R. Lv, X. Sun, N. Xiong and Y. Shi, A novel Weber local binary descriptor for fingerprint liveness detection, *IEEE Transactions on Systems, Man and Cybernetics: Systems*, vol. 50(4), pp. 1526–1536, 2020.

[30] C. Yuan, Z. Xia, L. Jiang, Y. Cao, Q. Wu and X. Sun, Fingerprint liveness detection using an improved CNN with image scale equalization, *IEEE Access*, vol. 7, pp. 26953–26966, 2019.

[31] C. Yuan, Z. Xia, X. Sun and Q. Wu, Deep residual network with adaptive learning framework for fingerprint liveness detection, *IEEE Transactions on Cognitive and Developmental Systems*, vol. 12(3), pp. 461–473, 2020.

[32] P. Zhang, F. Zou, Z. Wu, N. Dai, M. Skarpness, M. Fu, J. Zhao and K. Li, FeatherNets: Convolutional neural networks as light as a feather for face anti-spoofing, *Proceedings of the IEEE/CVF Conference on Computer Vision and Pattern Recognition Workshops*, pp. 1574–1583, 2019.

[33] Y. Zhang, S. Pan, X. Zhan, Z. Li, M. Gao and C. Gao, FLDNet: Light dense CNN for fingerprint liveness detection, *IEEE Access*, vol. 8, pp. 84141–84152, 2020.

[34] Y. Zhang, D. Shi, X. Zhan, D. Cao, K. Zhu and Z. Li, Slim-ResCNN: A deep residual convolutional neural network for fingerprint liveness detection, *IEEE Access*, vol. 7, pp. 91476–91487, 2019.

Chapter 6

A COMBINED FEATURE ENCODING NETWORK WITH SEMANTIC ENHANCEMENT FOR IMAGE TAMPERING FORENSICS

Yuling Luo, Ce Liang, Shunsheng Zhang and Sheng Qin

Abstract   Image tampering forensics is performed by analyzing images to locate the tampered regions. However, most image tampering detection methods lack locational accuracy and are effective only for specific types of tampering. To address these problems, this chapter proposes a method that employs an encoder-decoder network structure with combined multiple feature encoding to segment tampered regions of an image from untampered regions. Three features, obtained using constrained convolution, steganalysis rich model filtering and common convolution, are combined. During the encoding stage, ring residual units are used to extract features. The combination of multiple features and the ring residual units makes the proposed method most suitable for image tampering detection. Channel attention with a soft threshold function is used to reinforce semantic information in the decoding stage. Experiments with three image forensic datasets, NIST16, COVERAGE and CASIA, demonstrate that the proposed method exhibits strong performance in terms of the F1 score and localization of tampered regions.

Keywords: Image tampering, encoder-decoder, combined features, semantics

1.   Introduction

Digital image editing software is often used by unscrupulous individuals to tamper with images for purposes of fraud, harassment and blackmail. It is imperative to develop image forensic techniques that can effectively detect tampered images created by sophisticated image editing software.

ⓒ IFIP International Federation for Information Processing 2022
Published by Springer Nature Switzerland AG 2022
G. Peterson and S. Shenoi (Eds.): DigitalForensics 2022, IFIP AICT 653, pp. 107–121, 2022.
https://doi.org/10.1007/978-3-031-10078-9_6

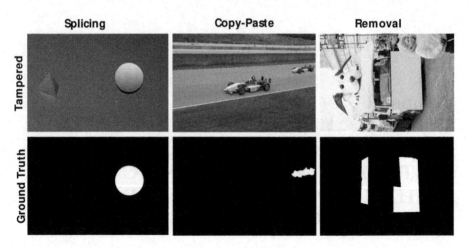

Figure 1. Image tampering using splicing, copy-paste and removal.

In general, image tampering involves image splicing, copy-paste and removal. The first row in Figure 1 shows tampered images created by the three techniques and the second row shows the corresponding ground truth masks of the images. Splicing adds an object or part of an image to another image. Copy-paste adds an object from an image to another area of the same image, resulting in two similar objects. Removal eliminates an area of an image or hides certain objects in an image.

Early research on image tampering detection developed algorithms that relied on prior knowledge about the questioned images. For example, Luo et al. [11] analyzed the error distributions caused by one or two image compressions to detect tampering. Ferrara et al. [7] examined the interpolated characteristics of color filter arrays to discover tampered regions in images. Mahdian and Saic [12] analyzed the noise distributions of images to detect tampered regions. The principal limitation of these and other algorithms based on manually-designed features is that they can detect tampered images only under specific conditions.

Recently, deep learning methods that leverage convolutional neural networks (CNNs) have demonstrated good performance in various image recognition tasks [8, 10]. However, image tampering detection is more challenging than image recognition because it requires finding subtle traces of tampered regions in images. Wu et al. [15] computed correlations between pairs of pixels in images to locate tampered regions; however, the approach only focuses on copy-paste tampering. Zhou et al. [19] analyzed red-green-blue (RGB) and noise streams to detect image tampering. Bi et al. [5] employed a network based on ring residual units to improve feature extraction and distinguish between tampered and untampered regions of images; however, the method is only applicable to image splicing tampering detection. Bappy et al. [2, 3] employed resampled features combined with a long short term memory (LSTM) network to detect various types of image tampering. However, their original method described in [2] localizes tampering at the image block level, which reduces its accuracy. Although the new method of Bappy et al. [3] achieves pixel-level localization, its accuracy still needs to be improved.

In summary, most state-of-the-art image tampering detection methods focus on specific types of tampering and/or have inaccurate localization. To address these limitations, this chapter proposes a generalized image tampering detection network structure. First, convolutional combinations are used to obtain combined features that contain adequate information about different types of image tampering. Next, ring residual units are used for encoding. Following this, channel attention with a soft threshold function for semantic information enhancement is employed to make the network more focused on tampered regions. Finally, decoding yields a mask with the tampered regions. The experimental results demonstrate that the proposed method outperforms baseline methods with F1 scores of 0.892 with the NIST16 dataset [13], 0.568 with the COVERAGE dataset [14] and 0.441 with the CASIA v1 dataset [6].

2. Proposed Method

The proposed method is designed to identify tampered regions in images. Figure 2 shows the network structure underlying the method. It is inadequate to use common convolution to detect image tampering traces. To address this problem, the proposed method extracts the residual features of a tampered image via constrained convolution. Constrained convolution suppresses the influence of image content on the tampered traces.

The proposed method also leverages noise features extracted by steganalysis rich model (SRM) filtering to identify noise inconsistencies between the real and tampered regions of an image. Common convolution is used to extract image texture features from the RGB channels. All these features are fused to obtain rich information. The ring residual unit enhances feature extraction to further discern differences between the untampered and tampered image regions. Additionally, channel attention with a soft threshold function (SSE) is employed to enhance semantic information in the decoding stage. The overall network is end-to-end trainable.

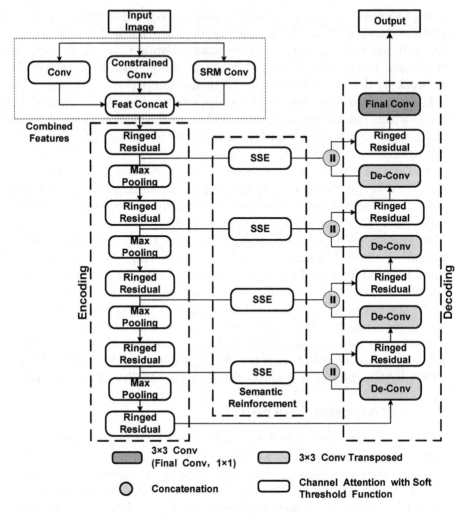

Figure 2.   Network structure.

2.1   Combined Feature Extraction

Combined feature extraction is performed using constrained convolution and steganalysis rich model convolution:

- **Constrained Convolution:** Image manipulation usually leaves specific traces of the types of image editing. Common convolution tends to learn the content of an image, but is unsuitable for learning subtle tampering traces. To address this limitation, Bayar and Stamm [4] proposed a constrained convolutional neural network for general-purpose image manipulation detection. Constrained con-

$$\frac{1}{4}\begin{bmatrix} 0 & 0 & 0 & 0 & 0 \\ 0 & -1 & 2 & -1 & 0 \\ 0 & 2 & -4 & 2 & 0 \\ 0 & -1 & 2 & -1 & 0 \\ 0 & 0 & 0 & 0 & 0 \end{bmatrix} \quad \frac{1}{12}\begin{bmatrix} -1 & 2 & -2 & 2 & -1 \\ 2 & -6 & 8 & -6 & 2 \\ -2 & 8 & -12 & 8 & -2 \\ 2 & -6 & 8 & -6 & 2 \\ -1 & 2 & -2 & 2 & -1 \end{bmatrix} \quad \frac{1}{2}\begin{bmatrix} 0 & 0 & 0 & 0 & 0 \\ 0 & 0 & 0 & 0 & 0 \\ 0 & -1 & 2 & -1 & 0 \\ 0 & 0 & 0 & 0 & 0 \\ 0 & 0 & 0 & 0 & 0 \end{bmatrix}$$

Figure 3. Stegananalysis rich model filter kernels.

volution suppresses the content of an image while adaptively learning the low-level residual features of tampered traces. It provides better generalization and robustness characteristics than common convolution.

The constrained convolutional layer is described as follows:

$$W_k(0,0) = -1$$

$$\sum_{m,n \neq 0} W_k(m,n) = 1$$

where W_k is the kth convolutional kernel and $(0,0)$ is the center coordinate of W_k.

During each iteration, W_k is normalized by updating the center position of each convolution filter to -1. The remaining partial position weights are divided by the sum of the weights other than the center position.

- **Steganalysis Rich Model Convolution.** Steganalysis rich model filtering is widely used in steganalysis to capture manipulation cues. While paying attention to the surface traces of an image, more attention should be paid to the statistical information within the image. Noise flow was proposed by Zhou et al. [19] to discover noise inconsistencies between real and tampered image regions with the noise features extracted via steganalysis rich model filtering. Steganalysis rich model filtering improves detection accuracy by analyzing the noise distribution within an image. The noise features may be extracted effectively using a steganalysis rich model filter with three kernels [19]. Figure 3 shows the three kernels of the steganalysis rich model filter.

As described above, two different features can be used for tampering detection. In this research, three different fused features are obtained from tampered images using a custom convolution of the two features as

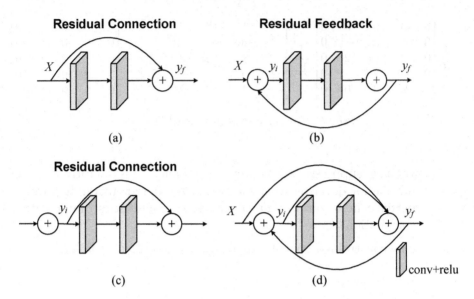

Figure 4.   Ring residual unit connections, feedback and overall structure.

well as common convolution. Wu et al. [16] state that such rich features are very effective at training image tampering detection models.

2.2   Encoding Network

The encoding network is constructed with ring residual units [5] and pooling layers. As shown in Figure 2, five ring residual units are cascaded with four pooling layers. The channels obtained, from the top to bottom of the encoding network, are 32, 64, 128, 256 and 256. Finally, a $16 \times 16 \times 256$ feature map is obtained.

A ring residual unit [5] is employed as the basic encoder. As shown in Figure 4(d), a ring residual unit comprises two residual connections and one feedback propagation. In the first residual connection shown in Figure 4(a), the feature map x is input to the ring residual unit. The output y_f is obtained by two convolution operations, a shortcut and an add operation. The size of each convolutional kernel is $3 \times 3 \times c$ (c is the number of convolutional kernels). In the residual feedback shown in Figure 4(b), the output y_i is obtained by backward propagation of y_f. In the second residual connection shown in Figure 4(c), the final output is obtained with y_i as input.

The outputs y_f and y_i are given by:

$$y_f = F(x) + x$$
$$y_i = (S(y_f) + 1) \times x$$

where $F(x)$ is the output of two convolutions, x is the input, y_f is the output after the first residual connection, S is the sigmoid activation function. The final output y_i is computed as the sum of the y_f outputs processed by the S function in the residual feedback multiplied by the input x.

2.3   Decoding Network

The decoding network is also formed by ring residual units, and each decoder has a corresponding encoder. The decoding process performs upsampling on the feature maps, which is a deconvolution operation with a 3×3 convolution kernel. Four deconvolution blocks are mapped to the corresponding encoders, where the four deconvolution blocks yield feature maps of sizes $16 \times 16 \times 256$, $32 \times 32 \times 128$, $64 \times 64 \times 64$ and $128 \times 128 \times 32$, respectively. Finally, differences between the tampered and non-tampered regions are identified using the ring residual unit.

2.4   Semantic Reinforcement

Pooling layers are widely used in convolutional neural networks to reduce overfitting. However, a pooling operation reduces the size of the feature map, causing some key information to be lost. To address this issue, an attention mechanism is utilized to enhance the semantic information extracted by the encoder for the corresponding decoding process.

Attention mechanisms can focus on important regions in a feature map. Channel attention [9] yields a set of weights that explain the importance of feature map channels. However, channel attention only focuses on channel information. As discussed in [17], a soft threshold function can be regarded as a nonlinear layer embedded in a deep neural network to eliminate unimportant features. Therefore, channel attention with a soft threshold function is used to focus on relevant regions of the feature map and further weaken the unimportant regions.

The soft threshold function is given by:

$$y = \begin{cases} x - \tau, & x > \tau \\ 0, & |x| \leq \tau \\ x + \tau, & x < -\tau \end{cases}$$

where x is the input feature, y is the output feature and τ is the threshold value.

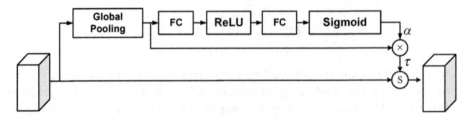

Figure 5.   Structure of channel attention with a soft threshold function.

Figure 5 shows the structure of channel attention with a soft threshold function. Global pooling is applied to the feature map to obtain a one-dimensional vector. Next, the one-dimensional vector is applied to the two-layer fully-connected (FC) network with a rectified linear unit (ReLU) and subsequently passed to a sigmoid function to obtain the weight parameter α for each channel. The threshold τ is computed as:

$$\tau_c = \alpha_c \times x_c$$

where τ_c is the threshold of the cth feature map channel, α_c is the weight parameter of the cth channel and x_c is the mean value of the cth channel obtained by global average pooling.

The threshold is positive and stays within a reasonable range. Attention with the soft threshold makes the feature map focus on the channel information and also designates regions below the threshold in each channel as irrelevant regions, weakening the focus on irrelevant regions.

3.   Experiments and Results

This section describes the experimental setup and metrics, datasets and results.

3.1   Experimental Setup and Metrics

An Nvidia GTX 2080 Ti GPU was used to execute the image tampering detection method. The parameters of the network were initialized with random values and optimized by stochastic gradient descent using a batch of 10 samples, momentum of 0.9, weight decay of 0.0005 and initial learning rate of 0.001. Cross-entropy was employed as the loss function.

The metrics used to evaluate the effectiveness of the detection method included the precision P, recall R and F1 score $F1$. The metrics were computed as follows:

Table 1. Training and testing dataset splits.

Dataset	Synthetic	NIST16	COVERAGE	CASIA
Training Set	65 K	404	375	5,123 (v2)
Testing Set	–	160	125	921 (v1)

$$P = \frac{TP}{TP + FP}$$
$$R = \frac{TP}{TP + FN}$$
$$F1 = \frac{2 \times P \times R}{P + R}$$

where the true positive TP is the number of pixels correctly detected as tampered, false negative FN is the number of pixels incorrectly detected as real, false positive FP is the number of pixels incorrectly detected as tampered, and $F1$ is the summed average of the precision P and recall R.

3.2   Datasets

The network was pre-trained using a synthetic dataset from [3] comprising approximately 65 K images with 1024×1024 pixels.

The detection method was evaluated using three image forensic datasets. The NIST16 dataset [13] includes images with three types of tampering, splicing, copy-paste and removal. The original COVERAGE dataset [14] comprises only 100 images, primarily images with copy-paste tampering; since this dataset was too small, it was augmented via image flipping to bring the total up to 500 images. The CASIA dataset [6] has two versions, CASIA v1 and CASIA v2. The CASIA v2 is usually used for fine-tuning and CASIA v1 is used for testing. During the training, all the images were resized to 256×256 pixels. Table 1 provides details about the datasets, including their training and testing splits.

3.3   Experimental Results

This section presents the results of four evaluations of the proposed detection method: ablation, comparisons of pixel-level accuracy against different methods, comparisons of F1 scores and area under curve (AUC) values against different methods, and qualitative evaluation.

Table 2.   Comparison of precision, recall and F1 scores for the NIST16 dataset.

Method	Precision	Recall	F1 Score
Base	0.840	0.800	0.819
Base-Combined	0.870	0.846	0.857
Base-SSE	0.885	0.858	0.871
Proposed Method	0.914	0.871	0.892

The proposed method was compared against traditional detection methods based on feature extraction as well as advanced methods based on deep learning, specifically, ELA [11], NOI [12], CFA [7], FCN [10], Encoder-Decoder [1], J-LSTM-Conv [2], RGB-N [19], LSTM-EnDec [3] and I-DeepLabv3 [18]. Comparisons were performed based on pixel-level accuracy, F1 score and area under curve.

Ablation.   The validity of the proposed method was evaluated by comparing it against baseline methods. The Base method uses only ring residual units [5]. The Base-Combined method uses encoding with combined features and ring residual units. The Base-SSE method uses semantic reinforcement with the soft threshold function and ring residual units.

Table 2 shows the precision, recall and F1 scores obtained for the NIST16 dataset. The Base-Combined method (using combined features) outperforms the Base method by 3% to 4.6% for all three metrics; this is because combined features convey more tampering information than individual features. The F1 score of the Base-SSE method (using semantic reinforcement) outperforms the Base method by 7% because it focuses on more important regions and compensates for information loss due to downsampling. Table 2 shows that the proposed model method has the best results (underlined) for all three metrics.

Accuracy Performance Comparisons.   Image tampering detection requires a mask expressing the tampered regions in order to be implemented using a full convolutional structure. Fully convolutional networks (FCNs) [10] and encoder-decoders [1] have been proposed to obtain masks for semantic segmentation. However, Table 3 shows that it is inadequate to use such methods to detect tampered images due to their low pixel-level accuracy results (74.28% and 82.96%). Indeed, with the best pixel-level accuracy of 98.00% (underlined), the proposed method outperforms the FCN and Encoder-Decoder methods with the NIST16 dataset. Note that the dash symbol (−) in Table 3 denotes that

Table 3. Comparison of pixel-level accuracy results.

Method	NIST16	COVERAGE	CASIA
FCN[10]	74.28%	–	–
Encoder-Decoder[1]	82.96%	–	–
J-LSTM-Conv[2]	84.60%	88.76%	–
LSTM-EnDec[3]	94.80%	88.76%	–
Proposed Method	98.00%	91.55%	86.02%

no results were provided by the developers of the specific method for the given dataset.

The proposed method also fares well in comparison with the J-LSTM-Conv [2] and LSTM-EnDec [3] methods. The pixel-level accuracy results of the proposed method are 13.4% and 3.2% better than the J-LSTM-Conv and LSTM-EnDec methods, respectively, for the NIST16 dataset. The proposed method also has the best result (underlined) with the COVERAGE dataset. The reason is that the combination of ring residual units and multiple features enables the proposed method to better locate tampered regions in images.

Other Performance Comparisons. It is not enough to evaluate image tampering detection methods using pixel-level accuracy alone. Therefore, the F1 score and area under curve metrics were used to compare the proposed method against other competing methods.

Table 4. Comparison of F1 scores.

Method	NIST16	COVERAGE	CASIA
ELA[11]	0.236	0.222	0.214
NOI[12]	0.285	0.269	0.263
CFA[7]	0.174	0.190	0.207
RGB-N[19]	0.772	0.437	0.408
I-DeepLabv3 [18]	–	–	0.423
Proposed Method	0.892	0.568	0.441

Table 4 shows the F1 score comparison. The proposed method yielded F1 scores of 0.892 and 0.568 with the NIST16 and COVERAGE datasets, respectively, which constitute 17.0% and 13.1% improvements over the RGB-N method [19]. Note that the dash symbols (–) are assigned to the I-DeepLabv3 method because its developers did not publish results for the NIST16 and COVERAGE datasets.

Table 5. Comparison of pixel-level area under curve results.

Method	NIST16	COVERAGE
ELA[11]	0.429	0.583
NOI[12]	0.487	0.587
CFA[7]	0.501	0.485
J-LSTM-Conv[2]	0.614	–
RGB-N[19]	0.934	0.817
LSTM-EnDec[3]	0.794	0.712
Proposed Method	0.973	0.897

Table 5 shows the area under curve results for the proposed method and other methods. The proposed method has the best results (underlined) for the two datasets used in the evaluation. Note that the dash symbol (–) is assigned to the J-LSTM-Conv method because its developers did not publish results for the COVERAGE dataset.

Based on the F1 score and area under curve results in Tables 4 and 5, it can be concluded that the proposed method outperforms traditional methods because they manually extract specific features and can only target specific types of tampering. The proposed method also outperforms the deep learning methods in terms of the F1 score and area under curve metrics for the NIST16 and COVERAGE datasets.

Qualitative Evaluation. Figure 6 shows sample detection results. The three rows (top to bottom) contain images or results corresponding to the three image tampering techniques, copy-paste, splicing and removal. The first and second columns (from left to right) show the tampered images and tampered region ground truth masks, respectively. The third and fourth columns show the masks predicted using only the ring residual units and the proposed method, respectively. The fifth column shows the probability heat maps.

The qualitative results of tampered localization in Figure 6 compare the localization between the Base method (constructed using only ring residual units) and the proposed method. The ground truth column shows masks that indicate the tampered regions of the images (white portions). The images in the heat map column convey the probabilities of detecting tampered regions. As seen in Figure 6, unlike the proposed method, the Base method incorrectly identifies some small regions as tampered regions or does not detect tampering around the boundaries of tampered regions.

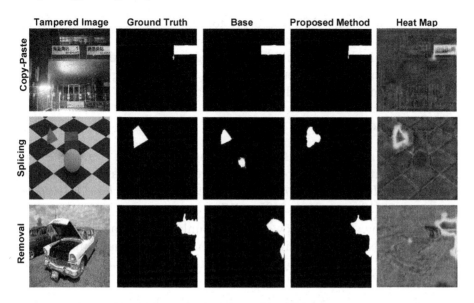

Figure 6. Example detection results.

Additionally, when the proposed method was evaluated using the NIST16 testing set comprising the three types of tampered images, it yielded F1 scores of 0.9305 for splicing tampered images, 0.936 for copy-paste tampered images, and 0.8339 for removal tampered images. This amply demonstrates its effectiveness at detecting various types of image tampering. The strong results are obtained because the proposed method encodes rich features that can effectively and accurately detect tampered regions of images.

4. Conclusions

The image tampering detection method described in this chapter employs an encoder-decoder network structure with combined multiple feature encoding to segment tampered regions of an image from untampered regions. In particular, it employs combined features and ring residual units for encoding, which enable the effective extraction of tampered features. Furthermore, it incorporates semantic enhancement, which compensates for information loss due to downsampling and improves localization accuracy. The method also demonstrates its generalization capability by detecting tampered images created by different techniques with high accuracy. In a series of experiments, the proposed model outperforms state-of-the-art image tampering detection methods, achieving

F1 scores of 0.892, 0.568 and 0.441 for the NIST16, COVERAGE and CASIA v1 datasets, respectively.

The principal limitation with the image tampering detection method is its inconsistency at identifying small tampered regions. Future research will attempt to address this limitation.

References

[1] V. Badrinarayanan, A. Kendall and R. Cipolla, SegNet: A deep convolutional encoder-decoder architecture for image segmentation, *IEEE Transactions on Pattern Analysis and Machine Intelligence*, vol. 39(12), pp. 2481–2495, 2017.

[2] J. Bappy, A. Roy-Chowdhury, J. Bunk, L. Nataraj and B. Manjunath, Exploiting spatial structure for localizing manipulated image regions, *Proceedings of the IEEE International Conference on Computer Vision*, pp. 4980–4989, 2017.

[3] J. Bappy, C. Simons, L. Nataraj, B. Manjunath and A. Roy-Chowdhury, Hybrid LSTM and encoder-decoder architecture for detection of image forgeries, *IEEE Transactions on Image Processing*, vol. 28(7), pp. 3286–3300, 2019.

[4] B. Bayar and M. Stamm, Constrained convolutional neural networks: A new approach towards general purpose image manipulation detection, *IEEE Transactions on Information Forensics and Security*, vol. 13(11), pp. 2691–2706, 2018.

[5] X. Bi, Y. Wei, B. Xiao and W. Li, RRU-Net: The ringed residual U-Net for image splicing forgery detection, *Proceedings of the IEEE/CVF Conference on Computer Vision and Pattern Recognition Workshops*, pp. 30–39, 2019.

[6] J. Dong, W. Wang and T. Tan, CASIA image tampering detection evaluation database, *Proceedings of the IEEE China Summit and International Conference on Signal and Information Processing*, pp. 422–426, 2013.

[7] P. Ferrara, T. Bianchi, A. De Rosa and A. Piva, Image forgery localization via fine-grained analysis of CFA artifacts, *IEEE Transactions on Information Forensics and Security*, vol. 7(5), pp. 1566–1577, 2012.

[8] R. Girshick, Fast R-CNN, *Proceedings of the IEEE International Conference on Computer Vision*, pp. 1440–1448, 2015.

[9] J. Hu, L. Shen, S. Albanie, G. Sun and E. Wu, Squeeze-and-excitation networks, *IEEE Transactions on Pattern Analysis and Machine Intelligence*, vol. 42(8), pp. 2011–2023, 2020.

[10] J. Long, E. Shelhamer and T. Darrell, Fully convolutional networks for semantic segmentation, *Proceedings of the IEEE Conference on Computer Vision and Pattern Recognition*, pp. 3431–3440, 2015.

[11] W. Luo, J. Huang and G. Qiu, JPEG error analysis and its applications to digital image forensics, *IEEE Transactions on Information Forensics and Security*, vol. 5(3), pp. 480–491, 2010.

[12] B. Mahdian and S. Saic, Using noise inconsistencies for blind image forensics, *Image and Vision Computing*, vol. 27(10), pp. 1497–1503, 2009.

[13] Multimodal Information Group, Information Technology Laboratory, Nimble Challenge 2017 Evaluation, National Institute of Standards and Technology, Gaithersburg, Maryland (`www.nist.gov/itl/Iad/mig/nimble-challenge-2017-evaluation`), 2019.

[14] B. Wen, Y. Zhu, R. Subramanian, T. Ng, X. Shen and S. Winkler, COVERAGE – A novel database for copy-move forgery detection, *Proceedings of the IEEE International Conference on Image Processing*, pp. 161–165, 2016.

[15] Y. Wu, W. Abd-Almageed and P. Natarajan, Image copy-move forgery detection via an end-to-end deep neural network, *Proceedings of the IEEE Winter Conference on Applications of Computer Vision*, pp. 1907–1915, 2018.

[16] Y. Wu, W. Abd-Almageed and P. Natarajan, ManTra-Net: Manipulation tracing network for detection and localization of image forgeries with anomalous features, *Proceedings of the IEEE/CVF Conference on Computer Vision and Pattern Recognition*, pp. 9535–9544, 2019.

[17] M. Zhao, S. Zhong, X. Fu, B. Tang and M. Pecht, Deep residual shrinkage networks for fault diagnosis, *IEEE Transactions on Industrial Informatics*, vol. 16(7), pp. 4681–4690, 2020.

[18] Q. Zhao, G. Cao, A. Zhou, X. Huang and L. Yang, Image tampering detection via semantic segmentation network, *Proceedings of the Fifteenth IEEE International Conference on Signal Processing*, pp. 165–169, 2020.

[19] P. Zhou, X. Han, V. Morariu and L. Davis, Learning rich features for image manipulation detection, *Proceedings of the IEEE/CVF Conference on Computer Vision and Pattern Recognition*, pp. 1053–1061, 2018.

Chapter 7

DEEPFAKE DETECTION USING MULTIPLE FEATURE FUSION

Ya Zhang, Xin Jin, Qian Jiang, Yunyun Dong, Nan Wu, Shaowen Yao and Wei Zhou

Abstract   It is becoming increasingly easy to generate forged images and videos using pre-trained deepfake methods. The forged images and videos are difficult to distinguish with the human eye, posing security and privacy threats. This chapter describes a deepfake detection method that employs multiple feature fusion to identify forged images. An image is preprocessed to extract high-frequency features in the spatial and frequency domains. Two autoencoder networks are then used to extract the two features of the preprocessed image, following which the extracted features are fused. Finally, the fused feature is input to a classifier comprising three fully-connected layers and a max-pooling layer. The experimental results demonstrate that fusing two features yields an average detection accuracy of 98.62%, much better than using the features individually. The results also show that the method has superior accuracy and generalization capability than state-of-the-art deepfake detection methods.

Keywords: Deepfake detection, deep learning, multiple feature fusion

1.   Introduction

The term deepfake, denoting a synthetic fake image or video created using deep learning, first appeared in 2017 when a Reddit user named "deepfakes" posted a synthesized pornographic video with facial images of celebrities [11]. Conventional image manipulation is done manually using Photoshop, GIMP or other image editing software. However, a deepfake technique uses a large number of images or videos to train a deep learning model over multiple iterations to automatically generate fake images or videos. The forged deepfake images and videos are difficult to distinguish from real images and videos with the human eye.

© IFIP International Federation for Information Processing 2022
Published by Springer Nature Switzerland AG 2022
G. Peterson and S. Shenoi (Eds.): DigitalForensics 2022, IFIP AICT 653, pp. 123–139, 2022.
https://doi.org/10.1007/978-3-031-10078-9_7

Deepfake methods can be used to generate films and television clips, virtual fittings and restore portraits of historical figures, which have commercial value. However, deepfakes pose security and privacy threats and seriously pollute cyberspace. Fake news is known to have impacted political discourse in several countries and even undermined the legitimacy of elections [16]. Deepfakes have even greater impacts because the forged images and videos are so realistic that they often generate news stories themselves. Although a number of social media platforms have banned deepfakes, their creation and dissemination are exploding. Several deepfake pornographic videos have victimized famous female personalities.

Researchers have proposed a number of deepfake detection methods. Bayar and Stamm [2] developed a new type of convolutional layer designed to suppress image content and adaptively learn manipulation features. Zhou et al. [19] proposed a dual-stream detection method that uses a convolutional neural network to learn boundary features and leverages steganographic noise characteristics to identify deepfakes. Durall et al. [7] introduced a novel classification pipeline for artificial face detection using frequency domain analysis; the approach directly extracts image frequency domain features using a discrete Fourier transform to provide classifier inputs. More recently, deepfake detection methods based on Resnet-50, Xception and InceptionV3 that achieve better performance have been developed.

Most deepfake detection methods have problems. Some detection methods extract spatial or frequency domain features of images that, to some extent, ignore the diverse information existing in real and fake images. Other detection methods require large numbers of training samples. Yet other methods do not have a generalization capability or the capability is not documented. Indeed, the lack of generalization is a serious problem in deepfake detection methods.

To address the problems, the proposed deepfake detection method employs multiple feature fusion. It combines spatial and frequency domain features, enabling the effective detection of images and videos generated by a variety of deepfake methods while exhibiting good generalization performance. Additionally, the proposed detection method requires smaller training datasets than competing deepfake detection methods.

2.   Related Work

This section describes contemporary deepfake generation and detection methods. Also, it discusses the application of multiple feature fusion in image classification.

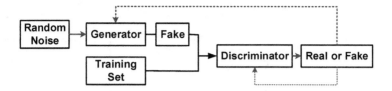

Figure 1. Basic generative adversarial network structure.

2.1 Deepfake Generation

Most contemporary deep generative models are based on generative adversarial networks (GANs) or autoencoder networks.

Goodfellow et al. [8] proposed the generative adversarial network concept, which is regarded as a breakthrough in the image generation field. Figure 1 shows the basic generative adversarial network structure. The core idea underlying a generative adversarial network is game theory. The generator is used to create fake images and a discriminator is used to distinguish real images from fake images. During the training phase, the generator and discriminator are optimized iteratively and the parameters are continuously updated until a Nash equilibrium is attained.

Collier et al. [5] proposed the progressively generative adversarial network (ProGAN). The key idea is to grow the generator and discriminator progressively. New layers are added starting with low resolutions and the model increasingly refines details as training progresses to achieve good generation performance. To improve the controllability of forged images, Karras et al. [9] proposed the StyleGAN model that is based on the progressively generative adversarial network. This alternative generator architecture borrows from work on style transfer, which can achieve good image generation effects. However, an obvious flaw with StyleGAN is that the generated images sometimes contain spot-like artifacts. Karras et al. [10] subsequently proposed StyleGAN2, which addresses the flaw in StyleGAN. Recently, Brock et al. [3] proposed BigGAN, a trained generative adversarial network with the largest scale yet attempted, and studied instabilities specific to the large scale. They demonstrated that the maximum performance improvement in a generative adversarial network can be achieved by increasing the number of parameters by two to four times.

An autoencoder comprises an encoder and decoder. Image features are compressed to low-dimensional space by the encoder and are subsequently reconstructed by the decoder. The autoencoder is iteratively trained many times until the output of the decoder is very close to the input of the encoder.

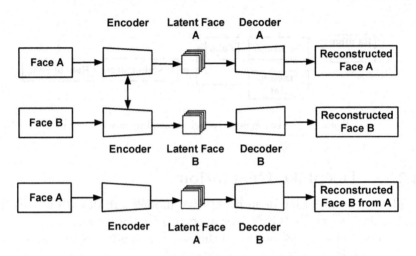

Figure 2. Deepfake face transformation using an autoencoder.

Figure 2 shows the deepfake face transformation process using an autoencoder. Two encoder-decoder groups are used to swap faces between source and target images, and the parameters are shared between the two encoders. The extracted features of Face A are connected with those of Decoder B to reconstruct Face B from the original Face A.

2.2 Deepfake Detection

Deepfake detection is an active area of research. Mo et al. [14] developed a modified convolutional neural network architecture with supervised learning that yielded good detection performance. Afchar et al. [1] proposed a method that automatically and efficiently detects tampered faces in videos. The method employs deep learning and two networks, both with a small number of layers, to focus on the mesoscopic properties of images. Kumar et al. [13] developed a multi-stream network that learns regional artifacts; specifically, a facial image is divided into multiple small patches that are sent to different Resnet-18 networks and ultimately to a fully-connected layer for weight distribution to obtain good detection results.

Other research has focused on preprocessing methods that improve deepfake detection performance. Nataraj et al. [15] extracted co-occurrence matrices on three color channels in the pixel domain and trained a deep convolutional neural network model to detect deepfake images generated by CycleGAN [20] and StarGAN [4]. Younus and Hasan [18] proposed a preprocessing method for deepfake video frames that leverages the Haar wavelet transform to discriminate between different types of edges; the method also determines the extent of blurred images.

Some researchers have attempted to improve generalization performance while enhancing deepfake detection accuracy. Cozzolino et al. [6] analyzed the generalization using a pair of datasets. To quickly adapt their detection network to new manipulation scenarios without retraining the entire network, they added a few images from the target domain to the source domain, which improved the generalization capability. Zhou et al. [19] developed a two-stream tampered face detection technique, where one stream detects low-level inconsistencies between image patches and the other stream explicitly detects tampered faces. The network was trained using FaceSwap and an evaluation using SwapMe demonstrated good performance.

2.3   Multiple Feature Fusion

Multiple feature fusion is finding increased applications in image recognition and classification. The approach is often more effective than using a single feature due to the complementary information provided by multiple features. Kikutani et al. [12] employed the weighted fusion of a global feature (color histogram) and local feature (bag-of-features model) for scene image representation and input the fused features into a classifier, significantly improving the recognition rate. Deepfake detection is essentially a two-class classification task. Inspired by the work of Kikutani and colleagues, the proposed method leverages multiple feature fusion for deepfake detection.

3.   Deepfake Image Detection Method

This section describes the proposed deepfake detection method, including its image preprocessing, image feature extraction and fusion, and classification components. Additionally, it specifies the optimized loss function and deepfake detection algorithm.

3.1   Method Overview

Since the fundamental concept is to combine multiple features of a source image, a dual-stream autoencoder network structure is used as the backbone network. Figure 3 provides an overview of the deepfake image detection method. First, high-frequency information and spectrum information of an image X_i are extracted and input to autoencoders. Next, the encoders with squeeze-and-excitation (SE) blocks are trained to extract the features of the preprocessed images, X_i^{high} and X_i^{freq},

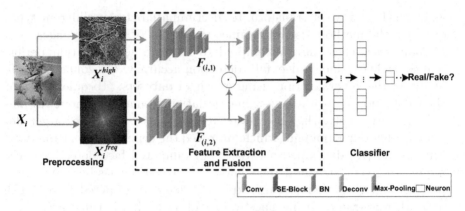

Figure 3.   Deepfake image detection method overview.

respectively. The encoders are subsequently used to fuse the extracted feature maps. Finally, the fused features are input to a classifier through a max-pooling layer.

3.2   Preprocessing

The low-frequency information associated with an image conveys its large-scale features whereas high-frequency information conveys the edges and details of the image. Deep image generation models often do not produce perfect image details. Therefore, given a source RGB image $X_i \in R^{W \times H \times 3}$ with width W and height H, the high-frequency information map X_i^{high} is extracted as follows:

$$X_i^{high} = X_i - X_i^{low}$$

where X_i^{low} is the low-frequency information map.

A Gaussian linear smoothing filter is very effective at suppressing normally-distributed noise. It is used to scan each pixel in an image X_i using a mask M to yield the low-frequency information map X_i^{low}:

$$X_i^{low} = X_i \cdot M$$

where $\cdot$ is the dot product and M is computed using the Gaussian function:

$$G(u, v) = \frac{1}{2\pi\sigma^2} e^{-(u^2+v^2)/(2\sigma^2)}$$

where σ is the standard deviation of the normal distribution.

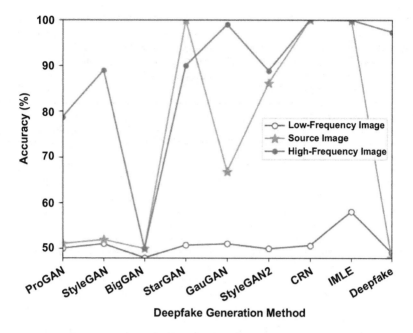

Figure 4. Preprocessing results using an Xception network.

The preprocessing operation was tested on an Xception network. Fake images were generated using multiple methods as in [17]. The methods included ProGAN, StyleGAN, BigGAN, StarGAN, GauGAN, Style-GAN2, CRN (cascaded refinement network), IMLE (implicit maximum likelihood estimation) and Deepfake. Figure 4 shows the preprocessing results obtained using an Xception network.

High-frequency information plays a positive role and low-frequency information plays a negative role in deepfake detection. Compared with the feature map extracted in the spatial domain, some image features are more prominent in the frequency domain. In particular, the repetitive nature and frequency features of images can be analyzed using the Fourier transform. The transformation indicates how the energy of a signal is distributed over a range of frequencies. The RGB domain image X_i is transformed to the frequency domain image as follows:

$$X_i^{\text{freq}} = F(X_i)$$

where X_i^{freq} is the frequency of image X_i and $F(\cdot)$ is the Fourier transform.

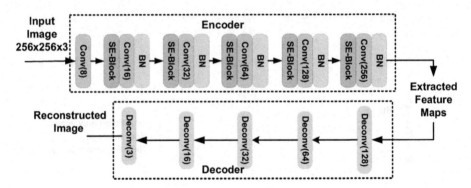

Figure 5. Autoencoder structure.

For a two-dimensional source image, the Fourier transform is computed as:

$$F(\mu, v) = \int_{-\infty}^{\infty} \int_{-\infty}^{\infty} f(x, y)e^{-j2\pi(\mu x + y)} dx dy$$

where x and y are time domain variables, μ and v are frequency domain variables, and $j^2 = -1$.

The high-frequency information is concentrated in the middle and the low-frequency information is distributed in the four corners of the frequency spectrum. To facilitate filter use, the spectrum is centered by the translation property of the two-dimensional Fourier transform. Finally, the centered image in input to autoencoder to extract the features.

3.3   Feature Extraction and Fusion

Figure 5 shows the autoencoder structure. A squeeze-and-excitation block (SE-block) can model the dependency between feature channels, which automatically provides the importance of the feature channels. Therefore, a squeeze-and-excitation block is added to an encoder to effectively extract image features.

The encoder comprises six modules. Except for the first module, which has a convolution layer, the remaining five modules all have a squeeze-and-excitation block before the convolution layer and a batch normalization (BN) layer after the convolution layer. A rectified linear unit (ReLU) can address the gradient disappearance problem and speed up training; hence, all the activation functions use a rectified linear unit in the encoder.

The decoder comprises five deconvolution layers. The activation function of each of the first four layers is a rectified linear unit. The tanh activation function is incorporated in the last deconvolution layer because

Table 1. Autoencoder settings.

	Type	Filter Size	Stride	Activation Function
	Conv2D	3×3	1	ReLU
	Conv2D	3×3	2	ReLU
Encoder	Conv2D	3×3	2	ReLU
	Conv2D	3×3	2	ReLU
	Conv2D	3×3	2	ReLU
	Deconv	3×3	2	ReLU
	Deconv	3×3	2	ReLU
Decoder	Deconv	3×3	2	ReLU
	Deconv	3×3	2	ReLU
	Deconv	3×3	2	Tanh

its range is [-1, 1]. Table 1 provides the details of all the autoencoder settings.

Given a source image X_i, features $F_{(i,1)}$ and $F_{(i,2)}$ are extracted from X_i^{high} and X_i^{freq}, respectively, as follows:

$$F_{(i,1)} = \text{Encoder}_1\left(X_i^{high}\right)$$

$$F_{(i,2)} = \text{Encoder}_2\left(X_i^{freq}\right)$$

where $\text{Encoder}(\cdot)$ is an encoder used to extract features.

Next, the features $F_{(i,1)}$ and $F_{(i,2)}$ are fused to create the fused features F_i:

$$F_i = F_{(i,1)} \cdot F_{(i,2)}$$

where $\cdot$ is the dot product.

Feature map pooling can reduce the feature dimensionality, compress data and parameters, reduce overfitting and improve the fault tolerance of the model. Max-pooling can reduce computations in the upper layers by eliminating the non-maximal values. Therefore, a max-pooling layer is incorporated in the model.

3.4 Classification

The classifier has three fully-connected layers with 512, 256 and two neuron nodes in successive layers. The first two layers use a rectified lin-

---

Algorithm 1: Multiple feature fusion deepfake detection.

Data: Environment E, Detection Image X and Label l.
Result: Trained Model Parameters θ.
Randomly generate environment;
Image Preprocessing
for *every image* **do**
    Obtain preprocessed results X_i^{high} and X_i^{freq};
    Resize X_i^{high} and X_i^{freq};
    Normalize data;
end
Network Training
for *every epoch* **do**
    Train the network using the stored environment E;
    for *every iteration* **do**
        if *environment is changed* **then**
            Generate network l' and $\hat{y}$;
            Find the global optimal position;
        end
        Perform action toward the global position
    end
end

---

ear unit activation function and the last layer uses the softmax activation function. Images are classified as real (0) or fake (1):

$$X_i = \begin{cases} 0 & \text{if } X_i \text{ is real} \\ 1 & \text{if } X_i \text{ is fake} \end{cases}$$

Finally, the deepfake detection result l' is computed as:

$$l' = Fc\,(F_{\mathrm{i}})$$

where $Fc(\cdot)$ denotes the classifier.

Algorithm 1 summarizes the deepfake detection algorithm.

3.5 Loss Function

The loss function L employed in this work has two parts, a cross-entropy loss L_{ce} and a reconstruction loss L_{re}:

$$L = \alpha L_{\mathrm{ce}} + \beta L_{\mathrm{re}}$$

where $\alpha = \beta = 1$.

Since deepfake detection is a two-class classification problem, cross-entropy can be used to measure the difference between two probability distributions. The cross-entropy loss L_{ce} is computed as:

$$L_{\mathrm{ce}} = -(l \log(p) + (1 - l) \log(1 - p))$$

Table 2. Dataset details.

Dataset	Sample Set Size	Testing Set Size
ProGAN	7,593	1,820
StyleGAN	9,582	2,400
BigGAN	3,200	800
StarGAN	3,200	800
GauGAN	8,000	2,000
StyleGAN2	13,143	3,192
CRN	10,212	2,552
IMLE	10,010	2,502
Deepfake	4,528	1,132

where l is the label of the real image and p is the probability of predicting the real image.

The reconstruction loss is the difference between the output data of the decoder and input data of the encoder. In this work, the L1 loss function is used to measure the difference between the input and output data of the autoencoder. The reconstruction loss L_{re} is computed as:

$$L_{re} = L^{l_1}(\hat{y}, y) = \sum_{i=0}^{T} |y - \hat{y}|$$

where y is the input data to the encoder and $\hat{y}$ is the output data of the decoder.

4. Experiments and Results

This section describes the experiments and the experimental results.

4.1 Dataset and Experimental Details

Nine datasets, each generated by a different deepfake image generation method, were employed in the experiments. Table 2 provides details about the nine datasets. Note that each dataset is assigned the name of the deepfake method used to generate its images. Real images and fake images account for 50% of each dataset.

In the experiments, each dataset was divided into a training set (80%) and testing set (20%). Figure 6 shows sample fake images (first row) and real images (second row). The two types of images cannot be distinguished by the human eye.

Figure 6. Sample fake (first row) and real images (second row) in the testing sets.

The accuracy metric was used to evaluate deepfake detection performance. Model training employed an Adam optimizer with a 1e-4 learning rate; the number of epochs was 50.

TensorFlow was used to define the layers of the various networks. The experiments employed an Nvidia 2080 Ti GPU with an Intel Core i7-8700K 3.70 GHz processor and 32 GB memory.

Table 3. Ablation experiment setup.

Features	High Frequency	Frequency Spectrum	Fused
High Frequency Feature	Y		
Frequency Spectrum Feature		Y	
Fused Features	Y	Y	Y

4.2   Ablation Experiment Results

An ablation experiment was conducted to validate the proposed deepfake detection method based on multiple feature fusion. Table 3 shows the experimental setup.

Table 4 shows the results of the ablation experiment. Note that the highest detection accuracy results are underlined. When the preprocessed high frequency and frequency spectrum features were employed as model inputs, average accuracy values of 97.10% and 90.41%, respectively, were obtained. However, after the two preprocessed features were extracted and fused, the average accuracy value increased to 98.62%. This result verifies the efficacy of multiple feature fusion in deepfake image detection.

Table 4. Ablatation experiment detection accuracy results.

Image Generation Algorithm	High Frequency Feature	Frequency Spectrum Feature	Fused Features
ProGAN	96.25	93.88	<u>99.34</u>
StyleGAN	<u>99.21</u>	96.92	98.96
BigGAN	95.00	95.88	<u>97.63</u>
StarGAN	<u>100.0</u>	50.00	<u>100.0</u>
GanGAN	96.25	83.95	<u>98.45</u>
StyleGAN	89.66	96.37	<u>95.33</u>
CRN	<u>100.0</u>	97.80	<u>100.0</u>
IMLE	99.88	99.37	<u>99.92</u>
Deepfake	97.69	99.53	<u>97.92</u>
Average	97.10	90.41	<u>98.62</u>

4.3 Comparative Experiment Results

Several classification models, such as InceptionV3, Resnet-50 and Xception, have achieved good deepfake image detection performance. This research implemented and trained several popular models and the model underlying the proposed deepfake detection method, and compared their performance for datasets with deepfake images created by different algorithms. Each model was trained using the training set of each dataset and tested using the testing set of the associated dataset.

Table 5 shows the detection accuracy results. As before, the highest detection accuracy results are underlined. The results reveal that the proposed method performs better than the other methods and its average accuracy over all the datasets reaches 98.62%. In fact, in the case of the StarGAN and IMLE datasets, the proposed method yielded accuracy values of 100%.

4.4 Generalization Experiment Results

Several researchers have not considered the generalization capability of their deepfake detection methods. A generalization experiment was conducted to compare the deepfake detection accuracy under generalization.

Table 6 shows the generalization performance results. As before, the highest detection accuracy results are underlined. The results reveal that the proposed method yields the highest average accuracy of 85.69% compared with the other deepfake detection methods when the ProGAN

Table 5. Comparative experiment detection accuracy results.

Image Generation Algorithm	Inception V3	Resnet-50	Xception	Meso [1]	Meso-Inception [1]	Proposed Method
ProGAN	53.47	53.09	51.05	55.39	61.18	99.34
StyleGAN	49.53	50.00	51.95	74.29	83.71	98.96
BigGAN	50.00	50.00	50.00	53.22	59.62	97.63
StarGAN	89.09	50.00	99.87	51.50	100.00	100.00
GauGAN	66.00	64.00	66.90	55.96	81.40	98.45
StyleGAN	83.18	80.85	86.15	63.31	90.29	95.33
CRN	99.88	99.88	100.00	63.79	99.73	100.00
IMLE	99.80	99.72	99.82	84.42	99.77	99.92
Deepfake	50.00	71.23	47.99	69.86	79.91	97.92
Average	71.22	68.75	72.64	63.53	83.96	98.62

Table 6. Generalization experiment detection accuracy results.

Method	ProGAN	Mixed
InceptionV3	50.00	53.83
Resnet-50	59.60	61.56
Xception	52.77	50.00
Meso [1]	54.88	60.31
Meso-Inception [1]	59.84	73.75
High Frequency	82.23	89.93
Frequency Spectrum	74.84	82.23
Proposed Method	85.69	95.42

training set was used as the source domain and tested against all the datasets. Additionally, when all the image samples were mixed into the training and testing datasets, the proposed method yields an average accuracy of 95.42%, which is much better than the other deepfake detection methods. Thus, the proposed deepfake detection method is superior to the other methods with regard to generalization capability.

5. Conclusions

The deepfake detection method based on multiple feature fusion detects deepfake images in datasets created using several deepfake image generation methods. The fusion of high-frequency spatial domain and frequency spectrum features of images is an innovative concept. Specifically, a dual-stream autoencoder network with squeeze-and-excitation blocks is trained and the fused features pass to the max-pooling layer before being input to the classifier. This multiple feature fusion strategy enables the deepfake detection method to exhibit superior average detection accuracy as well as generalization capability compared with a number of competing deepfake detection methods. Future research will continue to explore avenues for improving deepfake detection accuracy and generalization capabilities in the face of increasingly sophisticated deepfake image and video creation technologies and tools.

Acknowledgement

This research was supported by the National Natural Science Foundation of China under Grant nos. 62002313 and 62101481, Key Areas Research Program of Yunnan Province, China under Grant no. 202001BB050076, Science Research Foundation Project of the Yunnan Education Department, Yunnan Province, China under Grant no. 2021Y-025 and Key Laboratory in Software Engineering of Yunnan Province, China under Grant no. 2020SE408.

References

[1] D. Afchar, V. Nozick, J. Yamagishi and I. Echizen, MesoNet: A compact facial video forgery detection network, *Proceedings of the IEEE International Workshop on Information Forensics and Security*, 2018.

[2] B. Bayar and M. Stamm, A deep learning approach to universal image manipulation detection using a new convolutional layer, *Proceedings of the Fourth ACM Workshop on Information Hiding and Multimedia Security*, pp. 5–10, 2016.

[3] A. Brock, J. Donahue and K. Simonyan, Large-scale GAN training for high-fidelity natural image synthesis, *Proceedings of the Seventh International Conference on Learning Representations*, 2019.

[4] Y. Choi, M. Choi, M. Kim, J. Ha, S. Kim and J. Choo, StarGAN: Unified generative adversarial networks for multi-domain image-to-image translation, *Proceedings of the IEEE/CVF Conference on Computer Vision and Pattern Recognition*, pp. 8789–8797, 2018.

[5] E. Collier, K. Duffy, S. Ganguly, G. Madanguit, S. Kalia, G. Shreekant, R. Nemani, A. Michaelis, S. Li, A. Ganguly and S. Mukhopadhyay, Progressively growing generative adversarial networks for high resolution semantic segmentation of satellite images, *Proceedings of the IEEE International Conference on Data Mining Workshops*, pp. 763–769, 2018.

[6] D. Cozzolino, J. Thies, A. Rossler, C. Riess and L. Verdoliva, Forensic Transfer: Weakly-Supervised Domain Adaptation for Forgery Detection, arXiv: 1812.02510 (`arxiv.org/abs/1812.02510`), November 27, 2019.

[7] R. Durall, M. Keuper, F. Pfreundt and J. Keuper, Unmasking Deepfakes with Simple Features, arXiv: 1911.00686 (`arxiv.org/abs/1911.00686`), March 4, 2020.

[8] I. Goodfellow, J. Abadie, M. Mirza, B. Xu, D. Warde-Farley, S. Ozair, A. Courville and Y. Bengio, Generative adversarial nets, *Proceedings of the Twenty-Seventh Annual Conference on Neural Information Processing Systems*, pp. 2672–2680, 2014.

[9] T. Karras, S. Laine and T. Aila, A style-based generator architecture for generative adversarial networks, *Proceedings of the IEEE/CVF Conference on Computer Vision and Pattern Recognition*, pp. 4396–4405, 2019.

[10] T. Karras, S. Laine, M. Aittala, J. Hellsten, J. Lehtinen and T. Aila, Analyzing and improving the image quality of StyleGAN, *Proceedings of the IEEE/CVF Conference on Computer Vision and Pattern Recognition*, pp. 8107–8116, 2020.

[11] H. Khalil and S. Maged, Deepfake creation and detection using deep learning, *Proceedings of the International Mobile, Intelligent and Ubiquitous Computing Conference*, pp. 1–4, 2021.

[12] Y. Kikutani, A. Okamoto, X. Han, X. Ruan and Y. Chen, Hierarchical classifier with multiple feature weighted fusion for scene recognition, *Proceedings of the Second International Conference on Software Engineering and Data Mining*, pp. 648–651, 2010.

[13] P. Kumar, M. Vatsa and R. Singh, Detecting Face2Face facial reenactment in videos, *Proceedings of the IEEE Winter Conference on Applications of Computer Vision*, pp. 2578–2586, 2020.

[14] H. Mo, B. Chen and W. Luo, Fake face identification via convolutional neural network, *Proceedings of the Sixth ACM Workshop on Information Hiding and Multimedia Security*, pp. 43–47, 2018.

[15] L. Nataraj, T. Mohammed, B. Manjunath, S. Chandrasekaran, A. Flenner, J. Bappy and A. Roy-Chowdhury, Detecting GAN-generated fake images using co-occurrence matrices, *Proceedings of the IS&T International Symposium on Electronic Imaging*, article no. 532, 2019.

[16] A. Pal and A. Chua, Propagation pattern as a telltale sign of fake news on social media, *Proceedings of the Fifth International Conference on Information Management*, pp. 269–273, 2019.

[17] S. Wang, O. Wang, R. Zhang, A. Owens and A. Efros, CNN-generated images are surprisingly easy to spot... for now, *Proceedings of the IEEE/CVF Conference on Computer Vision and Pattern Recognition*, pp. 8692–8701, 2020.

[18] M. Younus and T. Hasan, Effective and fast deepfake detection method based on Haar wavelet transform, *Proceedings of the International Conference on Computer Science and Software Engineering*, pp. 186–190, 2020.

[19] P. Zhou, X. Han, V. Morariu and L. Davis, Two-stream neural networks for tampered face detection, *Proceedings of the IEEE Conference on Computer Vision and Pattern Recognition Workshops*, pp. 1831–1839, 2017.

[20] J. Zhu, T. Park, P. Isola and A. Efros, Unpaired image-to-image translation using cycle-consistent adversarial networks, *Proceedings of the IEEE International Conference on Computer Vision*, pp. 2242–2251, 2017.

Chapter 8

IDENTIFYING DESIRED TIMESTAMPS IN CARVED DIGITAL VIDEO RECORDER FOOTAGE

Divam Lehri and Anyesh Roy

Abstract Closed-circuit television cameras conduct round-the-clock surveillance to capture video evidence of illegal activities and suspects. The camera outputs are processed and stored on hard drives in standalone digital video recorders. As closed-circuit television cameras operate continuously, video files are constantly stored on the hard drives, with the new files periodically overwriting older files. The partially-overwritten files, which are present in slack space, can be recovered via data carving. However, the majority of the recovered video files are often fragmented. Unlike a normal video stream, a recovered video stream comprises frames that are not in chronological order. As a result, it is very tedious for a digital forensic professional to manually locate frames of interest.

This chapter describes a method for identifying timestamps in carved digital video recorder footage. Experimental results using a Python implementation demonstrate the efficiency of timestamp identification and its effectiveness at recreating video footage.

Keywords: CCTV forensics, Digital video recorder, file carving, timestamps

1. Introduction

Closed-circuit television (CCTV) cameras perform round-the-clock surveillance and store video footage on digital video recorder hard drives. Recovering video footage from digital video recorders is challenging due to their proprietary filesystems and video file formats. The inability of standard media players to decode and play videos with proprietary file formats also hinders investigations. Digital forensic professionals often have a hard time searching for and downloading media players in the hope of playing videos with odd file formats. The use of non-standard

© IFIP International Federation for Information Processing 2022
Published by Springer Nature Switzerland AG 2022
G. Peterson and S. Shenoi (Eds.): DigitalForensics 2022, IFIP AICT 653, pp. 141–152, 2022.
https://doi.org/10.1007/978-3-031-10078-9_8

container formats for videos also means that common video repair utilities are of little use in dealing with corrupted videos [11].

The video files on a digital video recorder hard drive are fragmented because they are stored as blocks in a non-contiguous manner for better memory utilization [13]. Park and Lee [10] have shown that data fragments are stored in unused areas of a digital video recorder filesystem. Additionally, because a closed-circuit television camera operates continuously, video footage files are constantly stored on the hard drive. A digital video recorder is often configured to perform automatic overwriting by default after a specific period of time or when the storage capacity limit is reached. As a result, new video files overwrite the older files on the hard drive.

Overwritten files, deleted files and files in proprietary formats can be recovered via data carving. The advantage of data carving over traditional recovery techniques is that it is independent of the filesystem. However, the majority of recovered video files are fragmented and most file carvers are not robust enough to handle even small amounts of fragmentation [2].

A digital video recorder typically has a high-capacity hard drive ranging from 1 TB to 6 TB. As a result, large numbers of video files are recovered after carving. When a digital video recorder begins to overwrite footage in previous blocks, the earliest footage is in the top block and the latest footage is in the bottom block. Additional overwriting leads to the earliest footage being located below the latest footage, which provides unexpected results during file carving [4, 9]. Also, the carved files are often corrupted or have unordered frames.

In normal closed-circuit television camera footage, a video file contains frames with timestamps in chronological order. However, this is not the case with carved footage because multiple video fragments reside in slack space. As a result, a carved video file has frames with unordered event timestamps and interrupted channel sequences.

Figure 1 shows consecutive frames from a carved video file from a digital video recorder. The first frame on the left occurs in the video at duration 4:10 with event timestamp 20/04/2020 23:46:46 Channel:CAM2. The next frame on the right occurs at duration 4:11 with event timestamp 08/05/2020 15:08:01 Channel:CAM7.

Carved fragments must be restructured and merged to create a complete video file. In such situation, a digital forensic professional has to manually play every video file on the digital video recorder to search for footage with the desired date-time values. A video clip of just a few minutes can have several hundred frames. As a result, it is very tedious

Figure 1. Consecutive frames from a carved video file.

for a digital forensic professional to manually locate and reorder frames to recreate video footage.

This chapter describes a method for identifying timestamps in carved digital video recorder footage. Experimental results using a Python implementation demonstrate the efficiency of timestamp identification and its effectiveness at recreating video footage.

2. Related Work

Digital forensics research has focused on recovering overwritten fragments from digital video recorders, but most research efforts involve manual reverse engineering of the filesystems, which is time-consuming and requires significant knowledge about the filesystems, video formats and codecs. Several forensic tools leverage databases containing signatures of known video formats to eliminate the manual determination of the filesystem structure prior to data carving. Some tools, notably Magnet DVR Examiner [9] and FTK Custom Carver [5], support a variety of proprietary video formats. However, the identification of video footage timestamps at the byte level is a complex task and poses several challenges to digital forensic professionals.

Ariffin et al. [1] developed a technique for carving video files with timestamps from digital video recorders that use proprietary file formats. The technique examines a cloned copy of a digital video recorder hard drive in hexadecimal format and probes for file signatures. The signatures of the video header, video footer, channel and event timestamp (date and time) are identified by searching for repeating patterns in the bytes of a video file. A desired event timestamp is located by decoding it to a Unix 32-bit timestamp and then converting it to the hexadecimal format. Following this, the hard drive is searched for the hexadecimal bytes. For example, the event timestamp 20/04/2020 23:46:46 is decoded to the Unix timestamp 1587426406, which is converted to hexadecimal 0x66\0x34\0x9E\0x5E (little endian).

Van Dongen [15] published a case study involving the recovery of overwritten videos in a Samsung digital video recorder using database file (DB) signatures. An image of the digital video recorder hard drive was created and processed using FTK. The filesystem turned out to be the Linux-based ext3, which is recognized by FTK. Analysis revealed that, due to its proprietary video format, the MPEG_STREAM file found in one of the partitions could not be played using a standard player and no information about the header was available. Database (DB) files in another partition were found to serve as bookkeeping records for the video footage and contained pointers to locations in the MPEG_STREAM file. Van Dongen examined the structure of the DB file signatures and attempted to recover overwritten fragments of the files in unallocated space to recover the overwritten video recordings.

Interpreting file data structures, headers and footers to recover files is referred to as manual carving. Manual data carving requires considerable time and knowledge about the filesystem, video format and codec. Such carving is hindered by the fact that most digital video recorders have proprietary filesystems without any documentation.

Other challenges are determining the byte order (little or big endian), limited knowledge of video file signatures at the byte level and finding media players that support proprietary file formats. Moreover, standard filesystems contain hexadecimal flags for partition types that are located in the master boot record. Sector 0 of a drive contains its master boot record, which has a simple code between hexadecimal 1BE and 1FF (decimal 446 to 511) that indicates the partition type [3]. Many digital video recorders do not have a hexadecimal flag and, even if a flag is present, it may not be identifiable because the filesystem is proprietary. For example, Gomm et al. [6] discovered that a Ganz digital video recorder hard drive does not contain a magic marker, indicating that it does have an industry-recognized filesystem. Additionally, when video files are fragmented, additional effort is required to parse and restructure the video footage, which are difficult to do manually.

This research stands out from related work in that it identifies timestamps in the video frames of carved digital video recorder files at the pixel level instead of the byte level.

3.   Method and Implementation

The method for identifying timestamps extracts frames from carved digital video recorder files and records when the frames appear in the video. After all the frames from a video are extracted, optical character recognition (OCR) is applied to each frame to retrieve the date and time

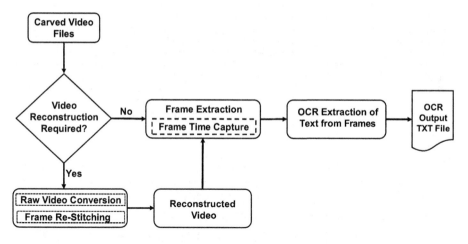

Figure 2. Detailed method workflow.

information contained in the frame. The method also reconstructs videos in situations where carved videos have corrupted headers or proprietary codecs. The reconstructed videos can then be replayed by a standard media player. Third-party applications such as Stellar Video Repair [14] and Yodot MOV Repair [16] may be used in conjunction with the method to repair corrupted videos. If a video has low resolution or poor quality, it is necessary to execute various image enhancement operations such as grayscaling and de-noising the extracted frames.

The method is implemented in Python (version 3.7.5). It works in conjunction with the FFmpeg library (version N-100029) and EasyOCR Python module (version 1.2.5.1). The EasyOCR Python module for performing optical character recognition is available at [12]. Image enhancement operations are provided by the Python OpenCV library.

The Python script, which provides a command line interface, executes on Windows, Macintosh and Linux machines. The script supports multiple instances, enabling multiple video files to be processed simultaneously. To achieve the best performance, a computing system with a CUDA-powered graphics processing unit is recommended. The script has been evaluated on an EDAS FOX forensic workstation with 12 Core Intel Xeon 2.4 GHz processors, 64 GB RAM, NVIDIA GEForce GTX 750 Ti Graphics Card and running the Windows 10 Pro operating system.

4. Detailed Method Workflow

Figure 2 shows the detailed method workflow. The video files retrieved after carving are supplied as inputs to the Python script. If the script is unable to process the input video file, it throws an error and the video

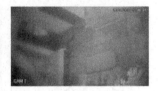

Figure 3. Frames `out90.png` (left), `out91.png` (center) and `out92.png` (right).

file undergoes reconstruction; otherwise, the frames from the input video file are extracted. During frame extraction, the script simultaneously captures the time duration at which each frame occurs in the video file. The time duration values are used to name the extracted frames.

Figure 3 shows frames named `out90.png`, `out91.png` and `out92.png` based on their durations in the video. The video frame rate must be known in order to interpret their durations. In the example, the video frame rate is one frame per second. Thus, the frame named `out90.png` has a duration of $90/1 = 90$ seconds, which means that it appears 1 minute and 30 seconds into the video.

Naming frames in this manner renders the search for frames highly efficient. Also, a digital forensic professional does not have to watch an entire video when a frame with the desired timestamp is found via optical character recognition because the duration at which the frame appears in the video is already known.

Video reconstruction is required when video files are unplayable due to their proprietary formats or missing or corrupted header structures. The reconstruction procedure is performed in a forensically-sound manner, ensuring that all the frames in the original video are preserved.

Video reconstruction involves two approaches: (i) video conversion or (ii) frame re-stitching:

- **Video Conversion:** Video conversion transforms the raw bitstream (H.264 format) extracted from an unplayable video file to a container format. A custom frame rate can be specified when converting the video to the container format. The container serves as a wrapper that encapsulates the raw bitstream along with other bundled elements such as the codec, metadata and, most importantly, header structures. A video file is playable upon conversion because it is equipped with a new container with all the necessary structures. If the header structures are missing, a video cannot be decoded and is, therefore, unplayable.

  Figures 4 and 5 show the differences between carved and normal videos with the same container format. Figure 4 shows the hexa-

```
00000000: 6c52 4d46 7e2d 3fe8 60b5 7cdf b3a0 e6ed   lRMF~-?.`.|.....
00000010: a6f3 2ec1 8705 caf4 d527 c706 36bf 6f41   .........'..6.oA
00000020: 9782 d3ad 4830 1748 0162 8b05 6e5b a4e3   ....HO.H.b..n[..
00000030: a759 c9b1 88cd a0ce 2328 f709 cb22 6333   .Y......#(..."c3
00000040: 5b90 5fc6 aead 033b 4491 9328 a0f4 d26a   [._....;D..(...j
00000050: 6425 9829 23ce 341c 182a 94e6 153b 87d9   d%.)#.4..*...;..
00000060: 6389 1dc7 805e c749 3c11 a854 07a2 68ad   c....^.I<..T..h.
00000070: e5b8 532a 6361 1a8e 62b2 8691 f832 fbb1   ..S*ca..b....2..
00000080: 9873 5ada 0d94 c266 63ec da04 8cc5 00cc   .sZ....fc.......
00000090: de6b bee2 883a 262b c91c cb28 3846 5285   .k...:&+...(8FR.
000000a0: 5ade 4e95 94f3 e2aa 01fc ae4e 1526 eb61   Z.N........N.&.a
000000b0: a77e ee6c 4ed6 6c96 907b 1997 581b a3cb   .~.lN.l..{..X...
000000c0: 4ff8 c384 19d0 2a8b 0d8c 4ab2 95fa d0cb   O.....*...J.....
000000d0: 5b8f 6f57 037f 8164 cdca 4b81 661a 52ad   [.oW...d..K.f.R.
000000e0: 6b5b f570 8d7c 0700 61ae 5897 2ebe 88d8   k[.p.|..a.X.....
000000f0: 7eac 5af9 00a2 b875 680a 6e73 9bd8 922e   ~.Z....uh.ns....
00000100: 114d 4368 bc55 eeea f392 6d65 f1a2 a5f8   .MCh.U....me....
00000110: ef58 6d75 e9dd 6fd8 620b bcf1 7149 723e   .Xmu..o.b...qIr>
00000120: aced 87d7 a28e 8632 c0c1 72cc 08a7 0f93   .......2..r.....
00000130: 8c76 bb0b 919a 65d1 3f2f c565 43a6 8271   .v....e.?/.eC..q
00000140: 9093 3b33 cd7f 0435 2ea9 1635 9da0 f50e   ..;3...5...5....
00000150: d96c 1655 357d 29c8 472d aeca 39dc 66ba   .1.U5}).G-..9.f.
00000160: 1a00 a6ab cab2 7ac6 b8c1 f216 282f 73ab   ......z.....(/s.
00000170: 97df 7d19 a487 734a 9d56 216f caf3 5589   ..}...sJ.V!o..U.
00000180: ecfe 16f6 1dc9 b54e abc9 9205 42e2 7723   .......N....B.w#
00000190: 4c29 5823 20b9 5a06 aa19 ddb7 c57a 4b38   L)X# .Z......zK8
000001a0: 20ff 36e4 76f0 45ac 9b41 f502 73d9 c60c   .6.v.E..A..s...
```

Figure 4. Hexadecimal view of a carved video file in the RMF container format.

decimal view of a carved video file in the RMF container format. Although, the first byte contains the RMF structure, all the other header structures are missing, which renders the video unplayable. In contrast, the normal video file in Figure 5 is playable because it has all the RMF file header structures (RMF, PROP, CONT, MDPR and DATA).

- **Frame Re-Stitching:** Frame re-stitching extracts frames from a damaged video file and constructs a new video file, preferably in the MP4 format, from the extracted frames. As in the case of video conversion, a custom frame rate can be specified when converting a video to the MP4 format. Frame extraction employs the FFmpeg library, following which the script applies optical character recognition to the extracted frames.

The optical character recognition output has the Python list data type, which contains the frame timestamp and channel number, and other text content in the frame along with a confidence level.

```
00000000: 2e52 4d46 0000 0012 0000 0000 0000 0000   .RMF.........
00000010: 0006 5052 4f50 0000 0032 0000 0005 fb40   . PROP ..2.....@
00000020: 0005 fb40 0000 ac7f 0000 17ef 0000 022b   ...@..........+
00000030: 0000 2878 0000 0000 0000 0000 0000 0165   ..(x.........e
00000040: 0002 0003 434f 4e54 0000 0012 0000 0000   ... CONT .......
00000050: 0000 0000 0000 4d44 5052 0000 0074 0000   ..... .MDPR ..t..
00000060: 0000 0003 0d40 0003 0d40 0000 ac7f 0000   .....@...@......
00000070: 2f8e 0000 0000 0000 0000 0000 2878 1054   /...........(x.T
00000080: 6865 2056 6964 656f 2053 7472 6561 6d14   he Video Stream.
00000090: 7669 6465 6f2f 782d 706e 2d72 6561 6c76   video/x-pn-realv
000000a0: 6964 656f 0000 0022 0000 0022 5649 444f   ideo..."..."VIDO
000000b0: 5256 3130 0190 02d0 0019 0000 0000 0019   RV10..........
000000c0: 0000 0000 0008 1000 0000 4d44 5052 0000   ..........MDPR..
000000d0: 009b 0000 0001 0002 ee00 0002 ee00 0000   ................
000000e0: 0400 0000 0343 0000 0000 0000 0000 0000   .....C.........
000000f0: 2845 1054 6865 2041 7564 696f 2053 7472   (E.The Audio Str
00000100: 6561 6d14 6175 6469 6f2f 782d 706e 2d72   eam.audio/x-pn-r
00000110: 6561 6c61 7564 696f 0000 0049 2e72 61fd   ealaudio...I.ra.
00000120: 0004 0000 2e72 6134 01b5 3530 0004 0000   .....ra4..50....
00000130: 0039 0002 0000 0343 0005 1540 0015 f900   .9.....C...@....
00000140: 0015 f900 0001 0343 0000 0000 ac44 0000   .......C.....D..
00000150: 0010 0002 0449 6e74 3004 646e 6574 0000   .....Int0.dnet..
00000160: 0000 0000 0044 4154 4100 33fd e800 0000   .... DATA 3.....
00000170: 0002 2b00 0000 0000 0003 4e00 0100 0000   ..+.......N.....
00000180: 0000 0277 0bb1 4540 54e1 43f5 06f0 75c2   ...w..E@T.C...u.
00000190: c427 1859 fdf9 a477 f4dd 15ea c4f3 f9cf   .'.Y...w........
```

Figure 5.   Hexadecimal view of a normal video file in the RMF container format.

The list can be sliced to simplify the output. The timestamp values from the list are then saved in a text file. Performing string searches with the desired event timestamps in the text file reveals whether or not the input video file contains frames with the desired timestamps.

5.   Experimental Results

The experiments employed a TVT TD-2116TS digital video recorder with a 2 TB hard drive. The hard drive was imaged using the Ditto DX forensic tool in the E01 compression format and the image was processed using FTK. The disk image emerged as unallocated space in FTK, indicating that the filesystem was proprietary and unrecognizable by FTK. Nevertheless, FTK custom carvers were imported to carve the video files. Specifically, the signatures of well-known video formats were added to the custom carver and the maximum file size was set to 2 GB. The carving, which took around two hours to complete, yielded 658 video files, each of size 2 GB.

```
Python 3.7.5 (tags/v3.7.5:5c02a39a0b, Oct 15 2019, 00:11:34) [MSC v.1916 64 bit
(AMD64)] on win32
Type "help", "copyright", "credits" or "license()" for more information.
>>>
============================ RESTART: D:\OCR.py ===============================
Enter path of extracted frames
 Note: Output OCR text file will be saved in the same directory
 E:\carvedframes
OCR COMPLETED!
```

Figure 6. User interaction with the Python script.

The carved files were exported from FTK and saved on the computing system. However, attempts to play the videos on VLC and Windows media players resulted in errors. Upon searching for and trying other media players, it was discovered that the PotPlayer [7] could decode and play the videos. However, the timeline bars were missing during playback, possibly because some file structures were overwritten. Since the videos did not require reconstruction, frame extraction was performed as detailed in the previous section.

The Python implementation was applied to a digital video recorder with a different make and model to further validate its accuracy and functionality. In this case, a Hikvision DS-7A0BHGHI digital video recorder with a 1 TB hard drive was employed. The hard drive was imaged in the E01 compressed format and the image was processed using FTK. The image could be read by FTK because most Hikvision digital video recorders use Linux filesystems that are supported by FTK. File carving took about 1.5 hours and yielded 302 videos. The videos were playable on a VLC media player. However, five videos, which could not be reconstructed, were unplayable.

Frames were extracted from all the playable videos. Figure 6 shows a user interaction with the Python script. The script takes the path of the extracted frames as input and provides an alert when all the frames have been scanned.

Optical character recognition applied to the extracted frames yielded the output text file shown in Figure 7. The output text file contains the timestamps of all the frames along with the file names, which indicate the times (in seconds) of their occurrences in the video footage.

Experiments were conducted to evaluate the speed and accuracy of the Python implementation. The script, which was executed on the EDAS FOX forensic workstation described above, required 4 hours and 34 minutes to complete optical character recognition on 5,700 frames extracted from carved video footage. The workstation supported the execution of four instances of the script at a time. The execution of multiple instances of the script simultaneously on two forensic worksta-

```
20/04/2020  23:54:50    out437.png
20/04/2020  23:54:51    out438.png
20/04/2020  23:54:52    out439.png
20/04/2020  23:54:53    out440.png
20/04/2020  23:46:36    out441.png
20/04/2020  23:46:37    out442.png
20/04/2020  23:46:38    out443.png
20/04/2020  23:46:39    out444.png
20/04/2020  23:46:40    out445.png
20/04/2020  23:46:41    out446.png
20/04/2020  23:46:42    out447.png
20/04/2020  23:46:43    out448.png
20/04/2020  23:46:44    out449.png
20/04/2020  23:46:45    out450.png
20/04/2020  23:46:46    out451.png
20/04/2020  23:46:47    out452.png
08/05/2020  15:08:01    out453.png
08/05/2020  15:08:02    out454.png
08/05/2020  15:08:03    out455.png
08/05/2020  15:08:04    out456.png
08/05/2020  15:08:05    out457.png
08/05/2020  15:08:06    out458.png
08/05/2020  15:08:07    out459.png
08/05/2020  15:08:08    out460.png
08/05/2020  15:08:09    out461.png
08/05/2020  15:08:10    out462.png
08/05/2020  15:08:11    out463.png
08/05/2020  15:08:12    out464.png
08/05/2020  15:08:13    out465.png
```

Figure 7.   Output text file with frame timestamps and file names.

tions took around five days to complete optical character recognition on
302 videos.

6.   Conclusions

Recovering video footage from digital video recorders is hindered by
their proprietary filesystems and video file formats. Unlike a normal
video stream, carved video files are typically fragmented, comprising
frames with unordered event timestamps and interrupted channel sequences. As a result, it is very tedious for digital forensic professionals
to manually locate and reorder frames to recreate video footage.

The method described in this chapter identifies timestamps in carved
digital video recorder footage at the pixel level instead of at the byte
level. Specifically, it uses optical character recognition to capture timestamps and channel numbers present on frames, and automates the task
of searching for desired timestamps when recreating video footage.

Experimental results using the Python implementation demonstrate
the efficiency and effectiveness of the method. The Python implemen-

tation, which is open source and executes on Windows, Macintosh and Linux platforms, can handle carved video files from digital video recorders of diverse makes and models. The implementation is currently being used in a law enforcement laboratory, where it significantly reduces the time and effort needed to recover video footage in criminal investigations. To increase its dissemination and use, the codebase is published under an Apache 2.0 license and is available at SourceForge [8].

Although image processing techniques are integrated in the Python implementation and are customizable based on the noise and lightning present in video footage, low quality images reduce the accuracy of optical character recognition of video frame data and, thus, the efficacy of recreating video footage. Future research will attempt to employ deep learning techniques to enhance optical character recognition accuracy.

References

[1] A. Ariffin, J. Slay and K. Choo, Data recovery from proprietary formatted CCTV hard disks, in *Advances in Digital Forensics IX*, G. Peterson and S. Shenoi (Eds.), Springer, Berlin Heidelberg, Germany, pp. 213–223, 2013.

[2] M. Ashraf, Forensic Multimedia File Carving, Master's Thesis, Department of Computer and Systems Sciences, School of Information and Communication Technology, KTH Royal Institute of Technology, Stockholm, Sweden, 2012.

[3] Datarecovery.com, Hexadecimal Flags for Partition Type, Edwardsville, Illinois (`www.datarecovery.com/rd/hexadecimal-fla gs-for-partition-type/#:%7E:text=Hexadecimal%20flags%20 are%20values%20that,the%20hexadecimal20flags%20listed%2 0below.`), July 23, 2014.

[4] DME Forensics, Inaccessible data recovery with DVR Examiner, Golden, Colorado (`dmeforensics.com/inaccessible-data-recovery-dvr-examiner`), 2019.

[5] Exterro, Custom Carvers, Portland, Oregon (`support.ext erro.com/support/solutions/articles/69000765593-custom-carvers`), 2022.

[6] R. Gomm, N. Le-Khac, M. Scanlon and M. Kechadi, An analytical approach to the recovery of data from 3rd party proprietary CCTV filesystems, *Proceedings of the Fifteenth European Conference on Cyber Warfare and Security*, pp. 117–126, 2016.

[7] Kakao, Global PotPlayer, Jeju-si, South Korea (`potplayer.daum. net`), 2022.

[8] D. Lehri, CCTV Frame Timestamp Extractor, SourceForge (`www.sourceforge.net/projects/carvedvrtimestamps`), 2021.

[9] Magnet Forensics, Magnet DVR Examiner, Herndon, Virginia (`www.magnetforensics.com/products/magnet-dvr-examiner`), 2022.

[10] J. Park and S. Lee, Data fragment forensics for embedded DVR systems, *Digital Investigation*, vol. 11(3), pp. 187–200, 2014.

[11] N. Poole, Q. Zhou and P. Abatis, Analysis of CCTV digital video recorder hard disk storage system, *Digital Investigation*, vol. 5(3-4), pp. 85–92, 2009.

[12] rkcosmos, EasyOCR, GitHub (`github.com/JaidedAI/EasyOCR`), July 8, 2021.

[13] SalvationDATA Technology, [Case study] DVR forensics: Fragmented files (overwritten video clips) come alive with SalvationDATA patented technology, *SalvationDATA Blog*, Chengdu, China, September 27, 2019.

[14] Stellar Data Recovery, Video Repair Tool, Metuchen, New Jersey (`www.stellarinfo.com/disk-recovery/video-repair.php`), 2022.

[15] W. van Dongen, Case study: Forensic analysis of a Samsung digital video recorder, *Digital Investigation*, vol. 5(1-2), pp. 19–28, 2008.

[16] Yodot Software, Yodot Video Repair Software, Mountain View, California (`www.yodot.com/video-repair.html`), 2022.

IV

NOVEL APPLICATIONS

Chapter 9

IDENTIFYING THE LEAK SOURCES OF HARD COPY DOCUMENTS

Pulkit Garg, Garima Gupta, Ranjan Kumar, Somitra Sanadhya and Gaurav Gupta

Abstract Technological advancements have made it possible to use relatively inexpensive hardware and software to replicate and leak sensitive documents. This chapter proposes a novel canary trap method for determining the source of a leaked hard copy document. The method generates self-identifying documents that secretly encode unique information about the individuals who receive them by modifying the inter-word spacing in the original reference document. The encoded information is robust to changes introduced during printing, scanning and copying, rendering the method useful for hard copy as well as digital documents. Due to the lack of publicly-available datasets, a custom hard copy document leakage dataset comprising 100 scanned self-identifying documents encoded at four levels of robustness was created. The hard copy document leakage dataset was subsequently employed to evaluate the performance of the canary trap leak detection method.

Keywords: Hard copy documents, leak source identification, canary trap

1. Introduction

In today's data-driven world, it is important for organizations to safeguard their sensitive information from unauthorized access and dissemination. The unauthorized access and release of sensitive information can result in monetary losses, diminished reputation, legal exposure and potential shutdown of business activities. The impacts of information leaks from government organizations are much more severe; leaked military secrets can jeopardize national security.

Recent advancements in technology and the availability of sophisticated hardware and software have increased the likelihood and scope of information leaks. Also, due to the COVID-19 pandemic, most organiza-

© IFIP International Federation for Information Processing 2022
Published by Springer Nature Switzerland AG 2022
G. Peterson and S. Shenoi (Eds.): DigitalForensics 2022, IFIP AICT 653, pp. 155–167, 2022.
https://doi.org/10.1007/978-3-031-10078-9_9

tions have their employees working remotely, which means sensitive information is processed and stored outside secure internal environments. An authorized individual with malicious intent can easily share sensitive information with millions of people on the Internet within seconds. Therefore, it is imperative to prevent information leaks and identify the individuals responsible for information leaks.

A leaker can transmit sensitive information in several ways, by sharing printed documents, sending email, using web applications and copying the information to removable storage. However, the most common method for leaking sensitive information is via printed documents because they leave minimal evidentiary traces. Additionally, organizations often store sensitive information in documents that can easily be replicated using printers, scanners and copiers. The document replicas are subsequently passed physically or shared online using messaging software or social media platforms.

Organizations often employ canary traps to identify potential leak sources. An organization sets up a canary trap by generating multiple copies of a sensitive document (reference document), each with one or more unique attributes that identify the copy. Each user (suspect) receives one of the unique document copies. Later, if one of the users leaks a document copy, the organization can extract the unique information encoded in the copy to identify the source of the leak. Canary traps are appealing, but the unique document copies created by current techniques are visually distinguishable and lack robustness to errors introduced when printing, scanning or copying documents.

This chapter describes a canary trap method that employs self-identifying documents. The method creates unique document copies that are visually indistinguishable from the reference document and other document copies. The unique data in each document copy is then encoded as a Quick Response (QR) code, which is embedded in the copy as a binary string by modifying the inter-word spacing. QR codes with high (30%) error correction capabilities render the method robust to errors introduced when printing, scanning or copying the unique document copies.

Due to the lack of publicly-available datasets, a custom hard copy document leakage dataset was created to evaluate the performance of the canary trap leak detection method. The custom dataset comprises 25 reference Microsoft Word (DOCX) documents and 100 scanned self-identifying document copies. The 100 scanned self-identifying document copies were created by encoding each reference document at four levels of robustness.

2. Related Work

Several data leak prevention techniques have been proposed in the literature to identify the sources of leaks of printed documents. Kuraki and Nakagata [4] proposed multiple techniques to embed invisible data in printed documents. They used starlight patterns (holes in a tint-block background) and modified the shapes of printed characters such as font glyphs as well as figures and drawings. Kaneda et al. [2] embedded an electronically-readable watermark by superimposing single dot and double dot patterns in background blocks with 18×18 pixels. Kaneda et al. [1] subsequently enhanced their approach by introducing error correction capabilities using low-density parity checking (LDPC) codes. Safonov et al. [8] introduced clusters of black dots in documents that represented secret information while ensuring that significant distortions were not introduced in the documents; also, information was encoded at multiple locations in documents to render them robust to modifications and noise. Beusekom et al. [11] proposed a technique that utilizes machine identification codes to identify the printers used to generate printed copies of documents. Although these three techniques are data independent, starlight patterns, watermarking and machine identification codes are very small and they may vanish after multiple rounds of scanning or copying.

Researchers have also developed techniques that introduce changes in the foreground of documents (written text). Low et al. [6] proposed a watermark encoding algorithm that shifts lines and words in documents according to a watermark bit. It segments lines into three groups of words and shifts the central group to the left and right. However, this technique requires the original document to be present at the time of decoding.

Zou and Shi [13] developed a technique that adjusts the inter-word spacing between adjacent words. It divides each line into two parts so that the sum of inter-word spacing (say, s_1 and s_2) of the two parts are nearly equal. Later, the inter-word space is modified such that, if the encoded bit is one, then $(s_1 - s_2)$ is positive; otherwise, it is negative.

Varna et al. [12] proposed a data hiding technique that modifies the shapes of characters by adding or removing two pixels from the left strokes of characters and uses error-correcting codes to correct errors and erasures. Tan et al. [9] developed a watermarking technique that identifies rotatable strokes in Chinese characters and modulates their directions according to the payload watermarks; the technique sorts the centroids of the strokes and embeds payloads in sequential order to ensure the proper ordering of bits during decoding. Loc et al. [5] developed

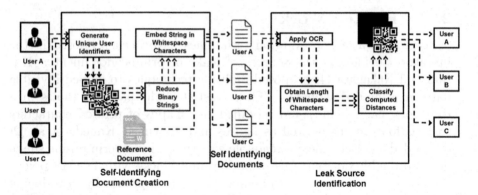

Figure 1. Leak source identification method overview.

a watermarking scheme that identifies stable regions in text documents (i.e., robust to noise during printing and scanning), further dividing them into strokes and fills; watermarks are encoded by computing the hiding factor for each fill region and assigning a zero or one accordingly. Nayak et al. [7] proposed a technique that embeds secret information in documents by changing the fonts of certain letters. Kozachok et al. [3] developed a technique that encodes watermarks by modifying line spacing within perceptual invisibility.

All the techniques described above are not robust against adversarial errors and have low data hiding capacities. In contrast, the proposed method employing self-identifying documents provides an optimal balance between data storage capacity and error robustness.

3. Proposed Method

Techniques for identifying the leak sources of digital documents are ineffective for hard copy documents because multiple iterations of printing, scanning or copying hard copy documents introduce noise and degrade document quality. To overcome this limitation and enhance robustness, the proposed method generates self-identifying copies of a reference document, each with unique encoded information tied to an individual user (suspect).

Figure 1 presents an overview of the proposed leak source identification method. The method involves two steps, self-identifying document creation and leak source identification. During the self-identifying document creation step, three self-identifying documents corresponding to a single reference document are created for users A, B and C. During the leak source identification step, the encoded information is extracted from each of the self-identifying documents that is uniquely associated

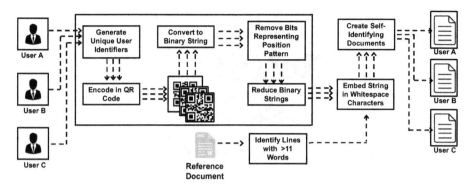

Figure 2. Self-identifying document creation.

with a user. The encoded information in the leaked document is then decoded to identify the leaker of the document.

3.1 Self-Identifying Document Creation

Figure 2 illustrates the creation of self-identifying documents, each document associated with a different user. The unique identifier created for a user is encoded as a QR code, which is subsequently converted to a binary string. The error correction capability of a QR code makes it possible to decode the extracted binary string even if the code is corrupted to a certain degree. The margins of the resulting document are also modified to compensate for the increased number of characters per line due to the addition of whitespace characters. This step is crucial to eliminate visual changes and increase the similarity between the reference and self-identifying documents. This work demonstrates the application of the method to Microsoft Word (DOCX) documents, but the method is readily applied to other document formats.

Binary String Generation. The assumption is that a sensitive document will be shared with a certain number of users. The initial task is to acquire unique distinguishing information for every user. This information may include the user name, organizational email address, identity number, IP address of the computing system being used, etc. However, this information cannot be encoded directly in the document given to the user. This is because a leaker might print, scan and/or copy the document with the encoding many times. As a result, the leaked document would contain noise that induces classification errors when decoding the leaked document. Therefore, the proposed method requires error correction capabilities.

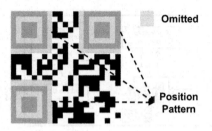

Figure 3.   Omission of position patterns to obtain a reduced binary string.

QR codes possess desirable characteristics such as high error correction and strong robustness to distortion, but still have small sizes (binary representations). QR codes encoded with the H error correction can tolerate errors up to 30%. Therefore, a Version 1 QR code is employed in an intermediate step. Specifically, the unique user identifier is encoded as a QR code, which is converted to a binary string (in row-major order) where a one represents a black pixel and a zero represents a white pixel. Since Version 1 QR codes have 21×21 pixels, the length of the generated string is 441 bits.

As mentioned above, the proposed method embeds the binary string corresponding to a QR code in a document by altering the inter-word spacing. Since the inter-word whitespace positions in a document are limited, it is necessary to reduce the size of the binary string that is generated.

Figure 3 shows how position patterns may be omitted to obtain a reduced binary string. The highlighted portions are known as position patterns and their relative locations and sizes remain the same for all the QR codes. Therefore, the pixels corresponding to the position patterns can be omitted, enabling the QR code size to be reduced by 192 bits, yielding a final string with 249 bits.

Binary String Encoding.   Upon inserting whitespace in a document, the cursor shifts by a constant amount to the right which is not altered by printing, scanning or copying. The whitespace is uneven only when the text in the document is justified (i.e., text is aligned with the left and right margins). For ease of analysis, it is assumed that the reference document is right-, left- or center-aligned. Since the changes in whitespace characters are hardly noticeable and robust to small errors, the whitespace is modified to encode the secret information.

Figure 4 shows self-identifying document text created from reference document text by encoding it with the string 01010101. The binary

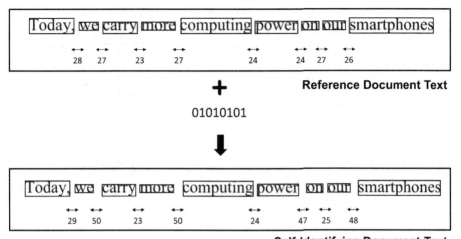

Figure 4. Self-identifying document text encoded with 01010101.

string 01010101 is encoded in the line of text such that, if a one is encountered, then the corresponding whitespace is doubled.

The proposed method uses two pointers to implement this task, one pointer for the original data and the other for the binary string to be inserted:

- The original data pointer is iterated over a line until a whitespace is encountered.

- The pointer to the binary string is read. If the value pointed to by the binary string pointer is a one, then an extra whitespace is added at the original data pointer location. If the value pointed to by the binary string pointer is a zero, no change is made.

- The original data pointer and binary string pointer are incremented to point to the next character and the preceding steps are repeated until the end of the binary string is reached.

- Thus, the line is modified by encoding the given binary string in the line.

Optimization. Due to optical character recognition (OCR) errors, the possibility exists that the decoding process may not detect all the whitespaces and skip some of them. This would cause the bits in the extracted binary string to shift towards the left, inducing a large error. For example, the original string 01010101 could be retrieved as 01001010. In

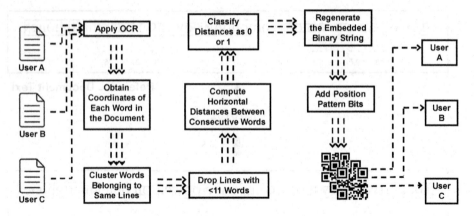

Figure 5. Leak source identification.

this case, the bit in the fourth position from the left in the original string is skipped. Therefore, every bit in the retrieved string starting with the fourth position onwards is misclassified. To limit such errors, the proposed method modifies only ten whitespace characters per line. Therefore, only lines with more than 11 words are encoded with the secret information.

The character count per line in a Microsoft Word document is not constant and depends on various uncontrollable factors. Adding whitespace characters in a line can cause the last few words to move to the next line. To maintain visual similarity with the reference document, the left and right margins of the self-identifying document are reduced accordingly.

3.2   Leak Source Identification

Leak source identification involves the extraction of the encoded binary string from the scanned image of a leaked document and the retrieval of the unique user identifying information by regenerating and decoding the QR code.

Figure 5 shows the steps involved in source identification. First, optical character recognition is performed and the coordinates of every word are determined. Next, the distances between consecutive words are computed, arranged in a sequential manner and classified as ones or zeros. Following this, position pattern bits are added to create the QR code. Finally, the QR code is decoded to identify the source of the leak.

Text Extraction.   The Tesseract open-source optical character recognition library [10] is used to extract the words in the scanned documents along with their bounding boxes. The coordinates of each word are computed and arranged sequentially from left to right and top to bottom as they appear in the document.

Binary String Retrieval. The horizontal distances between the bounding boxes of consecutive words are computed. If the distance exceeds the threshold value, the output bit is one; otherwise, the output bit is zero. The output bits are arranged as a one-dimensional array in row-major order to produce a binary string.

Unique Identifier Decoding. During the encoding process, the binary string representing the QR code is compressed by removing position pattern bits and the remaining information is encoded in the document. Since the relative position and size of the position pattern is the same for every QR code, the retrieved binary string is modified to obtain a valid version 1 QR code. Specifically, the binary string is reshaped as a 21 × 21 array corresponding to the QR code. The QR code is then decoded using ZXing, an open-source QR code library [14]. The source of the leak is identified using the QR code.

4. Document Dataset

Due to the lack of publicly-available datasets, a custom hard copy document leakage dataset comprising 100 scanned self-identifying documents encoded at four levels of robustness was created. Twenty-five reference documents with random text from the Internet were prepared using Microsoft Word 2016. The document text is in the Times New Roman font with a font size of 12. Figure 6(a) shows a sample reference document.

QR codes have four error correction (EC) levels, L, M, Q and H. Increasing the error correction capability decreases the storage capacity. To analyze the impact of the error correction levels on the proposed method, four self-identifying documents corresponding to the four error correction levels were created for each of the 25 reference documents. To model a real-world scenario, the self-identifying documents were printed and scanned at 300 dpi using an HP LaserJet P1007 printer and HP ScanJet Pro 2000 F1 scanner, respectively.

Table 1 summarizes the dataset content. Figures 6(b), 6(c), 6(d) and 6(e) show scanned samples of the self-identifying documents corresponding to error correction levels EC-L, EC-M, EC-Q and EC-H, respectively.

What is Statistics?

Statistics is the discipline that concerns the collection, organization, analysis, interpretation, and presentation of data. In applying statistics to a scientific, industrial, or social problem, it is conventional to begin with a statistical population or a statistical model to be studied. Populations can be diverse groups of people or objects such as "all people living in a country" or "every atom composing a crystal". Statistics deals with every aspect of data, including the planning of data collection in terms of the design of surveys and experiments.

(a) Sample reference document.

What is Statistics?

Statistics is the discipline that concerns the collection, organization, analysis, interpretation, and presentation of data. In applying statistics to a scientific, industrial, or social problem, it is conventional to begin with a statistical population or a statistical model to be studied. Populations can be diverse groups of people or objects such as "all people living in a country" or "every atom composing a crystal". Statistics deals with every aspect of data, including the planning of data collection in terms of the design of surveys and experiments.

(b) Sample self-identifying document (EC-L).

What is Statistics?

Statistics is the discipline that concerns the collection, organization, analysis, interpretation, and presentation of data. In applying statistics to a scientific, industrial, or social problem, it is conventional to begin with a statistical population or a statistical model to be studied. Populations can be diverse groups of people or objects such as "all people living in a country" or "every atom composing a crystal". Statistics deals with every aspect of data, including the planning of data collection in terms of the design of surveys and experiments.

(c) Sample self-identifying document (EC-M).

What is Statistics?

Statistics is the discipline that concerns the collection, organization, analysis, interpretation, and presentation of data. In applying statistics to a scientific, industrial, or social problem, it is conventional to begin with a statistical population or a statistical model to be studied. Populations can be diverse groups of people or objects such as "all people living in a country" or "every atom composing a crystal". Statistics deals with every aspect of data, including the planning of data collection in terms of the design of surveys and experiments.

(d) Sample self-identifying document (EC-Q).

What is Statistics?

Statistics is the discipline that concerns the collection, organization, analysis, interpretation, and presentation of data. In applying statistics to a scientific, industrial, or social problem, it is conventional to begin with a statistical population or a statistical model to be studied. Populations can be diverse groups of people or objects such as "all people living in a country" or "every atom composing a crystal". Statistics deals with every aspect of data, including the planning of data collection in terms of the design of surveys and experiments.

(e) Sample self-identifying document (EC-H).

Figure 6.   Document dataset samples.

Table 1. Dataset content.

	EC-L	EC-M	EC-Q	EC-H	Total
Self-Identifying Documents	25	25	25	25	100

5. Experimental Results

The decoding success rate and bit error rate metrics were employed to evaluate the performance of the proposed leak source identification method. The decoding success rate, which corresponds to the percentage of self-identifying documents that were decoded successfully, conveys the robustness of the method. The bit error rate, which measures the error (mismatch) in an extracted binary string, is computed as the percentage of white pixels in the XOR of the original and extracted QR code.

Table 2. Experimental results.

Evaluation Metric	EC-L	EC-M	EC-Q	EC-H
Decoding Success Rate (DSR)	80%	96%	96%	100%
Bit Error Rate (BER)	0.57%	1.39%	0.57%	0.44%

Table 2 shows the decoding success and bit error rates obtained for the scanned self-identifying documents, 25 documents at each of the four error correction levels. QR codes with EC-H yielded the best decoding success rate and bit error rate results. This is not surprising because EC-H has the highest error correction capability and lowest storage capacity. On the other hand, EC-L has the lowest error correction capability and highest storage capacity. Clearly, a tradeoff exists between accuracy and data capacity. Also, it is important to note that, although QR codes with EC-L have similar bit error rates compared with QR codes with EC-Q, they have lower decoding success rates. This is because QR codes with EC-Q are more robust than QR codes with EC-L.

The bit error rate of 1.39% is very high for QR codes with EC-M. Upon manual examination, it was determined that a single document contributed the most to the high bit error rate. Specifically, during the decoding process, optical character recognition interpreted two words separated by a hyphen as a single word. The misinterpretation reduced the word count in the line to ten (less than the minimum required count of 11 words), which caused the line to be skipped. The cascading effect led to an erroneous extracted string and high bit error rate.

Misclassifications caused by hyphens also occurred for some self-identifying document samples, but they did not lead to large errors because of the limited number of hidden characters per line. Except for the rare scenario where the hyphen misclassification reduced the word count in a line to under 11, the proposed method successfully decoded the extracted binary strings.

6. Conclusions

The canary trap method proposed for determining the source of a leaked hard copy document generates self-identifying documents that secretly encode unique information about the individuals who receive the documents by modifying the inter-word spacing in the original reference document. The method uses QR codes to provide robustness against errors introduced when printing, scanning or copying the self-identifying documents. Experimental results demonstrate that a decoding success rate of 100% was obtained for QR codes with the high (H) error correction level even after printing, scanning and copying the self-identifying documents, rendering the proposed method useful in real-world applications.

The canary trap method is unsuitable for justified documents with text aligned relative to the left and right margins. The space occupied by whitespace characters in a justified document is not the same every time; instead, it depends on the number of characters present in the line. Another problem is the anomalies introduced by optical character recognition when processing special characters such as hyphens. Future research will refine the canary trap method to handle justified documents and will optimize the optical character recognition process to address the anomalies caused by special characters in documents.

References

[1] K. Kaneda, H. Kitazawa, K. Iwamura and I. Echizen, A study of equipment dependence of a single-dot-pattern method for information hiding by applying an error-correcting code, *Proceedings of the Tenth International Conference on Intelligent Information Hiding and Multimedia Signal Processing*, pp. 497–501, 2014.

[2] K. Kaneda, F. Nagai, K. Iwamura and S. Hangai, A study of information hiding performance using a simple dot pattern with different tile sizes, *Proceedings of the Fourth International Conference on Intelligent Information Hiding and Multimedia Signal Processing*, pp. 323–326, 2008.

[3] A. Kozachok, S. Kopylov, A. Shelupanov and O. Evsutin, Text marking approach for data leakage prevention, *Journal of Computer Virology and Hacking Techniques*, vol. 15(3), pp. 219–232, 2019.

[4] V. Kuraki and V. Nakagata, Watermarking technologies for security-enhanced printed documents, *Fujitsu Science and Technical Journal*, vol. 43(2), pp. 197–203, 2007.

[5] C. Loc, J. Burie and J. Ogier, Stable regions and object-fill-based approach for document image watermarking, *Proceedings of the Thirteenth IAPR International Workshop on Document Analysis Systems*, pp. 181–186, 2018.

[6] S. Low, N. Maxemchuk, J. Brassil and L. O'Gorman, Document marking and identification using both line and word shifting, *Proceedings of the Fourteenth Annual Joint Conference of the IEEE Computer and Communications Societies*, vol. 2, pp. 853–860, 1995.

[7] J. Nayak, S. Singh, S. Chhabra, G. Gupta and M. Gupta, Detecting data leakage from hard copy documents, in *Advances in Digital Forensics XIV*, G. Peterson and S. Shenoi (Eds.), Springer, Cham, Switzerland, pp. 111–124, 2018.

[8] I. Safonov, I. Kurilin, M. Rychagov and E. Tolstaya, Embedding digital hidden data into hardcopy, in *Document Image Processing for Scanning and Printing*, I. Safonov, I. Kurilin, M. Rychagov and E. Tolstaya (Eds.), Springer, Cham, Switzerland, pp. 219–250, 2019.

[9] L. Tan, X. Sun and G. Sun, Print-scan resilient text image watermarking based on stroke direction modulation for Chinese document authentication, *Radioengineering*, vol. 21(1), pp. 170–181, 2012.

[10] R. Theis, `tess-two` version 9.1.0, GitHub (`github.com/rmtheis/tess-two`), 2015.

[11] J. van Beusekom, F. Shafait and T. Breuel, Automatic authentication of color laser print-outs using machine identification codes, *Pattern Analysis and Applications*, vol. 16(4), pp. 663–678, 2013.

[12] A. Varna, S. Rane and A. Vetro, Data hiding in hard-copy text documents robust to print, scan and photocopy operations, *Proceedings of the IEEE International Conference on Acoustics, Speech and Signal Processing*, pp. 1397–1400, 2009.

[13] D. Zou and Y. Shi, Formatted text document data hiding robust to printing, copying and scanning, *Proceedings of the IEEE International Symposium on Circuits and Systems*, vol. 5, pp. 4971–4974, 2005.

[14] ZXing Project Contributors, ZXing 3.4.1, GitHub (`github.com/zxing/zxing`), 2020.

Chapter 10

COMMUNITY DETECTION IN A WEB DISCUSSION FORUM DURING SOCIAL UNREST EVENTS

Ao Shen and Kam-Pui Chow

Abstract   Community detection, a network clustering method that identifies communities and reveals aggregated behavior, is an important topic in social network forensics. The purpose of social network forensics is to collect and analyze user information and content in social media. In recent years, much research has focused on social unrest events with the goal of accurately identifying key members in social networks. However, certain limitations exist with models that only use statistical properties of users and social networks, and do not consider the content of communications.

This chapter proposes a community detection model based on user attributes and communication content to analyze social unrest events. The investigation takes the form of a case study of users in a popular Hong Kong discussion forum, which includes potential event organizers and supporters. The results offer insights into engaging user behavior attributes and content features to identify user communities and community structures.

Keywords: Social network forensics, unrest events, community detection

1.   Introduction

Unrest events refer to manually-caused accidents, public health incidents and public security incidents that may result in serious social impacts and require emergency response measures [13]. Often, social unrest events escalate into conflict, violence and criminal activities [21]. Traditional crimes have been concealed with the development of the Internet [20], rendering conventional investigation methods difficult if not usable. When a social event is organized and the event details are disseminated using social media platforms, traces are buried in numerous

© IFIP International Federation for Information Processing 2022
Published by Springer Nature Switzerland AG 2022
G. Peterson and S. Shenoi (Eds.): DigitalForensics 2022, IFIP AICT 653, pp. 169–185, 2022.
https://doi.org/10.1007/978-3-031-10078-9_10

messages and posts. Social media forensics focuses on the extraction and analysis of user information from social media to identify, acquire and analyze user information for evidentiary purposes. Community detection, a network clustering method that identifies communities and reveals aggregation behavior, is an important topic in social network forensics. Forensic analyses of social unrest events often seek to identify key members in social networks [1, 6, 19]. Additionally, they help track protest movements, relationships between participants and community structures.

In 2019, a controversial extradition bill and police reaction to the resulting protests stirred extreme dissent in Hong Kong [22]. Massive demonstrations ensued, leading the Hong Kong Police to arrest 8,981 protesters between June 9, 2019 and May 29, 2020 [2]. Web discussion forums, anonymous and popular information dissemination platforms, became important channels for rapidly gathering and spreading information about planned protests.

This research does not focus on whether the protests were legal. Rather, it considers how law enforcement can leverage social media information related to social unrest events to maintain public safety [3]. Social media information has been well studied in disciplines such as law, sociology and psychology [5, 7, 21], but has not been studied adequately from the social network forensic perspective. Specifically, social media forensic techniques can be used to good effect to review and analyze social unrest events [17].

This research proposes a community detection model based on user attributes and communication content to conduct social network forensics and community detection during social unrest events. By examining social relationships and computing the similarities and connections between users, the model contributes to a deep understanding of user relationships and community structures. A case study involving LIHKG [11], a popular Hong Kong discussion forum, is employed to analyze the community of potential social unrest event organizers and supporters.

2.   Related Work

Social network forensics is an emerging field of digital forensics [15]. Research has focused on the challenges and limitations of social network forensics, especially related to evidence collection and jurisdictional issues [9]. Information in social networks of particular interest in forensic investigations includes users, relationships and content [21]. Several attempts have been made to develop social media models that support the automated analyses of social network information.

Okolica et al. [16] developed a probabilistic latent semantic index model that was applied to analyze the Enron email corpus and identify potential malicious insiders who felt estranged from the organization or had hidden interests in sensitive topics. Mulazzani et al. [12] determined important data sources and methods for analyzing social network user data in digital forensic investigations. They also generated graphs to show friends and other individuals who had relationships with persons of interest.

Catanese and Fiumara [4] developed a smartphone traffic visualization tool for reasoning about the potential criminal associations of suspects. They employed traffic graphs that displayed connections between individuals based on recorded phone calls. Statistical measures were used to identify anomalous users and clustering algorithms were employed to construct user groups.

Tian et al. [19] proposed a method for analyzing relationships in the WeChat social network and constructing social network diagrams expressing user intimacy. WeChat users were clustered based on the compactness of their accounts.

Al-Khateeb et al. [1] have studied social influence in social networks, focusing on cyber propaganda campaigns conducted by deviant groups on Twitter. They collected social network user attributes such as the numbers of friends, followers, mentions and replies, and employed a focal structure approach to identify the most influential users.

Chan et al. [6] observe that, while mob phenomena have been well-studied in sociology and public health, user classification based on social influence is most relevant in social network forensic investigations. They classified discussion forum participants based on their online behavior to detect potential flash mob organizers.

Analysis of the research literature reveals that the focus is on understanding statistical influences in social networks using graph-based or attribute-based methods. In contrast, the research described in this chapter demonstrates that post and tweet content are also essential in social network forensic investigations. Whereas classical social network analysis models only consider statistical relationships between replies, retweets, etc., the proposed model focuses on content that provides deep semantic understanding of the relationships between users in social network communities.

3. Community Detection Model

The proposed community detection model seeks to detect the similarities and connections between users at the statistical influence and

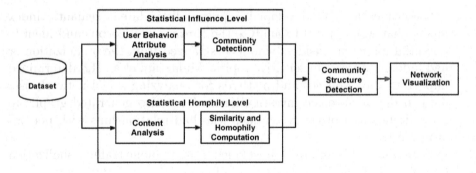

Figure 1.   Community detection model.

semantic homophily levels. Figure 1 presents an overview of the community detection model.

3.1   Statistical Influence Level

Social influence has traditionally been assessed by measuring an individual's impact on other people. This section describes how the attribute-based method and graph-based network method are employed to measure the statistical influence of users.

User Behavior Attributes. Weak ties usually occur between acquaintances and strangers with distant social ties and little interactions whereas strong ties occur between friends and family [18].

It is believed that weak ties build a social community structure. A discussion forum integrates weak ties so that more new information can be received from anonymous forum participants [10]. Table 1 specifies the attributes that measure the motivation and influence of each weak tie in the LIHKG Hong Kong discussion forum. The motivation indicator expresses the frequency with which a user attempts to spread information and promote an event. The influence indicator indicates the level of attention that the content posted by a user attracts other users.

Graph-Based Community Detection. A graph-based social network is a structured weighted graph $G = (V, E, W)$ comprising nodes V and edges E with weights W. Nodes refer to individuals or organizations whereas edges between nodes represent social relationships. When two individuals communicate with each other, the compactness between them is expressed by a weight. A social network is constructed where each node indicates a user, an edge between two nodes indicates the

Table 1. User attributes in the LIHKG discussion forum.

Category	User Behavior Attribute	Description
Motivation Indicator	Posts	Number of posts by user
	Self-replies	Number of replies by user to his/her own posts
Influence Indicator	Replies to others to posts by other users	Number of replies by user
	Replies from others	Number of replies to user received from other users

post-reply relationship between the two users, and the corresponding weight is incremented for every reply posted between the users.

In order to identify communities in a social network, a breadth-first search is used to traverse the social network and visualize the community graph.

The process of community detection begins by randomly selecting a user ID in the social network and locating its corresponding node in the community graph. Next, related nodes are traced using the edges connected to the selected node and other nodes connected to the nodes are identified; all these nodes form a community. Community detection terminates when every node has been allocated to a community.

3.2   Semantic Homophily Level

In order to conduct social network forensics at the semantic level, the similarity and homophily between posts created by users must be analyzed.

Content Analysis.   Content analysis is performed by extracting keywords from content using the BERT-CRF named entity recognition method [14]. The named entity recognition method converts the text of a post to a vector corresponding to the post with semantic information. The named entities (keywords) in the text are detected and classified as different entity types. The BERT-CRF method employs the BERT (bidirectional encoder representation from transformers) algorithm [8] and a CRF (conditional random field) layer [23]. The BERT pre-training language model encodes a single character to obtain the corresponding character vector with context-related semantic information. The semantic vector of the context information is input to the CRF layer for decoding. CRF is a standard sequence labeling algorithm that is used to label entities. The BERT-CRF model is trained with the default structure of the Chinese BERT-BASE model [8], which has 12 layers of transformer blocks and 12 attention heads. The length of the pre-training word vector is 768 dimensions and the batch size is 16 with the Adam optimizer and a learning rate of 1e-5.

Similarity and Homophily Computation. The similarity and homophily between users are computed by converting the user and posts created by the user to vector representations. The user post vector is the average of the vectors of all the posts created by the user:

$$\text{Vector(user post)} = \frac{\sum_{i=1}^{n} v_i}{n}$$

where user post represents the user who has created posts in the LIHKG forum, n is the total number of posts created by the user and v_i is the vector of each post created via content analysis. By incorporating the post vector in the computation of the user vector, it is possible to accurately reflect the relationships and semantic connections between users.

3.3   Community Structure Detection

To reflect the clustering of user communities in the social network graph, community detection engages the k-means algorithm to compute the relationships between users and place them in user communities. The vector associated with each user is the concatenation of the user attributes vector and user post vector. The specific user vector is computed as follows:

$$\text{Vector(user attributes)} = [attr1, attr2, attr3, attr4],$$

$$\text{Vector(user)} = \text{Vector(user attributes)} \oplus \text{Vector(user post)}$$

where Vector(user attributes) is the attribute vector of the user and $attr1$, $attr2$, $attr3$ and $attr4$ represent the number of posts, number of self-replies, number of replies to others and number of replies from others to the user, respectively. The k-means clustering algorithm is used to cluster users and detect communities. Thus, all the users are vectorized based on their user attributes and the content they posted. Finally, the users are classified into n clusters representing different types of nodes (users).

As shown in Figure 2, there are three types of nodes in a hierarchical community structure, core node (tree root), parent nodes and leaf nodes.

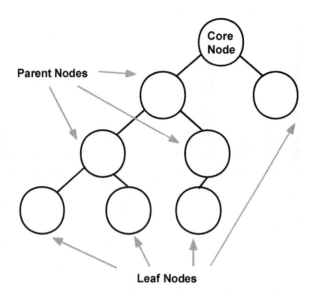

Figure 2. Hierarchical community structure graph.

The core node and parent nodes actively send and reply to posts whereas the leaf nodes only reply to posts from their parent nodes.

4. Experiments and Analysis

The application of the community detection model is illustrated using a case study involving the LIHKG discussion forum.

4.1 Data Collection and Labeling

The experimental data used to evaluate the performance of the proposed community detection model was collected from the Current Affairs Section of the LIHKG discussion forum from August 1, 2019 to August 11, 2020. Upon consideration of the ethical issues regarding data collection and the research purpose, only posts, replies, creation times and author IDs were collected. All sensitive and personal information was eliminated.

The dataset comprised 941,114 posts and replies, most of them written in Chinese and Cantonese. The frequent social unrest events that occurred all over Hong Kong during 2019-2020 renders the dataset ideal for studying patterns and characteristics of user communities, including potential unrest event organizers and supporters. Figure 3 shows the numbers of posts in the LIHKG discussion forum over August 1, 2019 to August 11, 2020.

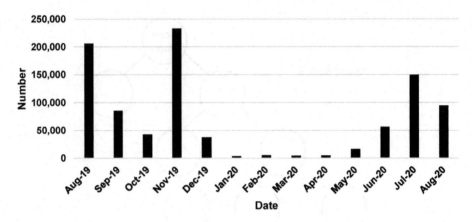

Figure 3. LIHKG forum posts from August 1, 2019 to August 11, 2020.

Since no authoritative real-world forensic dataset was available for named entity recognition, a portion of the data was labeled manually. In particular, 11,000 posts were randomly selected from the LIHKG forum dataset and manually assigned entity labels. Table 2 shows the named entity descriptions and examples.

4.2　Statistical Influence Analysis

Other social media platforms, such as Twitter and Facebook, maintain multiple relationships between users, including reply, forward, follow and like. However, the only action available to LIHKG discussion forum users is reply; this renders analysis and network generation much more accessible. Table 3 provides five examples of user attributes.

The attribute analysis results validate an earlier study that profiled event organizers in a Hong Kong discussion forum [17]. Some users generated large numbers of new posts and were very active at communicating with others. As a result, these users received more attention from other users as well as large numbers of replies (e.g., user IDs 5254 and 4018 in Table 3). Other users occasionally generated posts and actively replied to their posts, which contributed to their higher rankings; these users rarely contacted other users (e.g., user IDs 3242 and 52284 in Table 3). The two types of users correspond to potential event organizers or supporters.

In order to plot the social network in the discussion forum as a graph, users were designated as graph nodes. If a user replied to a post by another user, then a relationship was deemed to exist between the two users and an edge was constructed between the two nodes. Table 4 lists

Table 2. Named entity descriptions and examples.

Entity Type	Description	Example	Label
Person	Name of relevant person	Carrie Lam Cheng Yuet-Ngor (Chief Executive of Hong Kong), thug	\<PER\>
Time	Relevant date and time	17:05, Oct 20, 2020	\<TIM\>
Location	Protest addresses	Hong Kong, Airport, Cheung Sha Wan Station	\<LOC\>
Organization	Names of relevant organizations	Hong Kong Police, Government Central Committee	\<ORG\>
Crime	Nouns/expressions about crimes	Assault, riot, vandalism, fire	\<CRI\>
Action	Relevant verbs	Sit-in, destroy, gather, commit arson	\<ACT\>
Tool	Hazardous tools	Metal rod, petrol bomb, fire extinguisher, arms	\<TOO\>
Emotion	Emotional words about protests	Hatred, love, support	\<EMO\>
Other	Irrelevant words	The, a, is, are	\<O\>

Table 3. User attribute examples.

User ID	Posts	Self-Replies	Replies to Others	Replies from Others
5254	226	1,614	771	12,285
4018	145	1,185	437	3,668
3242	127	186	6	7,697
52284	96	639	4	3,639
104878	95	146	55	6,665

some frequent user-user pairs and the corresponding numbers of replies they sent to each other.

Next, it is necessary to examine the distribution of the user-user pairs. The statistical results reveal that among the 108,841 users with 526,599 user-user pairs, only 1.26% of the pairs have more than ten connections. Thus, the focus was on the 1.26% of the pairs and a graph was constructed to present the social network corresponding to these users.

Table 4. Examples of frequent user-user pairs.

User ID of Post	User ID of Reply	Frequency
17665	14395	2,085
11834	11834	1,932
17665	1984	1,835
5254	5254	1,614
4531	4531	1,443

Figure 4 shows the community detection results. Clear delineations of three communities, A, B and C, exist with almost no communications involving users outside each community. Communities A, B and C have 1,736, 145, and 575 users, respectively, covering 37.1% of the pairs with more than ten connections. According to the number of users in each cluster, community A has many more users than the other two communities. However, as discussed above, the contents of posts and replies are important to community detection as well as to analyzing the semantic relationships between users. Therefore, the next section presents the results of semantic homophily analysis on the user pairs.

4.3   Semantic Homophily Analysis

The labeled posts were used as the training dataset for the BERT-CRF model to identify entities from the posts. The manually-labeled data was randomly split into 80% and 20% for the training and testing datasets, respectively. As mentioned above, the user vector was obtained by concatenating the user attributes vector and user post vector.

The entities extracted by BERT-CRF can be treated as keywords in the content. To illustrate the importance and indispensability of considering content in social network forensics, a preliminary user-entity network was generated for location entities. Figure 5 shows the resulting user-entity network. The gray nodes represent the location entities extracted by BERT-CRF. The black nodes correspond to users who mentioned the social unrest events related to the locations in their posts. Some locations such as Airport, PolyU (Hong Kong Polytechnic University) and CUHK (Chinese University of Hong Kong) are highlighted. The most interesting aspect of the graph is that the users who mentioned Airport were not interested in the unrest events at universities (PolyU and CUHK). Likewise, users who mentioned universities in their posts rarely mentioned unrest events at the Airport. The main reason is that,

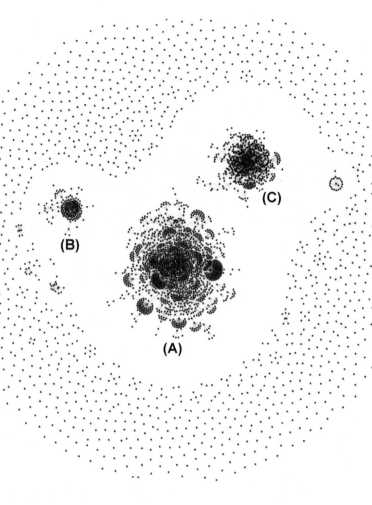

Figure 4. Community detection results.

during the period of the posts, all the universities in Hong Kong prohibited outsiders from entering their campuses. Therefore, it was almost impossible for outsiders to participate in campus unrest events.

4.4 Community Analysis and Visualization

In order to determine the community structure in the LIHKG discussion forum, an attempt was made to classify users into different groups. The community analysis involved three steps. First, the initial communities were identified by performing similarity clustering using k-means.

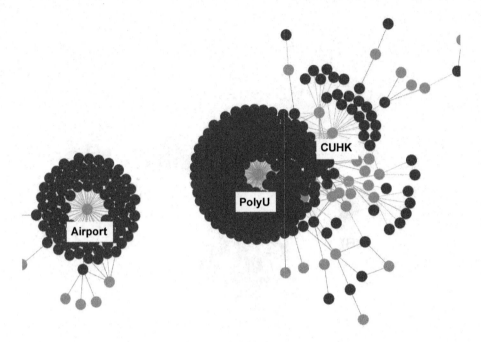

Figure 5.   User-entity network sample.

Next, the best number of clusters was computed based on the elbow method (four clusters in the experiment). Finally, the clustering result created during the first step was mapped to the social network. The mapping results reveal the community network and its structure.

To further analyze the user attributes and community structure, the clustering results were consolidated with community detection in the user-user network. Figure 6 shows the clustering results of communities A, B and C. The four grayscale colors represent the four clusters. Nodes with the same grayscale color are in the same cluster. Clusters 0, 1, 2 and 3 have 13, 52, 403 and 1,988 users, respectively. Figure 6 preliminarily illustrates that cluster 0 includes the core nodes in each community. User IDs 94, 1080 and 119, the core nodes in cluster 0, frequently communicated with other users. Nodes in cluster 1 are likely to be the parent nodes whereas clusters 2 and 3 comprise leaf nodes and several parent nodes that constitute the grassroots of the community. In this way, community structure can be employed to advance user analysis.

Table 5 shows the distribution of community users in each cluster. Cluster 0, the smallest cluster, includes the core users of each community. To compare the distributions of user attributes before and after adding the content analysis in the social network, the box plots in Figure 7

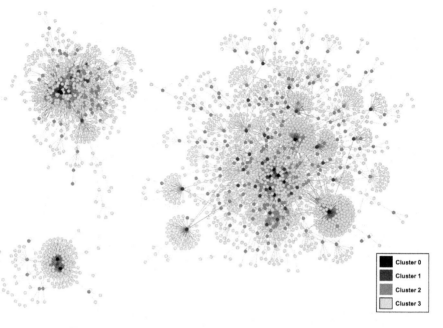

Figure 6. Clustering results of community structure.

Table 5. Community user distributions in clusters.

Community/Cluster	0	1	2	3	Total
A	6	27	275	1,428	1,736
B	1	1	22	121	145
C	6	24	106	439	575
Total	13	52	403	1,988	2,456

indicate the distributions of the four user attributes in different clusters. Specifically, the four plots represent the distributions of the four user attributes in clusters 0 to 3. Compared with other clusters, cluster 0, which includes the core users in each community, has the highest median value for all four user attributes.

Therefore, it can be assumed that the core members are not only a minority community, but are also most proactive and influential at organizing or supporting social unrest events. Since the clustering algorithm is based on user attribute similarity and content similarity, the users in cluster 0 usually posted similar content in the LIHKG discussion forum. To verify that the users in cluster 0 are potential organizers or support-

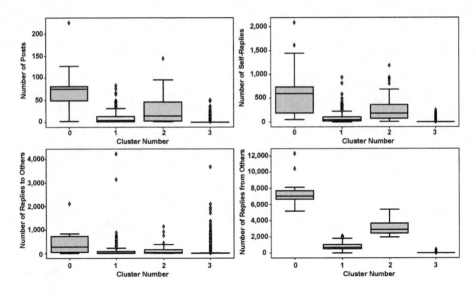

Figure 7. Attribute distributions in clusters.

ers of the unrest events, the numbers of crime, action and tool entities must be computed to evaluate if users mention the topics related to unrest events frequently. Indeed, the data analysis reveals that the users in cluster 0 posted the largest number of event-related topics (12,393), accounting for 51.2% of event-related topics.

5.   Conclusions

User relationship analysis and community detection are important tasks in social network forensics. The community detection model described in this chapter leverages statistical data about user attributes and semantic analysis of the communications between users. By mining and analyzing user relationships and community structure, users and communities with high levels of social influence are identified from among a massive number of users. The results provide valuable clues in social network investigations and can be used proactively to prevent social unrest demonstrations from going out of control.

Future research will attempt to integrate community structure and communication content, such as adding entities in the social network as a new type of node. Additionally, research will focus on topic extraction in social networks and user communities, and apply sentiment analysis to user communities.

References

[1] S. Al-Khateeb, M. Hussain and N. Agarwal, Leveraging social network analysis and cyber forensic approaches to study cyber propaganda campaigns, in *Social Networks and Surveillance for Society*, T. Ozyer, S. Bakshi and R. Alhajj (Eds.), Springer, Cham, Switzerland, pp. 19–42, 2019.

[2] A. Arranz, Arrested Hong Kong protesters: How the numbers look one year on, *South China Morning Post*, June 11, 2020.

[3] H. Arshad, A. Jantan and E. Omolara, Evidence collection and forensics on social networks: Research challenges and directions, *Digital Investigation*, vol. 28, pp. 126–138, 2019.

[4] S. Catanese and G. Fiumara, A visual tool for forensic analysis of mobile phone traffic, *Proceedings of the Second ACM Workshop on Multimedia in Forensics, Security and Intelligence*, pp. 71–76, 2010.

[5] J. Chan, A storm of unprecedented ferocity: The shrinking space of the right to political participation, peaceful demonstration and judicial independence in Hong Kong, *International Journal of Constitutional Law*, vol. 16(2), pp. 373–388, 2018.

[6] V. Chan, K. Chow and R. Chan, Profiling flash mob organizers in web discussion forums, in *Advances in Digital Forensics XII*, G. Peterson and S. Shenoi (Eds.), Springer, Cham, Switzerland, pp. 281–293, 2016.

[7] Y. Chen, The controversy of the Amendment of Anti-Extradition in Hong Kong – Threat to the people of Hong Kong, *HOLISTICA – Journal of Business and Public Administration*, vol. 10(3), pp. 133–142, 2019.

[8] J. Devlin, M. Chang, K. Lee and K. Toutanova, BERT: Pre-training of deep bidirectional transformers for language understanding, *Proceedings of the Conference of the North American Chapter of the Association for Computational Linguistics: Human Language Technologies, Volume 1*, pp. 4171–4186, 2019.

[9] M. Firdaus, Forensic Analysis of Social Media Data: Research Challenges and Directions, Department of Information Security, Graduate School, Pukong Natonal University, Busan, South Korea, 2020.

[10] M. Granovetter, The impact of social structure on economic outcomes, *Journal of Economic Perspectives*, vol. 19(1), pp. 33–50, 2005.

[11] LIHKG Discussion Forum, Hong Kong, China (lihkg.com/cate gory/1), 2016.

[12] M. Mulazzani, M. Huber and E. Weippl, Data visualization for social network forensics, in *Advances in Digital Forensics VIII*, G. Peterson and S. Shenoi (Eds.), Springer, Berlin Heidelberg, Germany, pp. 115–126 2012.

[13] S. Muthiah, B. Huang, J. Arredondo, D. Mares, L. Getoor, G. Katz and N. Ramakrishnan, Planned protest modeling in news and social media, *Proceedings of the Twenty-Ninth AAAI Conference*, pp. 3920–3927, 2015.

[14] D. Nadeau and S. Sekine, A survey of named entity recognition and classification, *Lingvisticae Investigationes*, vol. 30(1), pp. 3–26, 2007.

[15] A. Nikolaidou, M. Lazaridis, T. Semertzidis, A. Axenopoulos and P. Daras, Forensic analysis of heterogeneous social media data, *Proceedings of the Eighteenth Joint Conference on Knowledge Discovery, Knowledge Engineering and Knowledge Management*, pp. 343–350, 2019.

[16] J. Okolica, G. Peterson and R. Mills, Using PLSI-U to detect insider threats from email traffic, in *Advances in Digital Forensics II*, M. Olivier and S. Shenoi (Eds.), Springer, Boston, Massachusetts, pp. 91–103, 2006.

[17] A. Powell and C. Haynes, Social media data in digital forensic investigations, in *Digital Forensic Education*, X. Zhang and K. Choo (Eds.), Springer, Cham, Switzerland, pp. 281–303, 2020.

[18] M. Ruef, Strong ties, weak ties and islands: Structural and cultural predictors of organizational innovation, *Industrial and Corporate Change*, vol. 11(3), pp. 427–449, 2002.

[19] J. Tian, Y. Bi and J. Ma, Research on forensics of social network relationship based on big data, *Journal of Physics: Conference Series*, vol. 1584(1), article no. 012022, 2020.

[20] D. Wall, *Cybercrime – The Transformation of Crime in the Information Age*, Polity Press, Cambridge, United Kingdom, 2007.

[21] J. Wang, Hong Kong's Government faces resistance from within as dissent spreads. Organizers expect more than 1,000 civil servants to attend a rally despite the threat of consequences, *The Wall Street Journal*, August 2, 2019.

[22] Wikipedia Contributors, 2019-2020 Hong Kong protests, *Wikipedia* (en.wikipedia.org/w/index.php?title=2019%E2%80%932020_Hong_Kong_protests&oldid=1066507368), January 18, 2022.

[23] C. Wojek and B. Schiele, A dynamic conditional random field model for joint labeling of object and scene classes, *Proceedings of the Tenth European Conference on Computer Vision, Part IV*, pp. 733–747, 2008.

Chapter 11

ANALYZING THE ERROR RATES OF BITCOIN CLUSTERING HEURISTICS

Yanan Gong, Kam-Pui Chow, Hing-Fung Ting and Siu-Ming Yiu

Abstract   Bitcoin is a decentralized peer-to-peer cryptocurrency. Bitcoin's strong cryptography ensures anonymity that makes it possible to profit from crimes such as ransomware attacks and money laundering. Unfortunately, developments in blockchain technology make it almost impossible to identify the owners of Bitcoin addresses. Address clustering seeks to target the pseudo-anonymity by grouping Bitcoin addresses to eventually reveal real-world identities. However, none of the heuristic-based address clustering algorithms have been successfully admitted in court proceedings because they are heuristic in nature. According to the Daubert standard, for an algorithm to be admissible, it should have a known error rate. An error rate helps determine the extent to which a court can rely on the evidence, but no address clustering algorithm is able to report an error rate.

This chapter describes a simulation model for validating heuristic-based address clustering algorithms and obtaining the corresponding error rates. The evaluation results demonstrate that the model can simulate real-world transactions. Two heuristics, multi-input and one-time change, are applied. The multi-input and one-time change heuristics yield average error rates of 63.46% and 92.66%, respectively. The application of both heuristics yields the lowest average error rate of 57.47%.

Keywords: Bitcoin, simulation, heuristic-based address clustering, error rates

1.   Introduction

Bitcoin, currently priced in excess of $39,000 per unit [5], is a decentralized peer-to-peer cryptocurrency that has received considerable attention. Bitcoin is based on strong cryptography and has many advantages, including permissionless, confidential and decentralized transactions [25]. The anonymous nature of Bitcoin protects the privacy of

© IFIP International Federation for Information Processing 2022
Published by Springer Nature Switzerland AG 2022
G. Peterson and S. Shenoi (Eds.): DigitalForensics 2022, IFIP AICT 653, pp. 187–205, 2022.
https://doi.org/10.1007/978-3-031-10078-9_11

users and enables pseudo-anonymous financial transactions. Bitcoin wallets enable the cryptocurrency to be traded with new and unused Bitcoin addresses for every new transaction, which make it almost impossible to identify the actual owners of Bitcoin addresses. Bitcoin's secure, unrestrained payment method coupled with its anonymity hinders law enforcement investigations, making it possible to profit from crimes such as ransomware attacks and money laundering. According to the 2021 Crypto Crime Report from the blockchain data firm Chainalysis [7], in 2020, ransomware victims paid attackers more than $406 million worth of cryptocurrency.

De-anonymizing real-world identities in the Bitcoin ecosystem is an active area of research. Much effort has focused on address clustering [17]. The goal of address clustering is to break pseudo-anonymity by attempting to find correlations in clusters, Bitcoin addresses and IP addresses, eventually revealing the real-world identities of users.

Heuristic-based address clustering exploits the structural details of Bitcoin transactions [31]. Some address clustering algorithms group "unrelated" Bitcoin addresses and link them to criminal suspects. However, the limitation of heuristic-based clustering is that it is very difficult to evaluate the quality of the clustering results. In particular, heuristic approaches lack large-scale ground-truth labels that could be used to indicate which addresses belong to specific users [31]. Since the relationships derived between addresses may not be accurate, the collected evidence has not been admitted in court proceedings.

The Daubert standard is used by trial judges to assess the scientific testimony of expert witnesses [16, 18, 19, 27]. The standard specifies five criteria for determining admissibility: (i) whether the theory or technique can be and has been tested, (ii) whether it has been subjected to peer review and publication, (iii) its known or potential error rate, (iv) existence and maintenance of standards controlling its operation and (v) whether it has attracted widespread acceptance within a relevant scientific community. Unfortunately, heuristic-based address clustering does not meet the third Daubert criterion. This is because the nature of heuristics makes it very difficult to derive accurate error rates.

This chapter describes a simulation model for validating heuristic-based address clustering algorithms and obtaining their error rates. The model simulates real-world Bitcoin transactions and collects the required statistics at the same time. The distribution patterns of simulated transactions are similar to the distribution patterns of transactions in the real Bitcoin network. The simulation model enables the actual owners of generated Bitcoin addresses to be determined, enabling the error rates of heuristic-based address clustering algorithms to be measured.

2. Related Work

It is impractical to conduct experiments on the real Bitcoin network due to factors such as anonymity, time and cost. Therefore, a simulator that closely models the real Bitcoin network is required to better understand and evaluate network behavior. Existing simulators are broadly classified into two types, event-based simulators and virtualization-based simulators [1].

In an event-based simulator, state variables change in discrete time [3]. The simulator abstracts the node logic as a sequence of discrete events to simulate the Bitcoin network and the simulation time can jump to the start time of the next event. The Shadow-Bitcoin event-based simulator is scalable and supports multi-threaded applications [21]. Stoykov et al. [26] have developed the VIBES simulator that handles large-scale simulations with thousands of nodes, enabling users to explore node interactions and observe important features of the network in an intuitive manner. Faria and Correia [13] have implemented the BlockSim framework that provides a collection of base simulation models applicable to blockchains; the framework can be extended by users to evaluate their design and deployment decisions. SIMBA is an improved version of BlockSim that adds Merkle tree verification to each block to enhance simulation fidelity and support transaction authentication [14].

Virtualization-based simulators employ lightweight virtualization techniques. Chen et al. [8] have modeled a large-scale peer-to-peer network by simulating logical nodes that run a custom Bitcoin application. The framework, which deploys containers and a Docker platform as real Bitcoin miners, has been shown to achieve a good balance between simulation fidelity and cost. Alsahan et al. [1] have created a new simulation framework that integrates the Linux kernel traffic control (tc) tool to enable fast simulations of large-scale networks and specify different network topologies and Bitcoin mining difficulty levels.

Address clustering is another research topic that focuses on the important process of de-anonymizing Bitcoin users. The addresses that potentially belong to a specific user are associated by address clustering. Heuristic-based address clustering reasons about the relationships between Bitcoin addresses based on the structural details of transactions [31]. It is categorized as a heuristic technique because it takes advantage of the way in which typical wallet software creates transactions [23]. Meiklejohn et al. [20] have defined the multi-input heuristic in detail. In multi-input transactions, all the input addresses of a transaction are likely to be controlled by a single user because the transaction has to be signed using the corresponding private keys for all the inputs. This heuristic is also referred to as the common spending heuristic [12].

Meiklejohn et al. [20] proposed the one-time change address heuristic – if one Bitcoin transaction has a change, the address used to receive the change (change address) and all the input addresses may be controlled by the same user. Zhang et al. [31] specified the address-reuse-based change address detection heuristic [31], which is based on the change address heuristic. The heuristic modifies one condition to achieve more accurate identification because the change address heuristic depends on address reuse to identify change addresses. Nick [23] specified the consumer heuristic that considers redeeming transactions in consumer wallets and the optimal change heuristic based on Bitcoin client behavior.

Due to the diversity of simulated networks, including their scale, security, speed and cost, most simulations focus more on the implementation of network-level functionality (e.g., network protocols) or propagation performance (e.g., block/transaction propagation). Additionally, when evaluating the performance of a simulated model, the measurements usually concentrate on network delays and propagation times. In other words, most simulations do not pay enough attention to the structural details of simulated Bitcoin transactions. In contrast, this research seeks to validate heuristic-based address clustering algorithms and measure their error rates. Since heuristic methods exploit structural details of Bitcoin transactions such as the numbers of input/output addresses and address reuse, a simulation model is developed that captures real-world Bitcoin transactions and collects required data such as user wallet information and the structural details of transactions.

3.   Real-World Bitcoin Transaction Investigation

The distribution of transactions in the real Bitcoin network needs to be investigated in order to create a high-fidelity simulation. As of June 16, 2021 (05:32:18 UTC), there were a total of 687,775 (block height of 0-687774) blocks in the Bitcoin blockchain. Parsing the chain revealed that 649,569,196 transactions were contained in the blocks. This investigation covers the distributions of four types of blockchain transactions, the distributions of different numbers of inputs and outputs in blockchain transactions and the address reuse rates. Additionally, the number of transactions generated per block in the real Bitcoin blockchain is also examined.

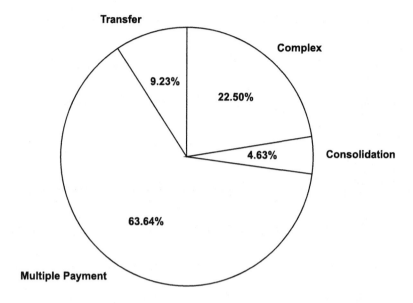

Figure 1. Transaction type distribution (real Bitcoin blockchain).

3.1 Transaction Distribution

Heuristic-based clustering algorithms have specific requirements regarding the numbers of input/output addresses in transactions. For example, the multi-input heuristic algorithm that clusters addresses in a multi-input transaction requires the number of input addresses to be greater than one. Therefore, the transactions are not classified into standard and non-standard transactions according to Bitcoin scripts [4].

Depending on the numbers of inputs and outputs, there are four types of transactions, transfer, multiple payment, consolidation and complex transactions [10]. A transfer, or full payment, means that the entire amount from one address is transferred to another address; a transfer transaction only has one input address and one output address. A batch payment, which often has lower transaction fees, is a multiple payment transaction with a single input and multiple outputs. A consolidation transaction receives multiple inputs to one address in a single transaction; thus, it has multiple inputs and one output. A complex transaction has multiple inputs and outputs.

First, the numbers of the four types of transactions and their proportions in the real Bitcoin blockchain were examined. Figure 1 shows the distributions of the four types of transactions. Multiple payments have the largest number of transactions, accounting for 63.64% of the

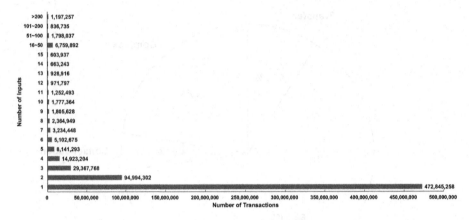

Figure 2.   Distribution of the numbers of inputs (real Bitcoin blockchain).

total transactions. Complex transactions constitute the second largest type of transactions, 22.50% of the transactions. Transfer transactions constitute the third largest type and consolidation transactions have the least number of transactions, just 4.63% of the total transactions.

Next, the distribution of the numbers of inputs and outputs in transactions was examined. Figure 2 shows that the majority of transactions have only one input, accounting for 72.79% of all transactions. Figure 3 shows that the majority of transactions have two outputs, 75.83% of all transactions. Also, transactions with one to six inputs and transactions with one to five outputs constitute more than 96% of all transactions. This means that the vast majority of transactions have one to six input addresses and one to five output addresses.

Finally, the numbers of transactions in each block were examined. About one-half of all blocks have one to 500 Bitcoin transactions.

3.2   Address Reuse

Heuristic-based clustering algorithms rely on address reuse. The one-time change heuristic, for example, identifies the change address from the outputs based on the number of occurrences of each address. An address is considered to be an old address if it has already appeared as an output address in at least one transaction in the blockchain. If the address appears as an output address for the first time in the entire blockchain, then it is considered a new address. Users are advised to use a new Bitcoin address whenever they receive a new payment to protect their privacy, but it is still common to reuse old addresses to receive Bitcoin payments [15].

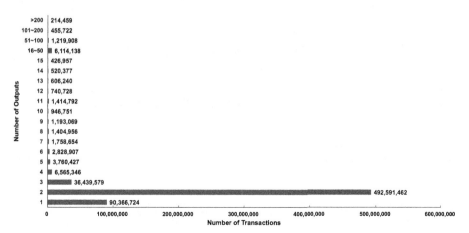

Figure 3. Distribution of the numbers of outputs (real Bitcoin blockchain).

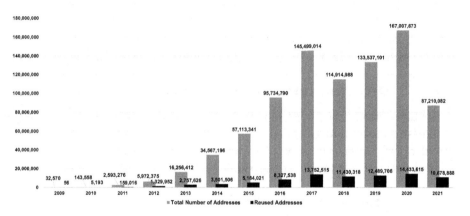

Figure 4. Address statistics.

Bitcoin was created in 2008 and first used in 2009 [2]. Therefore, the reuse of Bitcoin addresses since 2009 is investigated. Figure 4 shows the reused address statistics and the total number of addresses for each year from 2009 to 2021.

Figure 5 shows the address reuse rates from 2009 to 2021. The address reuse rate increased during the first four years. The reuse rate dropped to 10.1296% in 2014 and has hovered around 10% for the next seven years. However, there was a slight increase in the address reuse rate to 12.245% in 2021. The change is expected because complete Bitcoin address data for 2021 was not available when conducting the research described in this chapter. However, according to data for the previous years, the final reuse rate of 2021 may also be around 10%. All in all, since 2014,

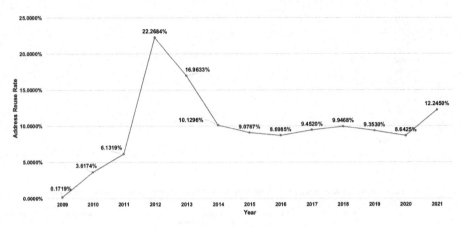

Figure 5. Address reuse rates.

the Bitcoin address reuse rate has been around 10%. Therefore, a 10% address reuse rate was employed to simulate the real Bitcoin network.

4.   Bitcoin Network Simulation

This section describes the Bitcoin network simulation used to validate heuristic-based address clustering algorithms. In addition to simulating real-world transactions, it collected user wallet information and structural details in Bitcoin transactions.

4.1   Simulator Architecture

The simulation model is based on Simchain [24]. Various improvements and modifications were introduced in Simchain to generate the four types of Bitcoin transactions. Also, a coinbase transaction was generated automatically when a new block was created.

Bitcoin mixing services, which were introduced to improve transaction anonymity, are frequently used for money laundering, complicating the task of tracking illegal funds [29]. By combining different inputs and outputs in a transaction, mixing makes it more difficult to uncover the relationships between outputs and inputs [30]. Mixing services also affect the results of address clustering algorithms. Therefore, to make the simulation as close as possible to the real-world Bitcoin network, transactions from multiple nodes to multiple nodes were generated, as in the case of Bitcoin mixing services.

All the nodes in the simulation were full nodes with four functions, wallet, routing, consensus and storage [24]. The wallet function stores

```
Basic info of Peer 21: peer(82, 39)
Balance is 1057.6849841605979BTC
Address list: ['1NYzbn8pzf7AcMPM5DeQN1RVyQCGuQvjjb', '1QCcz9pp4jasEUC2WXGX9uExf3KPMnJRLY', '18ZuLMHk
'1CEGzmMWduA23JDNjqb1sdwKPxcRVrhGCP', '17Z6eH9t6GeN184JrXn7FmsVcwLv26Nfnc', '13MYbD984ou9CoJK9QzCsjb
'1wjMU43Srxc8F5VrCsFGq9DszsewF3ug9', '16i47ZyuapieUXmssb4fuZNmZpVRzvD2qS', '12gqsfFzAoyR8X75M6kQLaVN
'1Paf2dBo6cajL9pPqYFa57AY4wfgMnEV9v', '1PnE9Um7a5QCnE2HjwKWGx7rdedxZ2soDm', '17ATctN93dKzQNGyooNkbf4
'1L3GtbSyPtLXYfYHCxzKMGDvbChzMBESNw', '12oxKm1QBgGnF6Phtw6hMCNma5zbvb72fV', '1EVoohLhJSxy2JnEk7JC5SK
'1BuPjQUatZtkL5e7ZdrpuuzgZYDxYer4e5', '1EBH7EwZmsjsde5L5UQjnyB4r9mowrnRrG', '1K6qHagdwsb7ZQoZRUJJbng
'1PaEBLkix5jvB6wevLUqH3VyxyLSAZX9cJ', '1Kfj9RgUypv12onRtRQPRcX3FEuowma6Fz', '19eW9NaQtSMw8Tyb9dBtcSf
'1L6Qe2bwuH2t5QhhYN5nYimbXcwfrzp6tx', '1PuLEFjctqgq2Lfz2FEnuhJQn5NqJAuqsq', '1K5iSRSmXrDmV62xbLaWrPb
'1DreuDho3ojRcpUhU8rGC4We47seEpqAHw', '172SYZZVytPnRTYBzD8UyEc3z6iES3QLSD', '1D1cxH5fcuJztaEPcnAeEHU
'1CnNmiiq1Hn62SeF8CMQseTedqiFDnhY7K' '1113dISFcMNTRuREYVI5dEzzFliryi3QCM' '1Ch91imnSDhcSacdYVSR33R
```

Figure 6. File `basicdata.log`.

Bitcoin key pairs and the corresponding addresses; it can also be used to query information such as the wallet balance at a node. The routing function supports the communication of information between nodes in the simulated network; also, it verifies the validity of transactions. The storage function maintains all the blockchain data such as valid transactions and unspent transaction outputs (UTXOs). The consensus function implements the same proof-of-work (PoW) consensus algorithm as the real Bitcoin network.

SHA-256 double hashing [11] was used in the simulation; specifically, after performing the SHA-256 operation on an input, another SHA-256 operation was performed on the hashed result to produce the output. The simulation employed elliptic-curve cryptography, in fact, the same secp256k1 elliptic curve as the real Bitcoin network.

4.2 Bitcoin Network Simulation

The experiments simulated a Bitcoin network with 300 nodes. The initial balance at each node was 1,000 BTC. The transaction fee was 0.01% of the input amount. The mining reward of 6 BTC was paid to the winning miner. Based on previous investigations, a 10% address reuse rate was set in the simulation. When setting up transactions from multiple nodes to multiple nodes, the maximum number of outputs was limited to six. This is because only 2.62% of real Bitcoin transactions have output addresses greater than six. The number of transactions generated per block was adjusted to match the probability distribution in the real Bitcoin network. The simulation generated 12 blocks and 11,796 transactions.

While real-world Bitcoin transactions were being simulated, generated data, such as user wallet information and transaction details, was recorded in three log files:

- **basicdata.log:** This file saves basic information about user wallets, such as the address list and balance (Figure 6). Note that "Peer" refers to a Bitcoin node.

Figure 7. File `bitcoin.log`.

- **bitcoin.log:** This file maintains the simulation logs. Figure 7 shows some logs in the file, such as which node created and broadcasted a transaction, the number of nodes conducting mining and when a new block was created. Note that "pid" denotes a peer identifier.

Figure 8. File `detaildata.log`.

- **detaildata.log:** This file holds details about each transaction. Referring to the real Bitcoin transaction structure [2], a Bitcoin transaction has the txid (hash of transaction), vin, vout and used UTXO set. Thus, the file saves the txid, vin, vout, vin size, vout size and used UTXOs of each transaction as shown in Figure 8.

4.3   Evaluation Metrics

Before validating heuristic-based address clustering algorithms, the simulated Bitcoin network was evaluated to check whether it generates transactions that are as close as possible to real-world Bitcoin transactions. Since the investigation of real-world Bitcoin transactions covers:

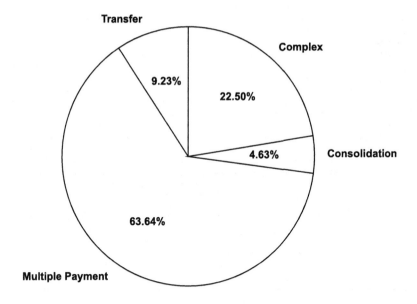

Figure 9. Transaction type distribution (simulated Bitcoin blockchain).

(i) distribution of the four types of transactions across the blockchain, (ii) distribution of different numbers of inputs and outputs, and (iii) address reuse rate, the evaluation metrics were selected based on these three criteria. In addition, the number of transactions generated per block was also checked to see if it followed the probability distribution in the real network.

The simulation generated 11,796 transactions. Figure 9 shows the distribution of the four types of transactions. Note that multiple payments constitute the highest proportion of transactions (63.14%), followed by complex transactions and transfer transactions. Consolidation transactions constitute the lowest proportion of transactions.

Figures 10 and 11 show the distributions of the numbers of inputs and outputs, respectively. The largest proportion of transactions have one input and the largest proportion of transactions have two outputs. The simulated network has a total of 29,005 addresses with a reuse rate of 9.7880%. The number of transactions in each block follows the probability distribution in the real network. The distribution patterns of the simulated transactions are similar to the distribution patterns of real Bitcoin network transactions. The address reuse rate of 9.7880% in the simulation is also close to the 10% address reuse rate in the real Bitcoin network. Thus, the simulation effectively models real-world Bitcoin transactions.

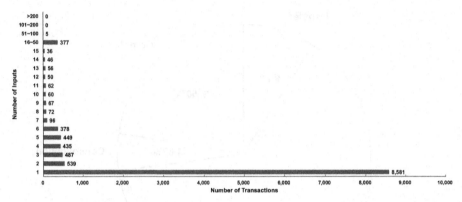

Figure 10.   Distribution of the numbers of inputs (simulated Bitcoin blockchain).

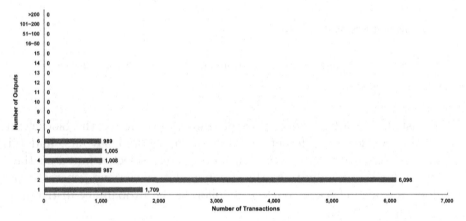

Figure 11.   Distribution of the numbers of outputs (simulated Bitcoin blockchain).

5.   Validation of Heuristic Algorithms

The multi-input and one-time change heuristics, which rely on the numbers of input and output addresses and address reuse [20] are commonly used for Bitcoin address clustering [22]. However, because they are heuristic in nature, the clustering results may have errors. For example, the multi-input heuristic usually comes with the assumption that a transaction was created by a single user. However, in the real world, combining multiple payments from different spenders in a single transaction is permitted, as in the case of CoinJoin [9] and PayJoin [28]. This results in false positives. Although the one-time change heuristic is based on different conditions, change addresses in the real Bitcoin network may not be identified due to address reuse or other reasons; this can lead to false negatives. Alternatively, paying money to two payees without any change leads to false positives.

The actual owners of all the addresses in the simulated Bitcoin network can be identified because all the required data, such as wallet information, is saved. It is also possible to determine which addresses belong to specific users in order to obtain the real clusters. Applying the heuristic algorithms to the addresses yields heuristic clusters. By comparing the heuristic clusters against the real clusters, the quality of heuristic clustering can be evaluated. In particular, the validation results are expressed in terms of the error rates.

5.1 Error Rates

Every node in the simulated network has a wallet and generates transactions. Thus, every node has a corresponding real cluster that contains owned Bitcoin addresses. The weight of a real cluster is used to find the corresponding heuristic cluster. For example, if a point represents a given cluster and if another cluster (another point) has at least one identical address as the given cluster, then there is an edge between the two clusters (points). The weight of the edge is the number of identical addresses owned by the two clusters [6]. If a real cluster corresponds to multiple heuristic clusters, then the heuristic cluster with the highest weight is the best match. This cluster is designated as the heuristic cluster corresponding to the real cluster.

Let R_i denote a real cluster derived from a user wallet and let H_i denote a heuristic cluster generated by the heuristic algorithm that corresponds to the real cluster R_i based on the highest weight criterion. Then, the accuracy of the cluster match is given by:

$$\text{Accuracy}_i = \frac{|\, H_i \cap R_i \,|}{|\, R_i \,|}$$

where $|\, H_i \cap R_i \,|$ is the number of correctly-clustered addresses appearing in clusters H_i and R_i and $|\, R_i \,|$ is the number of addresses in the real cluster R_i.

The error rate of the cluster match is given by:

$$\text{Error Rate}_i = 1 - \text{Accuracy}_i.$$

If N is the total number of clusters, then the average error rate is given by:

$$\text{Average Error Rate} = \frac{1}{N} \sum_{i=1}^{N} \text{Error Rate}_i.$$

Table 1. Experimental results.

	MI Heuristic	OTC Heuristic	MI + OTC Heuristics	Real Clusters
Clusters	1,023	908	1,017	300
Addresses (Largest Cluster)	9,954	58	12,266	131
Addresses/Cluster (Avg)	17	4	18	97
Average Error Rate	63.46%	92.66%	57.47%	NA

5.2   Validation Results

Heuristic-based address clustering algorithms were applied to all the Bitcoin addresses in the simulated Bitcoin network. Specifically, three address clustering experiments were performed. The first experiment used the multi-input (MI) heuristic, the second used the one-time change (OTC) heuristic and the third used the multi-input and one-time change (MI + OTC) heuristics. The simulated network had a total of 29,005 addresses. The simulated network was determined to have 300 real clusters because each node in the simulated network had a wallet and generated transactions.

The experimental results are summarized in Table 1. The following details are especially relevant to the validation:

- **Multi-Input Heuristic:** In this experiment, transactions have to be signed with the correct private keys. If a transaction has more than one input, then all its input addresses may belong to the same user [20]. The application of this heuristic yielded a total of 1,023 clusters. The largest cluster contained 9,954 Bitcoin addresses, but most of the clusters had only two addresses. On average, each cluster contained 17 addresses. The average error rate using the multi-input heuristic was computed as 63.46%.

- **One-Time Change Heuristic:** In this experiment, if one Bitcoin transaction has a change, then the address used to receive the change (change address) and all the input addresses may be controlled by the same user [20]. Ermilov et al. [12] have suggested limiting the transactions to have exactly two outputs to obtain more precise identification. Therefore, the one-time change heuristic was executed on transactions with exactly two outputs. A total of 908 clusters were generated. The largest cluster contained 58 Bitcoin addresses, but most of the clusters had two addresses. On

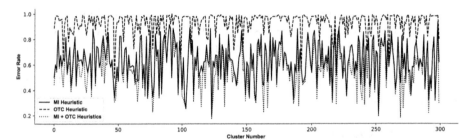

Figure 12. Error rates.

average, each cluster contained four addresses. The average error rate using the multi-input heuristic was computed as 92.66%.

- **Multi-Input and One-Time Change Heuristics:** In this experiment, the multi-input heuristic was applied first following which the one-time change heuristic was applied. A total of 1,017 clusters were generated. The largest cluster contained 12,266 Bitcoin addresses, but most of the clusters had two addresses. On average, each cluster contained 18 addresses. The average error rate using the multi-input and one-time change heuristics was computed as 57.47%.

Figure 12 shows the error rates for each real cluster in the three experiments. The one-time change heuristic has the highest average error rate and the multi-input heuristic has the second-highest error rate. However, using both the heuristics reduces the error rate and provides the highest accuracy. In order for the one-time change heuristic to identify change addresses more accurately, the additional condition that all transactions should have two outputs was imposed, but the average error rate still reached 92.66%. This is because the heuristic relies on the occurrences of an address to distinguish the change address. However, with developments in Bitcoin wallets, new unused Bitcoin addresses for receiving Bitcoins for new transactions are usually generated automatically. In short, if a transaction has two new output addresses, it is not possible to determine the change address based on this heuristic.

The error rates for all three experiments are not low. There are two possible reasons. First, heuristic-based clustering algorithms consider address reuse to group Bitcoin addresses, but with the increase in security awareness, the address reuse rate in the blockchain has dropped below 10%. Second, various anonymity enhancing technologies such as mixing services and privacy improvements for Bitcoin wallets have been introduced. These technologies interfere with the effectiveness of address clustering. Therefore, to render heuristic-based clustering algorithms admissible in court, it is necessary to develop correspondingly effective address clustering methods based on new developments in blockchain technology. The anticipated smaller and measurable error rates will increase the likelihood that address clustering algorithms will ultimately become admissible.

6. Conclusions

Address clustering targets the pseudo-anonymity by grouping Bitcoin addresses to eventually reveal real-world identities. However, none of the heuristic-based address clustering algorithms has been successfully admitted in court proceedings because the algorithms are heuristic in nature. According to the Daubert standard, for an algorithm to be admissible, it should have a known error rate. Computing the algorithm error rates enables a court to determine the degree to which it can rely on the proffered evidence.

A simulation model was employed to analyze the error rates of two commonly-used Bitcoin address clustering heuristics, the multi-input and one-time change heuristics. The simulation effectively models real-world Bitcoin transactions and collects statistics that enable the determination of the ground truth. The ground truth, which identifies the owners of the generated Bitcoin addresses, enables the error rates of the heuristic-based address clustering algorithms to be determined. Experimental results reveal that combining the multi-input and one-time change heuristics yields the lowest average error rate of 57.47%. In contrast, using the multi-input and one-time change heuristics individually yields average error rates of 63.46% and 92.66%, respectively. These relatively high error rates, which are likely due to low address reuse rates and anonymity enhancing technologies, render it necessary to develop more effective address clustering methods based on new developments in blockchain technology.

Future research will focus on incorporating network-level functionality such as network protocols and propagation performance to create better, multi-functional simulations. Additionally, efforts will be made to develop more effective address clustering methods.

Acknowledgement

This research was supported by the HKU-SCF FinTech Academy 2021/22 R&D Funding Scheme.

References

[1] L. Alsahan, N. Lasla and M. Abdallah, Local Bitcoin network simulator for performance evaluation using lightweight virtualization, *Proceedings of the IEEE International Conference on Informatics, IoT and Enabling Technologies*, pp. 355–360, 2020.

[2] A. Antonopoulos, *Mastering Bitcoin: Unlocking Digital Cryptocurrencies*, O'Reilly Media, Sebastopol, California, 2014.

[3] J. Banks, J. Carson, B. Nelson and D. Nicol, *Discrete-Event System Simulation*, Prentice Hall, Upper Saddle River, New Jersey, 2010.

[4] S. Bistarelli, I. Mercanti and F. Santini, An analysis of non-standard transactions, *Frontiers in Blockchain*, vol. 2, article no. 7, 2019.

[5] Blockchain.com, Bitcoin BTC USD39,431.96, Miami, Florida (`www.blockchain.com/prices/BTC`), April 25, 2022.

[6] F. Cazals, D. Mazauric, R. Tetley and R. Watrigant, Comparing two clusterings using matchings between clusters of clusters, *ACM Journal of Experimental Algorithmics*, vol. 24, article no. 1.17, 2019.

[7] Chainanalysis Team, Ransomware 2021: Critical mid-year update, Chainanalysis, New York (`blog.chainalysis.com/reports/ransomware-update-may-2021`), May 14, 2021.

[8] C. Chen, Z. Qi, Y. Liu and K. Lei, Using virtualization for blockchain testing, *Proceedings of the International Conference on Smart Computing and Communication*, pp. 289–299, 2017.

[9] CoinJoin, CoinJoin Bitcoin Mixer (`coinjoin.io/en`), 2022.

[10] T. Cotten, An overview of Bitcoin transaction types, *Cotten.IO Blog* (`blog.cotten.io/an-overview-of-bitcoin-transaction-types-f22677b8e5a9`), December 11, 2018.

[11] N. Courtois, M. Grajek and R. Naik, Optimizing SHA256 in Bitcoin mining, *Proceedings of the International Conference on Cryptography and Security Systems*, pp. 131–144, 2014.

[12] D. Ermilov, M. Panov and Y. Yanovich, Automatic Bitcoin address clustering, *Proceedings of the Sixteenth IEEE International Conference on Machine Learning and Applications*, pp. 461–466, 2017.

[13] C. Faria and M. Correia, BlockSim: Blockchain simulator, *Proceedings of the IEEE International Conference on Blockchain*, pp. 439–446, 2019.

[14] S. Fattahi, A. Makanju and A. Fard, SIMBA: An efficient simulator for Blockchain applications, *Proceedings of the Fiftieth Annual IEEE-IFIP International Conference on Dependable Systems and Networks – Supplemental Volume*, pp. 51–52, 2020.

[15] A. Gaihre, Y. Luo and H. Liu, Do Bitcoin users really care about anonymity? An analysis of the Bitcoin transaction graph, *Proceedings of the IEEE International Conference on Big Data*, pp. 1198–1207, 2018.

[16] D. Garrie and J. Morrissy, Digital forensic evidence in the courtroom: Understanding content and quality, *Northwestern Journal of Technology and Intellectual Property*, vol. 12(2), article no. 5, 2014.

[17] M. Harrigan and C. Fretter, The unreasonable effectiveness of address clustering, *Proceedings of the IEEE International Conferences on Ubiquitous Intelligence and Computing, Advanced and Trusted Computing, Scalable Computing and Communications, Cloud and Big Data Computing, Internet of People and Smart World Congress*, pp. 368–373, 2016.

[18] Legal Information Institute, Daubert Standard, Cornell Law School, Ithaca, New York (www.law.cornell.edu/wex/daubert_standard), 2022.

[19] J. Luu and E. Imwinkelried, The challenge of Bitcoin pseudo-anonymity to computer forensics, *Criminal Law Bulletin*, vol. 52(1), pp. 191–236, 2016.

[20] S. Meiklejohn, M. Pomarole, G. Jordan, K. Levchenko, D. McCoy, G. Voelker and S. Savage, A fistful of Bitcoins: Characterizing payments among men with no names, *Communications of the ACM*, vol. 59(4), pp. 86–93, 2016.

[21] A. Miller and R. Jansen, Shadow-Bitcoin: Scalable simulation via direct execution of multi-threaded applications, *Proceedings of the Eighth USENIX Conference on Cyber Security Experimentation and Test*, 2015.

[22] H. Mun, S. Kim and Y. Lee, A RDBMS-based Bitcoin analysis method, *Proceedings of the Twenty-Third International Conference on Information Security and Cryptology*, pp. 235–253, 2020.

[23] J. Nick, Data-Driven De-Anonymization in Bitcoin, Master's Thesis, Distributed Computing Group, Computer Engineering and Networks Laboratory, Swiss Federal Institute of Technology Zurich, Zurich, Switzerland, 2015.

[24] Y. Pei, Simchain, GitHub (github.com/YaoyaoBae/simchain), November 14, 2018.

[25] L. Peng, W. Feng, Z. Yan, Y. Li, X. Zhou and S. Shimizu, Privacy preservation in permissionless blockchain: A survey, *Digital Communications and Networks*, vol. 7(3), pp. 295–307, 2021.

[26] L. Stoykov, K. Zhang and H. Jacobsen, Demo: VIBES: Fast blockchain simulations for large-scale peer-to-peer networks, *Proceedings of the Eighteenth ACM/IFIP/USENIX Middleware Conference: Posters and Demos*, pp. 19–20, 2017.

[27] U.S. Supreme Court, Daubert v. Merrell Dow Pharmaceuticals, Inc., *United States Reports*, vol. 509, pp. 579–601, 1993.

[28] Wasabi Docs, PayJoin (`docs.wasabiwallet.io/using-wasabi/PayJoin.html`), June 5, 2021.

[29] J. Wu, J. Liu, W. Chen, H. Huang, Z. Zheng and Y. Zhang, Detecting mixing services via mining Bitcoin transaction network with hybrid motifs, *IEEE Transactions on Systems, Man and Cybernetics: Systems*, vol. 52(4), pp. 2237–2249, 2021.

[30] L. Wu, Y. Hu, Y. Zhou, H. Wang, X. Luo, Z. Wang, F. Zhang and K. Ren, Towards understanding and demystifying Bitcoin mixing services, *Proceedings of the Web Conference*, pp. 33–44, 2021.

[31] Y. Zhang, J. Wang and J. Luo, Heuristic-based address clustering in Bitcoin, *IEEE Access*, vol. 8, pp. 210582–210591, 2020.

Printed in the United States
by Baker & Taylor Publisher Services